1•2•3
Cook for Me

1·2·3
Cook for Me

Over 300 Quick, Easy, and Healthy
Recipes for Babies and Toddlers

Karin Knight, R.N.
and Jeannie Lumley

Authors of *The Baby Cookbook*

First published in the USA in 2006 by
Fair Winds Press, a member of
Quayside Publishing Group
33 Commercial Street
Gloucester, MA 01930

10 09 08 07 06   1 2 3 4 5

ISBN 1-59233-173-4

Library of Congress Cataloging-in-Publication Data
Knight, Karin.
  1, 2, 3, cook for me! : over 300 quick, easy, and healthy recipes for babies and
toddlers / Karin Knight with Jeannie Lumley.
     p. cm.
  Includes bibliographical references and index.
  ISBN 1-59233-173-4
  1. Cookery (Baby foods) 2. Quick and easy cookery. I. Lumley, Jeannie. II. Title.
  TX740.K57 2006
  641.5'6222--dc22

                                                                    2005036740

Cover design by Mary Ann Smith
Book design by Yee Design

Printed and bound in USA

The information in this book is for educational purposes only. It is not intended
to replace the advice of a physician or medical practitioner. Please see your
healthcare provider before beginning any new health program.

For Mirabai

Contents

Introduction

CONGRATULATIONS ON YOUR GROWING BABY! IT'S BEEN FIVE OR six months since you brought her home, and things are going well: You've got the bottle-feeding or breast-feeding down pat, your little one is sleeping through the night (well, maybe, almost), you've settled into a nice routine. But now, it seems that breast milk (or formula) just doesn't seem to be enough for your growing bundle. She wants more, and you need to feed her!

It can seem daunting, but it's not. *1, 2, 3, Cook for Me* is your one-stop book to guide you in the feeding of your baby, toddler, and young child. It is an indispensable nutrition guide and cookbook and an invaluable tool for teaching a new generation how and what to eat.

With my many years of research and teaching nutrition and healthy cooking, I am eager to share with you a commonsense approach to developing sound eating patterns for your baby, setting the stage for a lifetime of healthy eating habits.

In addition to dozens of recipes geared to the age of your child and easy-to-read nutritional information, I've also included chapters on introducing solids and weaning your baby and the choice of homemade vs. commercially prepared baby foods. And there are sections on allergies and food intolerance, choking hazards, oral health, weight concerns, and feeding a vegetarian baby.

Appreciating how busy many parents are, with little time for complicated cooking, *1, 2, 3, Cook for Me* offers a wide variety of quick and easy recipes geared specifically for your growing baby or toddler, along with family recipes that can be enjoyed by your toddler and the rest of the family. Time-saving suggestions for using quality, ready-made but healthy foods are also included. Most recipe ingredients can be found in supermarkets, but get to know your local health food and ethnic stores, as well as mega-warehouse stores, where you can buy high-quality foods in bulk for less.

Please be aware that the information in this book is for healthy infants, toddlers, and children. If you have any concerns about your child's health or diet, consult your pediatrician.

I hope you will continue to use this cookbook for your everyday family meals long after your child is past the toddler stage. You will be rewarded with the pleasure of knowing your whole family has the best possible nutrition you can give them for life.

Karin Knight, RN

P.S. At the beginning of each chapter, I have added a Mother Goose nursery rhyme. For generations, parents have been teaching their babies Pat-a-Cake, Pat-a-Cake, Jack and Jill, Little Jack Horner, Little Miss Muffet, *and many other rhymes. In addition to their charm, they teach babies and toddlers coordination, language, sounds, syntax, and the love of words, rhythms, and poetry. I chose Mother Goose because so many of the rhymes have to do with food.*

PART I

Nutrition for Your Baby or Toddler

———— 🍎 ————

We all know how important good nutrition is for the health and well-being of our children. But information on the subject can be confusing, overwhelming, and often contradictory. My goal is to define as simply as possible the elements that constitute "good nutrition." Understanding the value of each component to your baby or toddler's diet will go a long way toward setting your little one on a path to a well-balanced diet and a lifetime of healthy eating.

Healthy babies have innate instincts indicating hunger and fullness called *appestats*. If you allow your baby or toddler to follow his appestat, he will eat only as much as his body needs and won't develop habits of overeating later in life. Although portion sizes are given here as a general rule of thumb, remember that your child should decide how hungry he is and be allowed to eat accordingly.

As your toddler grows and his diet expands, encourage a liking for a wide range of foods, with emphasis on vegetables and fruits, whole-grain carbohydrates, and proteins from the dairy, meat, poultry, and legume groups. Use fat moderately, with a preference for monounsaturated fats.

As your toddler will share some of your meals at one year and eat family food by two years of age, serving quality food is important for the whole family.

PROTEIN

Fishy, fishy in the brook
Daddy catch him on a hook
Mommy fry him in a pan
Johnny eat him like a man

— FISHY, FISHY

What it does: Protein, the body's major building material, is important for growth, energy, and tissue repair. Our brains, muscles, blood, skin, hair, nails, and connective tissues are predominantly made of protein. Protein also transports hormones and vitamins through the bloodstream, builds muscle, forms antibodies for the immune system, forms glucose for energy, and plays an essential role in maintaining the body's fluid balance.

Kinds: All proteins are composed of amino acids (or "building blocks"), which can be either essential or nonessential. *Complete proteins* contain all the essential amino acids in the correct proportions and are found in animal products and soy products. *Incomplete proteins* contain fewer essential amino acids and come from plants. Combining different kinds of incomplete proteins can create a complete protein. (See "Sources of Protein" on page 14.)

Sources: Complete proteins are supplied by animal sources such as red meat, pork, poultry, milk, yogurt, cheese, eggs, and seafood. In addition, soy, although from a plant source, resembles animal protein and provides complete protein. Incomplete proteins come from plant sources such as beans, lentils, rice, bread, cereals, vegetables, grains, nuts, and seeds.

How much? Babies (six to twelve months) get most of the protein they need through nursing or formula (about 32 ounces for a six-month-old and about 24 ounces for an eleven-month-old); and the additional needed protein from solid food. Toddlers (one to two years) need 2 ounces of protein from the Protein Group and about 16 ounces whole milk a day. (More on this in "Twelve Months" on page 143.) Note that protein deficiency is rarely a problem for most non-vegetarian children; it is usually in conjunction with a lack of calories in the diet.

Sources of Protein

ANIMAL PRODUCTS	PORTION	PROTEIN	CALORIES	FAT
Chicken, 1/2 breast, no skin or bone, roasted	3 ounces	27 g	142	3 g
Lamb, leg, lean, roasted	3 ounces	24 g	162	7 g
Chicken, dark, skinless	3 ounces	23 g	175	8 g
Ground beef, lean, pan-fried	3 ounces	21 g	234	16 g
Pork loin, lean chop, pan-fried	3 ounces	21 g	190	9 g
Tuna, white, in water	3 ounces	20 g	109	3 g
Ham, boneless	3 ounces	19 g	150	8 g
Shrimp, cooked	3 ounces	18 g	84	1 g
Salmon, cooked	3 ounces	18 g	175	10 g
One egg, large, hard-cooked	2 ounces	6 g	80	5 g

DAIRY PRODUCTS	PORTION	PROTEIN	CALORIES	FAT
Cottage cheese, low-fat 2%	1/2 cup	16 g	100	2 g
Cottage cheese, creamed	1/2 cup	14 g	115	5 g
Yogurt, plain, low-fat	8 ounces	12 g	145	4 g
Whole milk, 1 cup	8 ounces	8 g	150	8 g
Skim milk	8 ounces	8 g	85	0.5 g
Yogurt, plain, whole milk	8 ounces	8 g	150	8 g
Cheddar cheese	1 ounce	7 g	114	9 g
American cheese	1 ounce	6 g	93	7 g

VEGETABLE PRODUCTS	PORTION	PROTEIN	CALORIES	FAT
Soybeans	1/2 cup, cooked	14 g	149	8 g
Tofu, firm	1/2 cup	10 g	97	6 g
Lentils	1/2 cup, cooked	9 g	115	<1 g
Kidney beans	1/2 cup, cooked	8 g	112	<1 g
Black beans	1/2 cup, cooked	8 g	113	<1 g
Split peas	1/2 cup, cooked	8 g	115	<1 g
Peanut butter	2 tablespoons	8 g	190	16 g
Chickpeas (garbanzo beans)	1/2 cup, cooked	7 g	134	2 g
Spaghetti, enriched (whole-wheat)	1 cup, cooked	6 g	197	1 g
Rice, white, long-grained	1 cup, cooked	4 g	220	trace
Corn	1/2 cup, cooked	3 g	88	1 g

VEGETABLE PRODUCTS	PORTION	PROTEIN	CALORIES	FAT
Bread, whole-wheat	1 slice	3 g	68	1 g
Soybeans	1 tablespoon, cooked	2 g	18	1 g
Broccoli	$^1/_2$ cup, cooked	2 g	22	trace
Lentils	1 tablespoon, cooked	1 g	14	0 g
Kidney beans	1 tablespoon, cooked	1 g	14	0 g
Split peas	1 tablespoon, cooked	1 g	14	0 g
Potato	$^1/_2$ cup, cooked	1 g	67	trace

Complementary Vegetable Proteins

To provide complete quality proteins from vegetable and dairy sources, combine an incomplete protein from Column 1 with another from Column 2.

GROUP	COLUMN 1	COLUMN 2
Legumes	Fava, kidney, white, black, lima, pinto, or navy beans, lentils, black-eyed peas, or tofu (soy)	Cheese, eggs, milk, yogurt, grains, or vegetables
Grains, including whole grains and grain products	Barley, buckwheat, bulgur, cornmeal, grits, oats, rye, rice, wheat, millet, kasha, polenta, or couscous	Dairy products, legumes, vegetables, nuts, or seeds
Vegetables	Asparagus, beets, broccoli, brussels sprouts, corn, cauliflower, chard, collard greens, kale, mustard greens, okra, spinach, potatoes, sweet potatoes, winter and summer squash, or yams	Dairy products, grains, legumes, nuts, seeds or nut butters
Nuts, seeds (finely ground or chopped), and nut butters	Almonds, Brazil nuts, cashews, filberts, pecans, pine nuts, peanuts, walnuts, pumpkin, safflower, and sunflower seeds, peanut butter, almond butter, or hazelnut butter	Dairy products, grains, legumes, or vegetables

If you are feeding your baby a vegetarian diet, or simply limiting the amount of animal protein she eats, she may not be getting enough complete protein. However, you can easily remedy this by combining different types of (incomplete) plant protein to produce complete proteins.

Here are some combinations of incomplete proteins that naturally complement each other to make high-quality protein.

- Peanut butter on whole wheat bread (Thinly spread the PB to avoid choking.)

- Corn or flour tortillas with refried beans

- Pasta with beans

- Black beans or black-eyed peas with rice

- Baked beans with corn bread

- Lentils with flat bread (chappati, pita, or tortilla)

- Chickpeas with bulgur wheat

- Tofu with vegetables and rice

Complementary incomplete proteins do *not* have to be served together at the same meal (on the same day is okay); however, it may be easier to combine them in a single meal.

CARBOHYDRATES

Sieve my lady's oatmeal,

Grind my lady's flour,

Put it in a chestnut,

Let it stand an hour.

—THE TAILOR OF GLOUCESTER

WHAT THEY DO: Carbohydrates provide the human body with energy. In the form of glucose, carbs are used for immediate energy needs. An important function of carbohydrates is to spare proteins from having to supply body energy, leaving them to fulfill their primary role in building and repairing body tissue.

KINDS: There are two kinds of carbohydrates, simple and complex. *Simple carbohydrates* are made up of simple sugars such as table sugar (sucrose), honey, corn syrup, and molasses. They provide quick energy, but they have little nutritional value and are often categorized as "empty calories." However, note that these sugars are also present in fruit, vegetables, and milk, which add necessary vitamins, minerals, and fiber to the diet. *Complex carbohydrates* contribute starch (a more efficient form of calories) and fiber to the diet, as well as protein and important vitamins and minerals. Complex carbohydrates are absorbed more slowly than simple carbohydrates, giving the body a more continuous source of energy.

SOURCES: Complex carbohydrates come from grains, beans and legumes, and vegetables.

- *Breads:* Whole-grain breads are good sources of complex carbohydrates. Multigrain, buckwheat, whole-wheat, barley, rye, and oat breads are good choices. Rice, corn, matzo, and white bread, along with crackers, pizza dough, buns, tortillas, and other flat breads, are also sources of carbs but not as nutritious as their whole-grain cousins, so give them to your child in moderation.

- *Cereals:* Whole-grain wheat, rye, oat, corn, rice, and barley cereals—cold or hot—are good sources of carbs, along with pasta (made from wheat, rice, or vegetables), polenta (cornmeal), rice (brown and white), couscous (made from semolina flour), and kasha (buckwheat).

- *Beans, Legumes, and Vegetables:* Dried beans, lentils, and peanuts are all good sources of complex carbohydrates, as are potatoes, sweet potatoes, yams, corn, and squash.

HOW MUCH? There is no RDA (recommended dietary allowance) for carbohydrates, but a balanced diet will provide an adequate supply.

DIETARY FIBER

Gee up, Neddy, to the fair

What shall we buy when we get there?

A penny apple and a penny pear

Gee up, Neddy, to the fair.

—GEE UP, NEDDY, TO THE FAIR

WHAT IT DOES: Fiber aids digestion, lowers blood cholesterol levels, and may reduce the risk of developing heart disease, obesity, and some types of cancer in later life. It also helps prevent constipation, a frequent problem for many children.

KINDS: Dietary fiber, which is found only in plants, is divided into two categories, soluble and insoluble. *Soluble fiber* dissolves within the digestive system and generally passes through the body without being absorbed. It expands and becomes gel-like on contact with water. Soluble fiber can help in lowering blood-cholesterol levels. *Insoluble fiber,* or roughage, passes through the intestines virtually unchanged. Insoluble fiber adds bulk, corrects the acid and alkaline balance in the body, and helps remove chemicals in

---

THE IMPORTANCE OF WHOLE GRAINS

Why are whole-grain foods so good for you? It's because grains that are left whole have not had any of their nutrient-rich layers removed. With white flour and other refined grains, the refining process discards the fiber-dense and antioxidant-rich bran and wheat germ layers to yield more delicate, but lower-nutrient flour. White flour may have some nutrients added, but they do not make up for all the important minerals and vitamins that were removed.

When buying bread, bread products, and cereals, look for whole-wheat flour, rolled oats, whole grain, or stone-ground whole grains as the first ingredient.

the intestines that may cause cancer and other health problems. A balanced diet with plenty of whole grains, vegetables, and fruits will easily provide both.

SOURCES: Soluble fiber is found in peanuts, lentils, beans, barley, oats, and oat bran. Other excellent sources of soluble fiber are fresh fruits and vegetables, especially blackberries, unpeeled apples and pears, avocados, peas, artichokes, parsnips, prunes, and dried dates.

Insoluble fiber is found in all whole grains, wheat bran, fruit and vegetable skins, corn kernels, and seeds. (See "Sources of Fiber" on page 17 for detailed information.)

HOW MUCH? Your child's age plus five will equal the amount of grams of dietary fiber he should eat each day. For example, a two-year-old should have about 7 grams fiber every day. However, it is not really necessary to calculate your child's fiber intake in grams. A minimum of three daily servings of green and/or yellow vegetables, two servings of fruit, and four to six servings of whole-grain bread, crackers, pasta, or cereal will provide an adequate amount of fiber. It's important to remember that those grain servings should be whole grains, which always have more fiber than products made with white flour. In ingredient labels, look for the words *whole wheat* or *whole grain*. (*Wheat flour* does not mean it contains whole wheat.) Limit giving your child products made with white flour.

Sources of Fiber

BEANS, RICE, LEGUMES, AND PASTA (cooked)	PORTION	AMOUNT OF FIBER
Lentils	1/2 cup	8.0 g
Kidney beans	1/2 cup	7.3 g
Black–eyed peas	1/2 cup	7.0 g
White beans	1/2 cup	7.0 g
Split peas	1/2 cup	5.0 g
Pinto beans	1/2 cup	4.0 g
Lima beans	1/2 cup	3.0 g
Spaghetti, whole-wheat	1 cup	2.3 g
Rice, brown long-grained	1/2 cup	2.0 g
Macaroni	1 cup	1.6 g
Tahini	1 tablespoon	1.4 g
Spaghetti, white	1 cup	1.1 g
Rice, white, long-grained	1/2 cup	0.3 g

GRAINS	PORTION	AMOUNT OF FIBER
Raisin Bran	1 cup	8.0 g
Grape-Nuts	1/2 cup	5.0 g
Shredded Wheat	1 cup	5.0 g
Oatmeal	1 cup	4.0 g
Whole-wheat bread	1 slice	2.0 g
Bran muffin	1 small	2.0 g
Fruit-filled cereal bar	1 bar	1.0 g
Stone-ground crackers	5 small	1.0 g
French bread	1 slice	0.7 g
Melba toast, wheat	1 slice	0.4 g
Wheat crackers	4 small	0.3 g

VEGETABLES (uncooked)	PORTION	AMOUNT OF FIBER
Avocado	1	5.0 g
Celery	1 stalk	1.1 g
Iceberg lettuce	1 1/2 cups	1.0 g
Tomato	1/2	1.0 g
Mushroom	1/2 cup	0.9 g
Green pepper	1/2 cup	0.5 g

Sources of Fiber

VEGETABLES (cooked)	PORTION	AMOUNT OF FIBER
Sweet potato, baked with skin	1 medium	4.0 g
Green peas	1/2 cup	3.6 g
Potato, baked with skin	1 medium	2.5 g
Brussels sprouts	1/2 cup	2.3 g
Spinach	1/2 cup	2.1 g
Broccoli	1/2 cup	2.0 g
Carrots	1/2 cup	2.0 g
Corn	1/2 cup	2.0 g
Green beans	1/2 cup	1.6 g
Asparagus	1/2 cup	1.0 g

FRUITS (uncooked)	PORTION	AMOUNT OF FIBER
Apple, with skin	1 medium	4.0 g
Blackberries	1/2 cup	4.0 g
Prunes, dried	3 medium	3.0 g
Kiwi	1 medium	3.0 g
Orange	1 medium	3.0 g
Pear	1 medium	3.0 g
Banana	1 medium	3.0 g
Strawberries	1 cup	3.0 g
Blueberries	1/2 cup	2.6 g
Fig, dried	1	2.3 g
Cranberries	1/2 cup	2.0 g
Grapefruit	1/2	2.0 g
Grapes	1 1/2 cups	2.0 g
Plums, pitted	2	2.0 g
Peach	1 medium	1.9 g
Apricots	3 medium	1.8 g
Cherries, pitted	10	1.2 g
Cantaloupe	1 cup	1.0 g
Watermelon	2 cups	1.0 g

FAT

Jack Sprat

    Could eat no fat,

      His wife could eat no lean;

        And so, betwixt the both of them,

          They lick'd the platter clean.

—JACK SPRAT

WHAT IT DOES: In the past few years, fat has become a villain in our diets and is probably one of the most misunderstood nutrients in food. But in fact, fat is important to good health and the enjoyment of food and also helps to regulate our eating habits.

With nine calories per gram, fat is the best supplier of energy to our bodies. It insulates against temperature changes, provides a protective cushion for our organs, and keeps skin and hair healthy. Nutritionally, fat also helps the body to absorb the four fat-soluble vitamins, A, D, E, and K. In addition, fat carries and enhances flavor in food, adding pleasure to eating. And because fat is digested and absorbed slowly and retards the emptying of the stomach, meals eaten with fat stay with you longer and turn off the desire to eat too much or too often.

KINDS: It's important to note that not all fats are created equal; some are much better for you than others. Even so, there should be no restrictions on any of the fats for infants and toddlers—except for trans fats, which should be avoided—because they need the calories during these crucial growing years. Fat also plays an important role in brain development during this time.

Polyunsaturated fats lower total blood cholesterol, but they also lower HDL (the "good" cholesterol). *Monounsaturated fats* are not considered harmful to your heart. Recent research suggests that monounsaturated fats may help lower blood cholesterol, thereby reducing risk of cardiovascular disease.

BUTTER VS. MARGARINE

Butter and margarine are major sources of dietary fat. Butter has 100 calories per tablespoon, 30 milligrams of cholesterol, and 7 grams of saturated fat per tablespoon. Margarine has from 45 to 100 calories per tablespoon, is cholesterol-free, and contains 1 to 2 grams of saturated fat per tablespoon. However, most supermarket margarines are made with partially hydrogenated vegetable oil, or trans fats, which should be avoided. Using butter for babies and toddlers is fine. If your family uses olive or canola oil, or margarine without trans fats, you can also use that for your toddler.

Too much *saturated fat* in an adult's diet may raise blood cholesterol levels, increasing the risk for heart disease. However, babies and toddlers need saturated fat to get enough calories for growth and development. Breast milk and whole milk are good sources of calories since infants and toddlers cannot eat meat, nuts, butter, or oil in adequate quantities to supply adequate calories.

Trans fats are considered very harmful, since they tend to act like saturated fat and raise LDL ("bad") cholesterol and also lower the HDL ("good") cholesterol. Trans fats are created when polyunsaturated vegetable oils are processed with hydrogen gas (hydrogenated) to harden them, resulting in a lard-like texture that is solid at room temperature.

SOURCES: Fats exist in both plants and animals. It is abundant in meats, dairy products, butter, shortening, salad and cooking oils, poultry, fish, and fatty vegetables such as avocados, soybeans, and olives. All fats in food are combinations of saturated, monounsaturated, and polyunsaturated fats. However, certain foods are higher in one type of fat than in others.

Good sources of *polyunsaturated fats* include sunflower, corn, soybean, cottonseed, and safflower oils. *Monounsaturated fats* are abundant in olive oil, canola oil, pecans, cashews, macadamia nuts, peanuts, pistachio nuts, and avocados. *Saturated fats* are found in large amounts in red meat, pork, cream, whole milk and whole milk dairy products, coconut milk, coconut oil, cocoa butter, and palm kernel oils.

Trans fats, the bad guys, are found in most vegetable shortenings and margarines and also in many snack foods, such as crackers, cookies, cakes, pastries, and chips, as well as fried foods and processed convenience foods such as frozen pizza, boxed macaroni and cheese, toaster pastries, etc. The good news is that as of January 2006, the amount of trans fats must be listed on the nutrition label of all foods and because of that many of the nation's food companies have been removing the partially hydrogenated oils (and therefore the trans fats) from their products. To know what you are buying, it is important to read labels. 🔍 *Look for no trans fats in the nutrition label and no partially hydrogenated oils in the ingredients list.*

How much? For the first six months, breast milk or infant formula contains all the calories and nutritional fat an infant needs. Between six months and a year, although your child will be getting additional calories and fat from the gradual introduction of solid foods, breast milk and formula will continue to provide most of the needed fat and calories.

From age one to two, fats should provide about half of your toddler's calories, which works out to be about 60 grams of fat each day, depending on his size. (As a very *general* guideline, figure that a toddler should get 40 calories a day for each inch of height, e.g. approximately 1160 calories a day for a 29-inch-tall toddler.)

Sample Meal Schedule for Toddlers (1 to 2 years old)

BREAKFAST	SERVING	CALORIES	GRAMS OF FAT
Cream of Wheat	2 tablespoons	16	0.00
Half-and-half	1 tablespoon	20	2.00
Applesauce	1 tablespoon	12	0.00
Whole milk	1/2 cup	75	4.00
SUBTOTALS		123 calories	6 grams

SNACK	SERVING	CALORIES	GRAMS OF FAT
Whole milk	1/2 cup	75	4.00
Whole wheat bread	1/4 cup slice	17	0.25
Butter	1 teaspoon	33	3.00
Strawberry jam	1 teaspoon	16	0.00
Peanut butter (natural) smooth	1 teaspoon	31	2.00
SUBTOTALS		172 calories	9.25 grams

THE IMPORTANCE OF FAT

Babies need fat in their diets for brain growth and development, and they get all they need from breast milk or formula. But as babies grow into toddlers, their nutritional requirements change. They have tiny stomachs and need foods that are dense in calories. And since snacks and meal portions are small, whole milk, whole-fat dairy products, and other fatty foods are necessary to provide the needed calories. Indeed, half of a toddler's calories should come from fat, so do not limit fatty foods, including full-fat cow's milk, which usually can be given instead of breast milk or formula after one year of age.

LUNCH

	SERVING	CALORIES	GRAMS OF FAT
Orange juice	1/2 cup	55	0.50
Egg, scrambled	1 egg	101	7.00
Parmesan, grated	1 tablespoon	23	1.50
Olive oil for frying	1 teaspoon	39	4.50
Avocado	1/4 avocado	80	7.50
Tomato	1/4 tomato	6	0.00
SUBTOTALS		304 calories	21 grams

SNACK

	SERVING	CALORIES	GRAMS OF FAT
Whole milk	1/2 cup	75	4.00
Cheerios	1/4 cup	25	0.00
Banana	1/3 banana	36	0.00
SUBTOTALS		136 calories	4 grams

DINNER

	SERVING	CALORIES	GRAMS OF FAT
Turkey patty	1 ounce	48	2.50
Olive oil for frying	1 teaspoon	39	4.50
Spaghetti or noodles	2 tablespoons	24	0.00
Olive oil for pasta	1/2 teaspoon	19	2.00
Parmesan, grated	1 teaspoon	23	1.50
Broccoli	1 spear	10	0.00
Carrot, cooked	3 inches	15	0.00
Butter	1 teaspoon	33	3.00
Vanilla ice cream	2 tablespoons	33	2.00
Fresh berries	2 tablespoons	10	0.00
SUBTOTALS		254 calories	15.5 grams

SNACK

	SERVING	CALORIES	GRAMS OF FAT
Whole milk	1/2 cup	75	4.00
Zwieback	1 piece	30	0.00
SUBTOTALS		105 calories	4 grams
DAILY TOTALS		**1,094 CALORIES**	**59.75 GRAMS**

CHOLESTEROL AND KIDS

High levels of saturated fat in an adult's diet can cause elevated blood cholesterol, which may increase the risk of cardiovascular disease, heart attack, and stroke. Because of this, health experts regularly encourage adults to limit their intake of dietary cholesterol and saturated fat.

However, according to the American Heart Association, ❗ **fat and cholesterol should not be restricted in the diets of children under two.** Babies and toddlers require more fat in their diets than older children and adults, and cholesterol is essential for babies' growth. Children from one to two years old should be given whole milk and whole-milk products, which contain the necessary amount of cholesterol for this age group. (In fact, breast milk has more cholesterol in it than does whole cow's milk.) Infants under one year of age should not be given whole milk. Babies should nurse or be given formula.

The family's best insurance against high cholesterol and too much saturated fat is to provide a balanced diet, rich in grains, vegetables, and fruits. Some lean meat, poultry, or fish, alternating or combined with legumes, and low or nonfat dairy products, will give adults and children over two all the fat and cholesterol they need.

Cholesterol/Fat/Calorie Content of Common Foods

Boldface numbers in the Cholesterol Table reflect extremely high levels of saturated fats, which should be used sparingly after two years of age. The values in these tables have been taken from the USDA Nutrient Database for Standard Reference.

MEAT, FISH, AND POULTRY					
FOOD	PORTION	CALORIES	POLY. FAT	MONO. FAT	SAT. FAT
Beef, lean, ground, pan-fried	3 ounces	235	0.56 gram	6.5 grams	**5.8 grams**
Beef, fatty chuck, pot roast,	3 ounces	282	0.74 gram	8.6 grams	**7.9 grams**
Chicken leg, dark meat, roasted	1 leg	181	1.8 grams	2.8 grams	2.1 grams
Chicken breast, white meat, roasted	1/2 breast	141	0.62 gram	1.0 gram	0.8 gram
Fish, halibut, cooked	3 ounces	119	0.7 gram	0.8 gram	0.3 gram

Food	Portion	Calories	Poly. Fat	Mono. Fat	Sat. Fat
Fish, sole, lean, cooked	3 ounces	99	0.5 gram	0.2 gram	0.3 gram
Fish, trout, cooked	3 ounces	127	1.5 grams	1.4 grams	1.3 grams
Lamb, leg, roasted	3 ounces	219	1.0 gram	5.9 grams	**5.8 grams**
Pork, lean chop, braised	3 ounces	212	1.0 gram	5.8 grams	**4.9 grams**
Turkey, ground, cooked	4 ounces	192	2.6 grams	4.0 grams	2.7 grams
Veal, ground, cooked	3 ounces	146	0.4 gram	2.4 grams	2.5 grams
Tuna, white, water packed	3 ounces	108	0.9 gram	0.6 gram	0.6 gram

DAIRY PRODUCTS

Food	Portion	Calories	Poly. Fat	Mono. Fat	Sat. Fat
Butter	1 tablespoon	101	0.4 gram	3.3 grams	**7.1 grams**
Cheese, cheddar, 1 slice	1 ounce	114	0.2 gram	2.6 grams	**5.9 grams**
Cottage cheese, 2% fat	4 ounces	101	0.06 gram	0.6 gram	1.3 grams
Cheese, ricotta, whole-milk	1/2 cup	215	0.4 gram	4.9 grams	**10.2 grams**
Cheese, mozzarella, whole-milk	1 ounce	90	0.2 gram	1.9 grams	**4.4 grams**
Egg, hard-cooked	1 large	77	0.7 gram	2.0 grams	1.6 grams
Ice cream, vanilla	1/2 cup	132	0.2 gram	2.0 grams	**4.4 grams**
Milk, whole	1 cup	148	0.3 gram	2.4 grams	**5.2 grams**
Milk, 2%	1 cup	121	0.1 gram	1.3 grams	2.9 grams
Milk, 1%	1 cup	102	0.09 gram	0.7 gram	1.6 grams
Milk, skim	1 cup	85	0 grams	0.1 gram	0.3 gram
Yogurt, plain, whole-milk	1 cup	150	0.2 gram	2.1 grams	**5.1 grams**
Yogurt, plain, low-fat	1 cup	155	0.1 gram	1.4 grams	2.4 grams
Yogurt, plain, skim	1 cup	136	0 grams	0.1 gram	0.2 gram
Peanut butter	2 tablespoons	189	4.4 grams	7.7 grams	3.2 grams

VITAMINS

WHAT THEY DO: Vitamins are organic substances that are required for the body's metabolic processes. They perform a wide variety of functions, from forming red blood cells to boosting the immune system to helping release energy from food. Thirteen vitamins are known to be essential for good health: Vitamins A, C, D, E, K, and eight B vitamins. (See "Fat-Soluble Vitamins" on page 26 and "Water-Soluble Vitamins" on page 28 for more information on the roles of individual vitamins.)

KINDS: Vitamins are divided into two categories, determined by how they are absorbed by the body: *water-soluble vitamins*, which include vitamin C and the eight B vitamins, and *fat-soluble vitamins*, A, D, E, and K. Fat-soluble vitamins are stored in the body and if taken in excess can build up toxic levels. Vitamins are stored in the body in varying amounts to meet general daily needs, with reserves for times when the diet may be inadequate.

SOURCES: The thirteen essential vitamins are found in a wide variety of foods and from daily exposure to direct sunlight (for vitamin D). (See "Fat-Soluble Vitamins" on page 26 and "Water-Soluble Vitamins" on page 28 for the best dietary sources for individual vitamins.)

HOW MUCH? Only very small amounts of vitamins are needed, but symptoms from vitamin deficiencies may develop if vitamins are lacking in adequate amounts. On the other hand, when taken in excess (as with supplements), some vitamins may be harmful. According to the American Academy of Pediatrics, healthy children do not need vitamin supplements, provided that they have a balanced diet of varied fruits and vegetables, whole-grain complex carbohydrates, fat, and protein. Indiscriminate use of supplements could result in toxicity. ⓘ **Vitamin supplements for infants and toddlers should not be used, except on the advice of your pediatrician.**

You shall have an apple,
You shall have a plum,
You shall have a rattle,
When papa comes home.

—DANCE TO YOUR DADDY

Sources of Vitamins

Here are guidelines of foods that are excellent, very good, and good sources of vitamins for your infant or toddler. Remove pits and seeds. Prepare all fruits and vegetables appropriately according to your child's age.

Fat-Soluble Vitamins

Vitamins A, D, E, and K need fat to be absorbed by the body.

VITAMIN A

WHAT IT DOES

Keeps skin, hair, nails healthy. Helps maintain gums, glands, bones, and teeth. Necessary for normal vision. Bolsters the immune system.

GOOD SOURCES

- Milk and milk products, butter, cheese, eggs, and fortified milk
- Beta-carotene converted to vitamin A

6 months to 1 year

EXCELLENT	VERY GOOD	GOOD
Carrots and sweet potatoes	Butternut squash, hubbard squash, red bell peppers, parsley, winter squash, romaine lettuce, broccoli, and pumpkin	Plantains, butter head lettuce, kale, green bell peppers, green beans, green peas, avocados, okra, rutabagas, crook neck and acorn squash

1 to 2 years

EXCELLENT	VERY GOOD	GOOD
Carrots and sweet potatoes	Mustard greens, spinach, butternut squash, hubbard squash, red bell peppers, parsley, winter squash, beet greens, basil, romaine lettuce, broccoli, and pumpkin	Plantains, butter head lettuce, tomatoes, kale, green bell peppers, green beans, green peas, asparagus, avocados, tomatoes, okra, rutabagas, asparagus, Swiss chard, collards, crookneck and acorn squash

VITAMIN D

WHAT IT DOES

Promotes calcium absorption. Builds and maintains bones and teeth.

GOOD SOURCES

6 months to 1 year

* Most formulas are fortified with vitamin D. If you are breast-feeding, ask your pediatrician if you need to supplement your baby's diet with vitamin D.

1 to 2 years

* Toddlers who drink vitamin D fortified whole milk will get an adequate amount of vitamin D. Naturally rich sources: fatty fish such as mackerel, salmon, and sardines; egg yolks.

* Fortified sources: milk and milk products, butter, cheese; some breakfast cereals.

* In addition, moderate exposure to sunlight without sunscreen is a good source of vitamin D.

VITAMIN E

WHAT IT DOES

Helps form red blood cells, muscles, and other tissues. Prevents cell damage. Preserves fatty acids.

GOOD SOURCES

In General

* Olive, safflower, soybean, and corn oils; whole grains; leafy vegetables such as Swiss chard, broccoli, spinach, mustard greens, and parsley; avocados; nuts and nut butters; some seafood.

VITAMIN K

WHAT IT DOES

Needed for normal blood clotting. Helps maintain healthy bones.

GOOD SOURCES

In General

* Green leafy vegetables such as spinach, kale, cabbage, lettuce, broccoli; potatoes; whole grains such as oats, wheat bran; soybeans

Water-Soluble Vitamins

VITAMIN B1 (THIAMIN)

WHAT IT DOES

Helps produce energy from carbohydrates. Promotes normal appetite, digestion, nerve function.

GOOD SOURCES

In General

- Pork, seafood, dried beans and peas, fortified grains and cereals

VITAMIN B2 (RIBOFLAVIN)

WHAT IT DOES

Helps produce energy from food. Maintains mucous membranes. Builds red blood cells. Keeps skin healthy.

GOOD SOURCES

In General

- Milk and dairy products, beef, lamb, dark meat of poultry, fortified cereals/grains, dark green leafy vegetables

VITAMIN B3 (NIACIN/NICOTINIC ACID)

WHAT IT DOES

Needed in many enzymes that convert food to energy. Helps ensure healthy skin, nervous system, and digestive tract.

GOOD SOURCES

In General

- Poultry and seafood, enriched breads, cereals and grain products, seeds, nuts, potatoes

VITAMIN B5 (PANTOTHENIC ACID)

WHAT IT DOES

Helps release energy from food.

GOOD SOURCES

In General

- Animal proteins, fresh vegetables

VITAMIN B6 (PYRIDOXINE)

WHAT IT DOES

Essential to protein metabolism and absorption and carbohydrate metabolism. Helps form red blood cells. Needed for healthy nervous and immune systems.

GOOD SOURCES

In General

- Meat, fish, poultry, nuts, whole grains, cereals, spinach, sweet and white potatoes, bananas, prunes, watermelon, dried peas and beans

VITAMIN B12

WHAT IT DOES

Helps manufacture red blood cells and DNA. Maintains healthy nervous system.

GOOD SOURCES

In General

- Foods of animal origin including organ meats, poultry, shellfish, seafood, cheese, yogurt, eggs, milk, and milk products

BIOTIN, A B VITAMIN

WHAT IT DOES

Needed for glucose metabolism and formation of certain fatty acids.

GOOD SOURCES

In General

- Meats, poultry, fish, eggs, nuts, seeds, legumes, vegetables
- Produced by intestinal bacteria

WHAT IT DOES

Needed to make genetic material (DNA, RNA). Needed to manufacture red blood cells.

GOOD SOURCES

6 months to 1 year

EXCELLENT	VERY GOOD	GOOD
Parsley, romaine lettuce	Beets, butter lettuce, avocados, broad beans, cauliflower, iceberg lettuce, peas, parsnips, broccoli, mixed greens, okra, green beans, snow peas, plantains, leeks, cabbage, and crookneck squash	Butternut squash, zucchini, winter squash, yams, rutabagas, carrots, kale, potatoes, kohlrabi, acorn squash, and sweet potatoes

1 to 2 years

EXCELLENT	VERY GOOD	GOOD
Parsley, asparagus, spinach, romaine lettuce; strawberries	Collard greens, beets, butter lettuce, mustard greens, basil, peas, avocados, brussels sprouts, parsnips, broad beans, iceberg lettuce, loose leaf lettuce (mixed greens), artichokes, broccoli, corn, okra, cauliflower, cabbage, spinach, green beans, snow peas, green bell peppers, plantains, radishes, leeks, and crookneck squash; blackberries	Butternut squash, zucchini, winter squash, yams, tomatoes, rutabagas, carrots, kale, potatoes, kohlrabi, acorn squash, and sweet potatoes

VITAMIN C (ASCORBIC ACID)

WHAT IT DOES

Helps bind cells together. Helps heal wounds. Strengthens blood vessel walls.

GOOD SOURCES

For infants 6 months to 1 year

EXCELLENT	VERY GOOD	GOOD
Guavas, kiwis, papayas, and cantaloupes; red, orange, yellow, and green bell peppers, and parsley	Raspberries, honeydew melons, pineapples, blueberries, grapes, and apricots; broccoli, kohlrabi, cauliflower, kale, snow peas, cabbage, romaine lettuce, and sweet potatoes	Plums, cherries, peaches, nectarines, bananas, apples, and pears; broad beans, rutabagas, butternut squash, potatoes, mixed greens, okra, peas, parsnips, turnips, yams, and plantains

For toddlers 1 to 2 years

EXCELLENT	VERY GOOD	GOOD
Guavas, kiwis, papayas, strawberries, oranges, lemons, limes, cantaloupes, grapefruits, and tangerines; red, orange, yellow, and green bell peppers, and parsley	Mangoes, raspberries, honeydew melons, blackberries, star fruit, pineapples, blueberries, grapes, and apricots; broccoli, brussels sprouts, kohlrabi, cauliflower, kale, snow peas, cabbage, garlic, mustard greens, beet greens, spinach, sweet potatoes, romaine lettuce, and radishes	Watermelon, bananas, cherries, plums, peaches, apples, nectarines, and pears; broad beans, tomatoes, Swiss chard, rutabagas, collard greens, mixed greens (loose leaf lettuce), basil, butternut squash, potatoes, okra, peas, parsnips, turnips, yams, plantains, asparagus, artichokes, and radishes

MINERALS

Z was once a piece of zinc,

Tinky,

Winky,

Blinky,

Tinky,

Tinkly minky, Piece of Zinc.

— z

WHAT THEY DO: Minerals perform many functions: They help build strong teeth and bones, maintain fluid balance, sustain a normal heartbeat, and transmit nerve impulses. (See "Major Minerals" on page 33 and "Trace Minerals" on page 34 for information on the functions of individual minerals.)

KINDS: Minerals fall into two groups: major and trace minerals. The six *major minerals* are calcium, phosphorus, magnesium, sodium, chloride, and potassium. The last three are known as electrolytes, which are essential for sustaining the body's proper fluid balance. The thirteen *trace minerals* are needed only in small amounts— but they are nutritionally important, especially iron and zinc.

SOURCES: The six major minerals and thirteen trace minerals are found in a wide variety of foods. (See "Major Minerals" on page 33 and "Trace Minerals" on page 34 for the best dietary sources for individual minerals.)

HOW MUCH? A varied and balanced diet usually provides adequate amounts of all essential minerals. However, infants and toddlers do have special requirements for iron, zinc, and calcium, which are needed to support the rapid skeletal muscle, bone growth, and expansion of blood volume during the two first years.

IRON DEFICIENCY

Iron-deficiency anemia is the most common nutritional deficiency in the United States. By six months, the iron supply infants are born with will be used up. After this time breast milk and non-iron-fortified formula may not be adequate sources of iron (and also zinc). After six months, keep an eye out for these symptoms of iron-deficiency anemia in your baby: tiredness, weakness, and increased susceptibility to infections. If you suspect your child is iron deficient, check with your pediatrician.

For infants and toddlers over one year old, $^1/_4$ to $^1/_2$ cup iron-fortified cereal a day should provide an adequate amount of iron. Vitamin C–rich juices or eating vitamin C–rich food with iron-fortified baby cereal enhances iron absorption. (But note that because of the danger of allergies, babies under one year should not eat citrus fruit.)

After age two, the growth rate slows, iron reserves begin to build, and the risk of iron deficiency decreases.

CALCIUM DEFICIENCY

Calcium deficiency can be a concern if a toddler is not getting enough breast milk, formula, or milk and has a low intake of dairy products and other calcium-rich sources. Lack of calcium in the diet can cause rickets, a childhood disorder involving softening and weakening of the bones. Be sure your child has a nutrient-rich diet, good eating patterns, and a diet rich in calcium, vitamin D, and phosphate.

ZINC DEFICIENCY

Zinc plays important roles in growth and development, immune response, neurological function, and reproduction. Some of the symptoms of mild zinc deficiency in infants and toddlers are diminished appetite, slow growth, increased infections and diarrhea, and a reduced sense of taste and smell. (See "Trace Minerals" on page 34 for information on good sources of zinc.)

IODINE DEFICIENCY

At one time, iodine deficiency disorder (IDD) was a serious problem, jeopardizing children's mental health in some states. But since the introduction of iodized salt, it is no longer a problem in this country. The World Health Organization is working worldwide to prevent IDD and its devastating effects.

The sodium content of salt does not change when iodine is added. Iodine is also found in seafood and vegetables grown in iodine-rich soil. Breast milk and iodine-fortified infant formulas are the best sources of iodine for infants.

Major Minerals

CALCIUM

WHAT IT DOES

Builds bones and teeth. Essential for blood clotting and nerve and muscle function.

GOOD SOURCES

6 months to 1 year

- Breast milk, infant formula, and calcium-fortified infant cereal; cheddar, ricotta, Swiss, mozzarella, and Parmesan cheeses; cottage cheese; yogurt; tofu (processed with calcium sulfate); dried figs; and parsley

1 to 2 years

- Milk, cream, ice cream, yogurt, cheeses, tofu (processed with calcium sulfate), dried figs, halibut, trout, beet greens, collard greens, spinach, basil, and parsley

PHOSPHORUS

WHAT IT DOES

Works with calcium, magnesium, and fluoride in bone growth, including teeth. Helps protect cells.

GOOD SOURCES

In General

- Milk and dairy products, egg yolks, meat, poultry, fish, and legumes

MAGNESIUM

WHAT IT DOES

Promotes bone growth. Essential in transmission of nerve impulses, muscle function, manufacture of protein, and DNA. Helps muscles relax after contractions.

GOOD SOURCES

In General

- Fortified whole-grain cereal and breads, green leafy vegetables, beans, nuts, and shellfish, yogurt, eggs, milk, and milk products

POTASSIUM

WHAT IT DOES

Works with sodium to regulate fluid balance. Essential for proper muscle function, especially of the heart.

GOOD SOURCES

In General

- Bananas, dates, cantaloupes, watermelons, mangoes, plantains, dried apricots, raisins, prunes, orange juice, grapefruit juice, avocados, potatoes and sweet potatoes, spinach, Swiss chard, broccoli, winter squash, parsnips, mushrooms, dry beans and lentils, sunflower seeds, milk, and yogurt

SODIUM

WHAT IT DOES

Helps maintain fluid balance.

GOOD SOURCES

In General

- Table salt, processed foods, and milk

CHLORIDE

WHAT IT DOES

Helps maintain acid-base balance of body fluids.

GOOD SOURCES

In General

- Table salt, processed foods, and milk

Trace Minerals

IRON

WHAT IT DOES

Necessary for the formation of hemoglobin in red blood cells, which carries oxygen to every cell in the body.

GOOD SOURCES

6 months to 1 year

- Iron-fortified infant formula, iron-fortified infant cereals, lentils and dry beans, soybean products, dried figs, dates, raisins, prunes, avocados, spinach, parsley, basil, green beans, and green peas

1 to 2 years

- Iron-fortified cereals, beef, pork, lamb, dark meat poultry, lentils, dry beans, soybeans, ground nuts and nut butters, dried figs, dates, raisins, prunes, avocados, brussels sprouts, green beans, green peas, Swiss chard, beet greens, spinach, parsley, and basil

ZINC

WHAT IT DOES

Essential for normal cell growth, wound healing, and sexual maturation. Also an essential component in many enzymes.

GOOD SOURCES

6 months to 1 year

- Zinc-fortified infant formula, zinc-fortified infant cereals, whole grains (except wheat), rolled oats, cheddar cheese, ricotta cheese, lentils, split peas, chickpeas, lima beans, green peas, spinach, and parsley

1 to 2 years

- Zinc-fortified cereals, rolled oats, whole grains (except wheat), shellfish, meats and poultry, yogurt, cheddar cheese, Parmesan cheese, mozzarella cheese, ricotta cheese, lentils, split peas, chickpeas, lima beans, green peas, spinach, parsley, and ground nuts and nut butters

SELENIUM

WHAT IT DOES

Helps vitamin E protect cells from damage.

GOOD SOURCES

In General

- Poultry, seafood, organ meats, red meat, egg yolks, whole-grain breads and cereals, mushrooms, onions, and garlic

IODINE

WHAT IT DOES

Essential for function of thyroid gland.

GOOD SOURCES

In General

- Iodized salt, seafood, and seaweed

FLOURIDE

WHAT IT DOES

Strengthens bones and teeth and enhances body's absorption of calcium.

GOOD SOURCES

In General

- Fluoridated water and tea

The other trace minerals (arsenic, chromium, cobalt, copper, manganese, molybdenum, nickel, silicon, tin, and vanadium) have a variety of metabolic functions. A balanced diet will provide sufficient amounts of these trace minerals.

WATER

If all the world were apple pie,

And all the sea were ink,

And all the trees were bread and cheese,

What should we have for drink?

— IF ALL THE WORLD WERE APPLE PIE

WHAT IT DOES: Water, the most abundant substance in our bodies, is essential to life. A newborn infant's body is 75 to 80 percent water. Water is necessary for digesting food, maintaining proper body temperature, transporting nutrients, eliminating waste products, and lubricating joints. Fluid requirements vary depending on climate, activity, body size, and age.

HOW MUCH? In the first six months, healthy infants do not normally need to be given water, since breast milk or formula provides all the fluid they need. In very hot weather, give your baby a small amount of water, but check with your pediatrician first as to how much is safe.

At six months, when your baby has started eating solid food and the prescribed requirement for nursing and formula has been met, water can be given from a bottle or cup to quench thirst.

From one year on, your toddler needs 2 cups (16 ounces, or 475 ml) of milk a day, after which you can use water if he is still thirsty.

Water for Infant Formula

The manufacturers of infant formula provide directions for mixing their products with water and usually do not specify the source of the water, as long as the water is safe to drink. In most situations, it is safe to mix formula using ordinary cold tap water that has been boiled for 1 minute.

Some water companies sell bottled water that is marketed for infants and for use in mixing with infant formula. The water

---

SAFE DRINKING WATER FOR CHILDREN

Most tap water is safe for both healthy adults and children. The United States has one of the safest water supplies in the world. The Environmental Protection Agency's (EPA) current drinking water standards are designed to protect children and adults. However, infants' and toddlers' immune systems are not yet fully developed. Consequently, they are more vulnerable to impurities in the drinking water. Certain microbes may induce diarrhea and vomiting, which could cause babies to become dehydrated. Young children may also be more susceptible to chemical contaminants (lead, nitrites, nitrates, copper, mercury, barium, cadmium, and pesticides) that affect learning, motor skills, and sex hormones during important stages of growth.

Since the water quality varies throughout the country, concerned parents should find out about the safety of their local water by calling the Safe Drinking Water Hotline, 800-426-4791, or the EPA Children's Environmental Health Hotline, 877-590-5437.

---

labeled specifically for infant use must meet the same standards as safe tap water, established by the Environmental Protection Agency. The label must also indicate if the bottled water is sterile. Water that is sterilized by the manufacturer and intended for use with infants must meet certain Food and Drug Administration standards. If the bottled water is not sterile, it should be boiled one minute before mixing it with the infant formula.

However, note that though sterilizing water does kill bacteria, it does not remove chemical contaminants such as lead, nitrates, copper, and mercury. There is no requirement that companies label their water to indicate the chemicals it contains (or does not contain), so there is no way of knowing if it is truly safe for infants or toddlers. The only advantage of bottled water marketed for babies is that parents don't have to sterilize the water themselves.

SALT

And I asked her how much she loved me.

And she said, "As much as fresh meat loves salt."

And I turned her away from my door,

For I thought she didn't love me.

And now I see she loves me best of all.

— CAP O' RUSHES

WHAT IT DOES: Salt (or sodium chloride) maintains fluid balance in the body and helps nerves perform properly.

SOURCES: Salt is found naturally in many foods and water.

HOW MUCH? ❗ **Salt should never be added to the food of babies under 12 months.** Breast milk and infant formula will provide all the sodium your baby needs. Once a healthy one-year-old starts to eat table food, very small amounts of salt will not be harmful. However, salt is an acquired taste, so use it sparingly. Use spices, herbs, and lemon juice to flavor the family recipes if desired, and add just enough salt to bring out the natural flavors without making the food taste salty.

SUGAR

God made the bees

And the bees make honey

The miller's man does all the work

But the miller makes the money.

—GOD MADE THE BEES

WHAT IT DOES: Sugar is a source of energy for the body. However, it is devoid of vitamins, minerals, or any other useful nutrients and is often referred to as providing "empty calories."

KINDS: *Sugar (table sugar)*, also called *sucrose*, comes from beets or sugarcane. *Molasses* is the concentrate that remains after sucrose is extracted from sugarcane. *Brown sugar* is white sugar crystals coated with molasses. *Maple sugar* and *maple syrup* are products of sap from the maple tree after boiling. *Honey* is produced by bees from the nectar of flowers. ❗ **The American Academy of Pediatrics recommends that honey not be given to infants younger than twelve months.** It has been associated with infant botulism, an illness that can be fatal for babies. Honey is often added to bread, jam, crackers, and other baked products, as well as ice cream or yogurt, so read labels carefully.

SOURCES: Sugars are simple carbohydrates that occur naturally in many foods such as fruit, vegetables, and milk. Refined sugars and other sweeteners are used extensively in processed food. In addition to those used in soft drinks, canned and frozen fruits, breakfast cereals, candy, jams, dairy desserts, fruit drinks, and baked goods, sugar is also found in ketchup, bread, canned vegetables, mustard, salad dressings, and many other unlikely products that we don't think of as being sweet. To make up for the flavor sacrificed by low-fat ingredients, some food manufacturers have increased the sugar content in their products. Consequently, consumption of sugar, honey, and other sweeteners has increased dramatically in the past decade.

HOW MUCH? All sugars, honeys, and syrups should be used in moderation. An excess of sugar in a baby's diet can cause diarrhea. Sugar also promotes tooth decay. All sugars are virtually identical nutrition-wise and supply about 4 calories per gram (with the exception of honey, which is higher in calories).

Babies and toddlers naturally love sweets. The challenge for parents is to find the best way to satisfy their child's sweet tooth without jeopardizing oral and general health. Naturally sweet fruits are always the best choice for desserts, as they also provide essential vitamins, minerals, and fiber—benefits not provided by most processed cookies, candies, and pastries.

Don't underestimate the importance of establishing good habits. If you emphasize fruits for snacks from an early age and don't keep cookies, candy, and sweet pastries in the house, your child will not get used to eating them and may not crave these sweets as he grows up. With any luck, fruits and berries will become his sweets of choice.

Juice and Sugar

Juices contain a lot of sugar, so from six months to two years of age, it is preferable to limit the amount to 4 ounces a day. Too much juice can fill small stomachs, leaving insufficient room for a balanced diet. Excessive amounts may cause cramping and diarrhea.

However, juice *does* provide essential vitamins, and it is one of the healthier ways of satisfying your baby's sweet tooth. For six- and seven-month-old babies, juices should be diluted with an equal amount of water. By eight months your baby may be given full-strength juice.

Although some pediatricians and nutritionists recommend serving children diluted juice for quenching thirst throughout childhood, I don't suggest using diluted juice as a drink. Having your child get used to drinking water when she is thirsty is much better. My recommendation of serving 4 ounces of 100 percent fruit juice that is rich in vitamin C counts as one serving from the Fruit Group, and it should be served only occasionally, not more than once a day.

🔍 **When buying juices, look for 100 percent fruit juice—check the label for the words *100 percent pure* or *100 percent juice*—with no sugar added.** This will ensure you are getting only pure fruit juice, not a sweetened juice beverage, diluted with water. There are a number of juices fortified with vitamin C made specifically for infants and toddlers. Should you choose to give your child adult juices, be sure they are vitamin C–fortified and that apple juice and cider have been pasteurized to eliminate harmful bacteria.

Steer clear of product names with the words *juice cocktail, juice punch, juice drink, juice sparkler, juice blend,* or *juice beverage* as these are terms used for sweetened and diluted juices. And be wary of products labeled *real fruit.* They can be misleading, as it means only that the fruit is real, not necessarily that the bottle contains 100 percent fruit juice.

Hidden Sugars

Remember that processed foods can contain large amounts of sugar. Be sure to read food labels carefully. Just because the ingredients list doesn't contain "sugar" doesn't mean that the product isn't loaded with sucrose. The following are different kinds of sugars to watch for in nutrition labels: glucose, dextrose, fructose, sucrose, maltose, lactose, honey, molasses, maple syrup, cane sugar, brown sugar, beet sugar, corn sugar, refined sugar, corn sweetener, corn syrup, high fructose corn syrup, and fruit juice concentrate.

A food is high in sugar when one of the above sugars is listed first or second on the label. Note that the amount of sugar and carbohydrates is also indicated in grams or milligrams on nutrition labels.

DAIRY PRODUCTS AND SUBSTITUTES

Milkman, milkman, where have you been?

In butter–milk channel up to my chin,

I spilt my milk and I spoilt my clothes,

And got a long icicle hung to my nose.

—MILKMAN, MILKMAN, WHERE HAVE YOU BEEN?

By the time your baby is one year old, you can start to give him 2 to 3 cups (16 to 24 ounces) whole milk each day. Whole milk is an important and inexpensive source of the fats, protein, calcium, and vitamins A and D your child needs. All cow's milk given to toddlers and young children should be pasteurized. Instead of giving your toddler a whole cup, which may fill up his little stomach and not leave room for any other food, give him 1/4 cup at a time throughout the day.

Whole-milk yogurt, cottage cheese, and ricotta cheese are all high in calcium and can be used liberally in your toddler's diet. Parmesan, mozzarella, and cheddar cheeses are also excellent sources of calcium and vitamin A. Ice cream, cream, and half-and-half have about the same amount of calcium as milk, but almost twice as much fat, cholesterol, and calories as whole milk. They can be used in a toddler's diet, but should be given in moderation. Remember, habits are quickly established but hard to change, so go easy on the high-fat and sweetened dairy products for your child. And keep in mind that once extra calories are not needed, frequent use of cream-based high fat and high cholesterol food will have to be modified.

Milk and Dairy Substitutes

Soy and coconut milk products are sometimes used as alternatives or in addition to whole milk and whole-milk products in toddler's and older children's diets. However, parents should always check with their pediatrician or a registered dietician first.

Soy milk is made from pureed soybeans and water. It is also available with added calcium. Soy dairy is the general term for soy-based yogurt, cream cheese, sour cream, and ice cream.

Soy margarine is a spread similar to butter, made from the oil of pressed soybeans.

Coconut milk is the extract pressed from grated coconut meat. It is very high in calories (552 in 1 cup). It does not have a significant amount of calcium, but it does contain some iron and vitamin C. Coconut milk has ten times as much saturated fat as whole milk, but no cholesterol. Coconut milk should not replace regular milk for toddlers, but its use in Asian recipes, particularly in Thai food, adds variety to the diet.

Rice milk and rice milk products have little nutritional value except for some carbohydrates and a large amount of folate. They are not good substitutes for regular milk, as they lack necessary fat, calcium, protein, vitamin A, and vitamin D. However, it is fine to use rice milk products occasionally as a treat or in smoothies.

WHAT ABOUT GOAT'S MILK?

After twelve months, when the digestive system has developed and the baby is eating a healthy diet, goat's milk may be beneficial. If you choose goat's milk for a one-year-old (or older), be sure it has been pasteurized.

WHAT ABOUT DRIED MILK?

There are a number of benefits of dried milk: It is less costly than liquid milk but has the same nutritional value, and it keeps for a long time. However, children up to age two should always drink full-fat milk, and it can be difficult to find dried whole milk; it is usually only available in low-fat and nonfat forms. If you can find dried whole milk (camping outfitters and bakers' suppliers sometimes carry it), by all means, serve it to your child. But you should not offer her dried nonfat or low-fat milk.

Lactose Intolerance

When the body lacks a needed enzyme (lactase) to digest the natural sugar in milk (lactose), some people may experience lactose intolerance. The most common symptoms are gas, bloating, and diarrhea. Infants are born with high levels of lactase, but by age three or four it has decreased, especially in people of Asian, African, southern European, and Native American ancestry. However, not all lactase-deficient people are lactose intolerant.

By age three or four, many children with lactose intolerance are also intolerant of soy products. Some, however, have only a partial intolerance and can handle milk and dairy products so long as only small amounts are served with food. Aged cheeses and yogurts are usually acceptable, because the lactose is broken down during the aging process.

Reduced-lactose and lactose-free milk is now readily available, as are lactase enzyme products that can be added to milk and dairy foods to make lactose digestible. Check with your pediatrician before giving this milk to your child.

PART II

Special Considerations

KEEPING WEIGHT PROBLEMS AT BAY

DURING THE PAST FEW YEARS, THERE HAS been much discussion among the medical profession, health organizations, and media about the dramatic increase in the number of overweight children in the United States. These concerns need to be addressed, especially in relation to feeding infants and toddlers.

Experts agree that children become overweight for a variety of reasons. The most common reasons are genetic factors, unhealthy food and eating patterns, and lack of physical activity.

There's not a lot parents can do about the genetic causes of obesity, but they *can* do much to help establish healthy exercise and eating habits, and the earlier you start the better!

ESTABLISHING A HEALTHY EATING PATTERN

One of the most valuable gifts a parent can give a child is the establishment of a healthy eating pattern. It is easier on both parents and children to establish healthy habits early, as eating patterns are ingrained through years of routine. It can be difficult for older children (and adults, for that matter) to modify unhealthy habits to maintain a healthy weight.

To develop healthy eating patterns in a child, parents need to be aware of the clues and signals that he is full, and then not force or encourage any more food after that. In addition, it almost goes without saying that limiting a child's consumption of empty calories of "juice" drinks, soda, cookies, candy, and other unhealthy snack foods goes a long way toward setting the stage for healthy eating throughout life.

THE APPESTAT

Recent research shows that infants are born with an instinct, referred to as their *appestat*, that sends a "stop eating" signal to the part of the brain that controls appetite. Trusting this inborn knowledge of how much food will satisfy his appetite lays the foundation for good eating habits

To heed their baby's appestat, parents should pay close attention to when she signals that she is full—and be equally attentive to when she signals that she is hungry. Here are clues that your child's appestat has told her that she's had enough:

NEWBORN

- Spits out nipple or falls asleep

SIX TO TWELVE MONTHS

- Turns head away to regulate pace or end feeding
- Refuses to open mouth
- Spits out food
- Stores food in mouth
- Pushes dish, cup, or bottle away

ONE TO TWO YEARS

- Shakes head no
- Puts hand over mouth
- Pushes away the hand that offers food
- Uses simple words like "No," "Don't," or "Away"
- Pushes away or throws plate, cup, or spoon

TWO TO THREE YEARS

- Combines words, "All done" or "Get down"
- Pushes away plate
- Tries to remove bib

THE PARENTS' ROLE

It cannot be emphasized enough that the type and quality of food that parents introduce from the beginning will shape their child's food preferences throughout life. It is therefore important to consistently provide a variety of healthy, tasty, and nutritious foods.

It is also important to teach your child how to feed himself as early as possible. Start giving finger foods by the eighth month. By the twelfth month, your child will begin to use a spoon and should be feeding himself independently by fifteen months of age.

Infants and toddlers who are allowed to follow their hunger and satiety cues, eating only as much as their bodies need for good health, will develop habits of moderation that should last a lifetime. However, as important as it is to let the child judge how much food he wants, it can be one of the most difficult things for a parent to do.

If a child's natural "appestat" breaks down because he is frequently encouraged to eat when he is full, feeding problems can develop and determining when and how much to eat may become a battle between parent and child. Remember that many parents tend to give infants and toddlers larger portions than necessary—and then expect them to finish all the food on their plates. Always start with small portions—the rule of thumb is 1 tablespoon of each food for each year of your child's age—and then let your little one tell you in his own way if he wants more.

Birth to six months: Nursing or formula provides all the nourishment an infant needs.

Although more research is necessary, there is evidence that breast-fed infants experience the variety of flavors of their mother's diet through breast milk, which may encourage better acceptance of solids during weaning. This is consistent with research showing that early experiences with a variety of flavors lead more readily to acceptance of new foods later.

Six to twelve months: Nursing or formula is still the primary source of needed fat, cholesterol, and calories. The introduction of vegetables, fruits, egg yolk, dairy products, beans, and legumes will be supplementary.

One to two years: Toddlers start to share foods from their parents' diet. This is a decisive time, as the family's eating habits will establish the kinds of food the child will choose for the rest of her life. Remember that toddlers need more dietary fat and cholesterol than adults. With the addition of whole milk and a few other high-fat foods, they may share the same meals as their parents—as long as the parents are following a healthy diet.

FAST FOOD AND JUNK FOOD

Fast food and junk food are the bugaboos of the establishment of a healthy diet. It's unfortunate that fast foods are a fact of life and, if given the choice, will usually be a child's preferred meal, but this is true only if he has been exposed to it early and often. So try to limit trips to the drive-up window.

Other kinds of junk food can derail a healthy diet because although cakes, cookies, and fatty snacks are okay as occasional treats, regular consumption leaves little room for nutrition-dense balanced meals the rest of the day. In addition, these foods generally have excessive calories and limited nutritional value.

Discourage a toddler from developing junk-food preferences by limiting potato chips, french fries, sugared cereals, cookies, pizza, milk shakes, cake, pie, artificially flavored fruit drinks, ice cream, deep-fried chicken, hot dogs, cheeseburgers, soda, and candy. Additionally, don't encourage your child to be inactive by letting him watch several hours of television each day, where such food choices are reinforced through advertising. All these factors may contribute to weight and health problems in children.

If you think that your toddler is too heavy, talk to your pediatrician. And be assured that generally, if the parents are not overweight, chubby toddlers (under two) will slim down as they grow and become more active.

ALLERGIES AND FOOD INTOLERANCE

The man in the wilderness asked me,

How many strawberries grew in the sea?

I answered him, as I thought good,

As many as red herrings grew in the wood.

— THE MAN IN THE WILDERNESS

Food intolerance is common among infants and toddlers, but it can be difficult to diagnose. The younger a child is when introduced to solid food, the greater the risk for intolerance or allergic reaction. If food allergies exist in your family, take careful note about what you eat while you are nursing and what type of solids you give your infant.

Because there are many different kinds of foods that cause intolerance or allergies, it is important to introduce new foods to your baby one at a time and watch for reactions. If you offer two or more new foods at the same time and there is a reaction, it will be difficult to determine which food caused the problem.

The risk of allergies and food intolerance lessens by the eighth or ninth month and continues to decrease after the first year until the third year when the risk levels off.

FOOD INTOLERANCE VS. FOOD ALLERGY

According to the American Academy of Pediatrics, true food allergies, which set the immune system into action, are rare. If you notice a reaction, it is more likely that your child is experiencing intolerance to a particular food or ingredient. Keep in mind that allergic reactions can happen immediately, but don't always happen the first time a food is given, so be aware that your child may develop an allergy to a food he previously tolerated. Consult your pediatrician to correctly identify if it is an intolerance or allergy. Food allergies can be life-threatening and it is critical to rule them out first.

Food Intolerance

These are the major symptoms of a food intolerance:

Diarrhea

Bloating

Gas

Should your child show these signs after eating a new food, immediately stop offering the food. Once you are assured it is intolerance and not an allergy (by checking with your pediatrician), try reintroducing that food a month or two later. If the intolerance recurs, it would probably be wise to wait until your baby turns one year old before offering that food again. If these symptoms continue after you have discontinued the newly introduced food, call your pediatrician.

True Food Allergy

A food that your child is allergic to will produce one or more of these symptoms:

Diarrhea

Skin rashes

Hives (itchy welts)

Vomiting

Difficulty breathing

Runny nose and tearing eyes

If your baby shows these symptoms after a new food, call your pediatrician immediately. The food should not be given again until your pediatrician has made a diagnosis. Note that if in addition to these symptoms, your child has a fever, it may not be a food allergy. But either way, you should check with a pediatrician.

PROBLEM FOODS

There are some foods that are likely to cause allergic reactions or intolerance problems in children who are susceptible. The following should not be offered to your baby until after twelve months.

- Nuts, peanut butter, and any food containing peanuts

- Cow's milk

- Egg whites and food containing egg whites, including cookies and cakes

- Citrus fruits and citrus juices (orange, lime, grapefruit, and lemon)

- Strawberries

- Garlic

- Shellfish (shrimp, crab, and lobster)

- Chocolate (cocoa) and any foods containing chocolate

- Mangoes

- Honey, which is often added to bread, jams, crackers, and other baked products, as well as ice cream or yogurt (❗**Honey may cause infant botulism, an illness that can be fatal.**)

- Any food containing additives, such as dyes, thickeners, preservatives, artificial flavors, and colors (Read food labels carefully.)

- Wheat (and wheat products) (If there are no known allergies of these products in the family, they can be introduced at nine months.)

- Soy (and soy products, including tofu) (If there are no known allergies of these products in the family, they can be introduced at nine months.)

CHOKING HAZARDS

Choking is a very real hazard to children under the age of three. Children should be constantly supervised while they are eating. In addition, don't let your toddler eat while running or playing and teach him to finish each mouthful before speaking. And it is not a good idea to allow your toddler to eat in the car; if he should choke, you may not be able to safely stop the car to help him.

Be careful with *firm or slippery foods* like hot dogs, hard candy, peanuts, cherries, cherry tomatoes, and grapes; they may be swallowed before they are fully chewed, get lodged in the throat, and cause choking. This can also happen with *small, dry, or hard foods* that are difficult to chew, like popcorn, potato and corn chips, nuts, seeds, small pieces of raw carrot, or large wads of melted cheese. Some common *sticky or tough foods* like peanut butter, tough meat, and uncooked raisins or other dried fruit can also easily lodge in the throat and block the airway.

CHOKING PREVENTION

Follow these guidelines when feeding your child to minimize the risk of choking.

- Cook food until it is soft enough to easily pierce with a fork.
- Cut foods into small pieces or thin slices small enough for easy chewing.
- Cut round foods, such as hot dogs or cooked carrots, into short strips rather than round pieces.
- Cut grapes in half and remove seeds, if any.
- Cut cherries in half and remove pits.
- Cut cherry tomatoes in quarters.
- Grind or mash and moisten food for young babies.
- Remove all bones from fish, poultry, and meat.
- Remove pits and seeds from fruit.
- Avoid nuts or seeds, such as sunflower or pumpkin, unless finely ground or chopped.
- Avoid peanut butter and other nut or seed butters, unless spread very thinly on crackers or mixed with hot or cold liquids and smoothies.
- Closely supervise mealtimes and encourage babies and toddlers to sit quietly while they eat.

CHOKING HAZARDS UNTIL THREE YEARS OLD

Be careful with firm or slippery foods; small, dry, or hard foods; and sticky or tough foods.

- Hot dogs
- Popcorn
- Whole nuts
- Whole seeds (pumpkin and sunflower seeds)
- Raw carrots (unless shredded)
- Raisins (uncooked or not soaked)
- Hard corn kernels
- Fruits with seeds or pits (cherries, apricots, peaches, nectarines, oranges, and grapes)
- Raw celery
- Fish with bones
- Tough meat
- Small or hard candy
- Whole grapes
- Whole cherry tomatoes
- Whole green beans
- Large chunks of any food (meat, potatoes, raw vegetables, fruit)
- Hard, uncooked peas

ORAL HEALTH

Thirty white horses

Upon a red hill,

Now they tramp,

Now they champ;

Now they stand still.

(The answer to this riddle: Teeth and gums.)

—THIRTY WHITE HORSES

There is a wide variation in the age that babies cut their first teeth, but the first teeth usually appear between five and seven months. Teething often causes problems like sore and painful gums, which may make babies cranky and irritable, reduce their appetite, or even cause diaper rash. Since so many teeth are cut during the first two years, there may be many trying times. A baby often has an elevated temperature during teething. A fever of 100°F (38°C) or higher, however, requires a call to the pediatrician. If feverish, give your baby plenty of liquids. It is important to get the fever down as quickly as possible, but do not give her any medicine without your pediatrician's advice. If your baby has diarrhea, cut out fruits, milk, and milk products until symptoms have disappeared, but do not eliminate or decrease breast milk or formula. Plain boiled rice or rice water can also be helpful.

For babies, rubbing the gums with a clean finger may ease some of his discomfort, and clean and frozen washcloths or terrycloth may be nice for him to chew on. Your baby may try to put hard objects in his mouth, so be careful that the object is not something he might choke on. Extra love, patience, attention, and cuddling will be needed at this time.

For toddlers, frozen berries, fruits, and some vegetables (cut into small pieces to prevent choking) and other cooked and frozen foods

CAVITY PREVENTION

A balanced diet is not only important to infants' and toddlers' general health, but also for their dental health. Baby and toddler tooth decay had until recently been blamed primarily on baby bottle tooth decay syndrome, cavities developed from allowing a child to drink from bottles of juice or milk while falling asleep, which can cause the liquid to pool in the mouth. A broader viewpoint now includes the following other causes of tooth decay and methods of prevention.

◆ Start early with good nutrition, eating habits, and oral hygiene.

◆ Don't dip pacifiers in sugar, honey, or juice. (Never give honey to a baby less than a year old under any circumstances.)

◆ Limit fruit juices to $1/2$ cup daily.

◆ Do not offer juice or other sweet liquids in a bottle; only in a cup. If you must give your baby something to suck on at bedtime for comfort, use only water or a pacifier.

◆ Use fluoride as prevention against cavities. (See "Fluoride Helps Prevent Tooth Decay" on page 53.)

◆ Pay an early visit to a pediatric dentist.

like mini waffles are popular during teething, as they soothe swollen gums. If you feel your child might need medication for relief, ask your pediatrician.

TEETH CARE, SIX TO TWELVE MONTHS

During this time, your baby will generally cut about eight teeth. These primary teeth are important for chewing food, speech, and good appearance. Baby teeth also help reserve space in the jaws for permanent teeth—all significant reasons for keeping them healthy. As soon as the teeth break through, clean them daily with a damp cloth, gauze pad, or soft baby brush. Use only fresh water, no toothpaste. Daily cleaning is essential, as this is the time when solids and juices are added to the diet.

Oral bacteria feed on sugar and starches that are left on the teeth for more than 20 minutes, producing acids that destroy tooth enamel and cause cavities. Foods that tend to cling to baby teeth include sugary foods and high-starch snacks, such as dried fruit, crackers, breadsticks, and teething biscuits. Eating cheddar, Monterey Jack, or Swiss cheese immediately after sugary and high-starch foods may counteract some of the negative effects, but not as thoroughly as cleaning the teeth.

If your water supply is not fluoridated and the natural fluoride content of your water is low, your pediatrician may prescribe a fluoride supplement around six months. By your baby's first birthday, visit a pediatric dentist and ask for a demonstration and information on proper brushing techniques.

TEETH CARE, ONE TO TWO YEARS

Between a toddler's first and second birthdays, eight more primary teeth will likely appear, giving your child a total of sixteen teeth. By now, she should drink all her liquid from a cup.

Toddlers are not developmentally ready to brush independently yet, but now is the time to start an oral hygiene regime. Between eighteen months and two years, start teaching your toddler to spit out toothpaste. So long as it is not swallowed, use a pea-sized amount of fluoride toothpaste on the toothbrush, and, guiding his hand, help him brush his teeth. Training toothpaste without fluoride, which is safe to swallow, is also available for toddlers. A two-year-old may be able to hold a toothbrush, but he is not ready to brush independently yet.

Try not to give your child sugar-rich foods that stick to the teeth, such as mints, lollipops, or hard candy. Avoid soft sticky sweets such as toffee, fruit leather, and dried fruits (unless soaked and cooked). Instead of sweet snacks, offer cheese, raw vegetables, plain yogurt, or fresh fruit. Variety, moderation, and attention to healthful between-meal snacks will benefit oral and general health.

This is the age when a broad variety of foods is introduced. Keep in mind that calcium is necessary for healthy teeth and bones, so be sure to offer plenty of dairy products, such as whole milk, cheese, and yogurt; they are the best dietary sources of calcium. Calcium-processed tofu, calcium-fortified orange juice, and broccoli are also good choices. Also ensure that an adequate supply of vitamin D (through milk and sunlight) is provided, which helps to increase calcium absorption.

FLUORIDE HELPS PREVENT TOOTH DECAY

Fluoride, a trace mineral present in varying concentrations in soil and water, plays an important role in the maintenance of healthy teeth and bones. It contributes to the growth of new enamel and also strengthens it, making the teeth more resistant to decay.

According to the American Dental Association, research shows that fluoride reduces children's cavities by up to 50 percent. As a direct result of water fluoridation and over-the-counter fluoride products, half of all children entering first grade today have never had a single cavity, compared with 36 percent in 1980 and 28 per-

OCCASIONAL SWEETS

If your toddler does enjoy the occasional sweet, keep in mind that they are likely to be less harmful if eaten at mealtimes. Eating releases saliva, which helps wash food from the mouth. However, encouraging brushing after each meal is still the best way to keep your child's teeth healthy.

NO FLUORIDE IN THE WATER?

Your child may need fluoride supplements or topical applications to prevent tooth decay if you live in an area where the drinking water supply contains low levels of naturally occurring fluoride. Check with your pediatrician or a local pediatric dentist.

cent in the early 1970s. Note that research in areas where the drinking water is naturally rich in fluoride has confirmed the safety of fluoride in the water supply. Virtually all major health organizations endorse and support the use of fluoride as an important tool in promoting dental health.

As with other essential elements (such as iron and vitamins A and D), which are also necessary for the body's good health, fluoride can be toxic in excessive quantities. Its safety range, however, is very wide, and large amounts of fluoride would have to be ingested over an extended period of time to present a significant health problem. Slight discoloration or white spots on the permanent teeth are early indications of excessive intake of fluoride.

THE VEGETARIAN BABY

Blow, wind, blow! And go, mill, go!
That the miller may grind his corn;
That the baker may take it,
And into bread make it
And send us some hot in the morn.

—BLOW WIND BLOW

Going "veggie" or just "semi-veggie" is a choice many people are making these days, whether guided by moral or health concerns. No matter the motivations, there's no doubt that a vegetarian diet, properly executed, can be healthy and nutritious. However, there are some certain issues you'll need to address if you are planning on feeding your baby or toddler a vegetarian diet. But first, to avoid confusion, let's look at just what *vegetarianism* means.

Being a vegetarian means different things to different people. But to generalize, we can say that vegetarians fit into one of the following four groups.

SEMI-VEGETARIANS eat a diet that contains only a small amount of meat, poultry, or seafood. Some semi-vegetarians eat no red meat.

LACTO-OVO VEGETARIANS do not eat any meat, poultry, or seafood, but they do eat eggs (ovo) and dairy (lacto) products.

LACTO-VEGETARIANS do not eat any meat, poultry, seafood, or eggs, but they do eat dairy products.

VEGANS eat no animal products whatsoever—no meat, poultry, seafood, eggs, dairy products, or any foods that come from animals, including honey and gelatin.

As with a nonvegetarian diet, a vegetarian regime can be healthy or unhealthy for babies, depending on whether the diet is nutritionally adequate. But it is not at all difficult to provide good nutrition with the less-restrictive vegetarian diets. The guidelines and recipes in *1, 2, 3, Cook for Me* can make it easy to provide a healthy vegetarian diet. However, it is always wise to discuss your baby's diet with a pediatrician or registered dietician.

Here is a summary for using this book when feeding a vegetarian baby.

SEMI-VEGETARIAN AND LACTO-OVO VEGETARIAN: Until six months of age, babies should be given breast milk (or formula) only. After that, follow the directions in "Introducing Solid Food" (page 74) and the "Baby's Month-by-Month Feeding Guide and Recipes for Six to Twelve Months" (page 78). By the twelfth month, your baby can share family meals, with some modifications.

LACTO-VEGETARIAN: Until six months of age, babies should be given breast milk (or formula) only. After that, follow the directions in "Introducing Solid Food"(page 74) and the "Baby's Month-by-Month Feeding Guide and Recipes for Six to Twelve Months" (page 78), but omit eggs and recipes requiring eggs. By the twelfth month, your baby can share family meals, with some modifications.

From six to twelve months (introduced at the appropriate age):

+ Mashed avocado

+ Bean spreads with cheese

+ Mashed or pureed tofu

+ Mashed hard-cooked egg yolk

+ Soy or whole-milk yogurt

+ Whole-milk cream cheese

+ Mascarpone, ricotta, and cottage cheese, cheddar, Jack, Swiss, Parmesan, Romano, and soy cheese substitutes

+ Cooked dried fruits such as apricots, figs, raisins, and prunes

After twelve months, you can add the following:

+ Smooth nut and seed butters (natural only)

+ Whole milk fortified with vitamins A and D

+ Whole-milk dairy products

+ Soy milk fortified with calcium and vitamin D

+ Soy products

+ Whole eggs

+ Calcium-fortified orange juice

+ Textured vegetable protein (used as a meat substitute)

VEGAN: It's important to note that a vegan diet—the most restrictive—requires extra planning. If you are intent on feeding your child a vegan diet, it is best to consult your pediatrician or registered dietician.

NUTRITIONAL CONCERNS WITH A VEGETARIAN DIET

There are a few areas of concern that should be addressed if you are feeding your child a vegetarian diet.

NUTRITIOUS AND CALORIE-DENSE FOODS: Vegetarian diets tend to be high in fiber, consisting of a lot of grain foods, such as pasta, rice, breads, dry cereals, crackers, and teething biscuits, as well as fruits, vegetables, lentils, and beans. While a high-fiber diet is advantageous for most adults, it may present a problem for infants and toddlers. Large amounts of high-fiber foods will fill a baby's stomach, leaving insufficient space or appetite for more complete proteins, fat, cholesterol, and calorie-dense foods, which are very important to this age group.

To ensure that your child is getting enough protein, fat, calories, and nutrients (and not too much fiber), don't skimp on calorie-dense foods.

ZINC

From six to twelve months, the lacto-ovo, lacto vegetarian, and non-vegetarian diet is basically the same when it comes to zinc intake. After twelve months, the non-vegetarian toddler has meat, poultry, and fish, which adds zinc to his diet. The vegetarian toddler will have to add extra zinc by eating bran flakes, wheat germ, ground nuts and smooth nut butters, and dried agar in addition to the six-month list.

VITAMIN D

Vitamin D is obtained from D-fortified foods and sun exposure. Vitamin D is added to cow, soy, and rice milks and other milk substitutes, as well as some ready-to-eat cereals.

Exposing hands, arms, and face to the sun for five to fifteen minutes per day may provide sufficient vitamin D. However, if you use sunscreen on your baby six months and older (if you want to use sunscreen on a baby under six months you need a prescription from your pediatrician), the amount of vitamin D absorbed will be reduced. People with dark skin and people who live far north or in cloudy or smoggy areas may need increased exposure, but care should be taken to prevent sunburn.

(See "Sources of Vitamins" on page 26 for sources of vitamin D.)

VITAMIN B12

Vitamin B12 is found only in animal products—meat, poultry, shellfish, seafood, dairy foods, cheese, yogurt, eggs, milk, and milk products. It is also added to B12-fortified cereals, fortified soy milk and soy products, meat substitutes, and fortified nutritional yeast. Lacto-ovo and lacto-vegetarian babies usually get enough B12 from dairy products. Parents of vegan babies, however, should take extra care to make sure there is adequate amounts of B12 in the fortified foods they feed their child, or offer B12 supplements.

IRON-RICH FOODS

Six to twelve months, good sources of iron are:

- Iron-fortified baby cereal
- Egg yolks
- Tofu (prepared with calcium sulfate)
- Soybeans, garbanzo beans, lentils, navy beans, and lima beans
- Spinach, parsley, green beans, Swiss chard, and sea vegetables
- Dried figs, dates, prunes, and raisins

After twelve months, good sources of iron are:

- Bran flakes and other iron-fortified low-sugar dry cereals, oatmeal, Cream of Wheat, Malt-O-Meal Original, Hot Wheat Cereal
- Blackstrap molasses
- Some dried fruits (See "Minerals" on page 31.)
- Ground pumpkin seeds, ground nuts (pine nuts, cashews, almonds, macadamia, pistachio, walnuts, peanuts, and pecans), and smooth nut butters (sesame [tahini], peanut, and cashew)
- Dried agar (gelatin made from red algae)

SOY PRODUCTS

Protein-rich soy foods are also good sources of iron, calcium, and zinc, making them a staple of many vegetarian diets. Here are descriptions of some common soy products.

Tofu: soybean curd, made by adding nigari (evaporated seawater) to soy milk, similar to the curd-making process of cheese

Silken tofu: more finely textured than regular tofu

Soy nut butter: a spread made from roasted, ground soybeans, similar to peanut butter

Soy oil: cooking oil made from the pressed soybean

Tempeh: a cake of fermented soybeans with a nutty flavor and firm texture

Miso: fermented soybean paste, dissolved in water as a base for soups (Lighter miso is less strongly flavored than darker varieties.)

Textured vegetable protein (TVP): made from soybean flour and used as a meat substitute

TOFU

Tofu, one of the more common soy products, is rich in protein, contains all eight essential amino acids, and provides more than 35 percent of its calories in protein. Tofu is low in saturated fats and carbohydrates and has no cholesterol, preservatives, coloring, or additives. It contains lecithin and linoleic acid, which are important nutrients. A good source of calcium (when fortified), tofu also supplies sufficient amounts of choline and vitamin E. It is soft, very easily digested, and an excellent food for babies.

Like yogurt or cottage cheese, tofu is ready to eat and requires no preparation. It is versatile in cooking and can be steamed, microwaved, broiled, sautéed, toasted, or baked. Tofu can also be sliced, cubed, mashed, pureed, frozen, dried, or blended. Since it is almost tasteless, it mixes well with other ingredients and will pick up the flavor and aroma of whatever it is combined with.

To store tofu, place it in a clean container with some fresh water and store it in the refrigerator. If the water is changed every day, it will keep for a week. Tofu may also be frozen (although it may be a bit chewier when thawed): Just rinse it in water, wrap it in plastic, or freezer wrap, and freeze immediately. Thaw *completely* before using again.

Silken, soft tofu does not come in water. Follow the directions on the package for how to store silken tofu.

FISH AND SHELLFISH

There once was a fish.

(What more could you wish?)

He lived in the sea.

(Where else would he be?)

He was caught on a line.

(Whose line if not mine?)

So I brought him to you.

(What else should I do?)

—A FISH FOR YOU

Fish and shellfish are valuable parts of a healthy diet. They provide high-quality protein and omega-3 fatty acids and are low in saturated fat. However, according to the Natural Resources Defense Council (www.nrdc.org), most fish contain some mercury, and it has been shown that large amounts of mercury may harm an unborn baby or young child's nervous system. Therefore, young children should modify their intake of fish (along with women who are nursing, pregnant, or may become pregnant).

I recommend not feeding your child any fish until a year old. (See "Allergies and Food Intolerance" on page 46.) Then you can give 1 tablespoon of fish for each year of age.

Here are guidelines from the NRDC of the kinds of fish that are safe (and unsafe) for children and pregnant and nursing women to consume.

ENJOY THESE FISH

anchovies
butterfish
calamari (squid)
catfish
caviar (farmed)
clams
crab (king)
crawfish/crayfish
flounder

haddock
hake
herring
lobster (spiny/rock)
oysters
perch (saltwater)
pollock
wild salmon (not
farmed)

sardines
scallops
shad
shrimp
sole
sturgeon (farmed)
tilapia
trout (freshwater)
whitefish

EAT NO MORE THAN SIX 6-OUNCE SERVINGS PER MONTH

carp
cod
crab (blue)
crab (Dungeness)
crab (snow)
mahi mahi

monkfish
perch (freshwater)
skate
snapper
tuna (canned, chunk light)
tuna (fresh Pacific albacore)

EAT NO MORE THAN THREE 6-OUNCE SERVINGS PER MONTH

bass (saltwater)
bluefish
croaker
halibut

lobster (American/Maine)
sea trout
tuna (canned, white albacore)
tuna (fresh bluefin, ahi)

AVOID EATING

grouper
marlin
mackerel (king)
orange roughy

shark
swordfish
tilefish

1, 2, 3 Cook for Me contains only recipes with fish from the two safest levels of mercury content.

CANNED TUNA

The NRDC recommends that children avoid canned albacore or white tuna because the levels of mercury are quite high. In addition, parents should limit their children's consumption of canned light tuna to less than 1 ounce for every 12 pounds of body weight per week, in order to stay below the level of mercury the Environmental Protection Agency considers safe.

Safety Guidelines for Feeding Toddlers and Children Canned Light Tuna

CHILD'S WEIGHT	SAFE AMOUNT OF CHUNK LIGHT TUNA PER WEEK
24 pounds	Less than 2 ounces ($1/2$ cup or 4 tablespoons)
36 pounds	Less than 3 ounces ($3/8$ cup or 6 tablespoons)
48 pounds	Less than 4 ounces ($1/2$ cup or 8 tablespoons)
60 pounds	Less than 5 ounces ($5/8$ cup or 10 tablespoons)

PART III

Feeding Your Baby

HOMEMADE VS. STORE-BOUGHT BABY FOOD

Just walk down the "Baby Needs" aisle of any major supermarket, and you can see that a large selection of commercial baby food is available. Why not just use that? The jars seem cheap, and convenient as well. But the truth is store-bought baby food often offers poor value for the price and is generally insipid (try some and you'll see what I mean) and nutritionally inferior. Your baby deserves tasty and nourishing food, just as you do. Don't sacrifice the opportunity to start your baby on a healthy eating pattern that will last for a lifetime.

Commercial baby foods usually offer fewer nutrients per serving, simply because they contain less wholesome food. Manufacturers often dilute the ingredients with water or add nutritionless starch or flour to thicken food to a palatable consistency. As an example, a common type of baby food—Junior Chicken Egg Noodle Dinner—does not compare favorably with home-cooked chicken, noodles, and carrots. (See "Homemade vs. Store-Bought Ingredients" on page 64.) Homemade baby food doesn't contain any added water or fillers—unless you want it to—which is why the nutrients are higher in homemade baby food, sometimes dramatically higher across the board.

The choice does not have to be either/or. I realize that time is precious to parents today, and they are frequently overbooked with work, errands, and simply keeping the house in order. Understandably, convenience and time-saving can frequently trump our good intentions of feeding our children the healthiest food we can. Both homemade and store-bought baby foods have their value, and it is important to know what they are and to learn how to prepare homemade baby food correctly.

If you do buy commercially prepared foods for your baby, try to choose organic brands, (see "Organic Foods" on page 70) and when buying meat, selections that have just one ingredient—meat. Although the nutritional value in commercial strained chicken baby food is still not as high as home-cooked chicken, at least it is higher than in the Junior Chicken Egg Noodle Dinner.

Good, better best;
Never rest
Till "good" be "better"
And "better" "best."

—GOOD, BETTER, BEST

WHAT ABOUT ORGANIC BABY FOOD?

Organically grown commercial baby food is free from pesticides and other agricultural chemicals. Meats are free from added hormones, antibiotics, dyes, waxes, and other additives. So if you are going to use store-bought baby food, by all means, the organic and "all-natural" brands are the best choice. However, keep in mind that organic brands can be expensive, and they still do not taste as good as homemade.

HOMEMADE VS. STORE-BOUGHT INGREDIENTS

A jar of store-bought Junior Chicken Noodle Dinner contains the following ingredients (in order of prevalence):

Water, carrots, finely ground chicken, enriched egg noodles, rice flour, chicken fat, pear juice concentrate, onion powder, balsamic vinegar, and dried parsley.

Now, here is what's in your homemade chicken noodle dinner:

◆ Chicken: meat only, oven-roasted

◆ Carrots: boiled, drained, without salt

◆ Egg noodles: cooked without salt

Which dinner do you think is better for your baby?

Note that calories, fats, carbohydrates, protein, iron, zinc, vitamin B6, vitamin A, folate (folic acid), and cholesterol—all important nutrients that your baby needs at this age—are significantly higher in homemade baby food than in commercial foods.

Nutrition Analysis of Homemade and Commercially

CHICKEN	prepared baby food "Junior Chicken with Egg Noodles" 100 g	homemade roasted 100 g	prepared baby food "Strained Chicken" 100 g
Water	87.25 g	63.79 g	77.50 g
Calories	55	190	130
Protein	2.37 g	28.93 g	13.70 g
Fat	1.18 g	7.41 g	7.90 g
Carbs	8.79 g	0.00 g	0.10 g
Fiber	0.9 g	0.0 g	0.0 g
Sugars	1.07 g	-	-
MINERALS			
Calcium	21 mg	15 mg	64 mg
Iron	0.38 mg	1.21 mg	1.40 mg
Sodium	78 mg	86 mg	47 mg
Zinc	0.40 mg	2.1 mg	1.21 mg
VITAMINS			
Vit. C	0.1 mg	0.0 mg	1.7 mg
Vit. B6	0.05 mg	0.47 mg	0.20 mg
Folate	7 mcg	6 mcg	10 mcg
Vit. B12	0.01 mcg	0.33 mcg	0.40 mcg
Vit. A	1729 IU	53 IU	53 IU
Vit. E	0.176 mg	0.265 mg	0.400 mg
Cholesterol	9 mg	89 mg	61 mg

Reference: *USDA Nutrient Database for Standard Reference, Release 14 (July 2001).*

Prepared Chicken, Carrots, and Noodles

CARROTS		EGG
homemade boiled without salt	prepared baby food "Junior Carrots"	noodles boiled without salt
100 g	100 g	100 g
87.30 g	91.00 g	68.70 g
45	32	133
1.09 g	0.80 g	4.75 g
0.18 g	0.20 g	1.47 g
10.48 g	7.20 g	24.84 g
3.3 g	1.7 g	1.1 g
-	-	-
31 mg	23 mg	12 mg
0.6 mg	0.39 mg	1.59 mg
66 mg	49 mg	7 mg
0.3 mg	0.18 mg	0.62 mg
2.3 mg	5.5 mg	0.0
0.20 mg	0.08 mg	0.036 mg
13.9 mcg	17 mcg	64 mcg
0.00 mcg	0.00 mcg	0.09 mcg
24554 IU	11810 IU	20 IU
0.420 mg	0.520 mg	0.050 mg
0 mg	0 mg	33 mg

Note that the calcium value is relatively high in the commercial Strained Chicken, compared to homemade chicken. Because the commercial label only states "strained chicken," we do not know what part of the chicken has been ground, so it could include parts of a chicken that you would not normally cook at home.

Advantages and Disadvantages of Homemade and Store-Bought Baby Food

HOMEMADE	COMMERICALLY PREPARED
ADVANTAGES	**ADVANTAGES**
■ Better flavor.	■ Quick and easy.
■ Generally more nutritious than store-bought baby foods.	■ Safe because prepared under sanitary conditions.
■ Cheaper.	■ Some foods have been fortified with vitamins and minerals that otherwise might be missing in the diet.
■ Familiarizes your baby with family foods.	■ Consistency in quality.
■ Control of texture, making it more age-appropriate.	■ Practical when away from home.
■ Can be frozen.	■ Consistency in texture, which is a concern for infants at six months of age.
■ Control of ingredients (no added sugar, salt, or starches should be given in the first year), including what part of poultry and meats.	■ Good variety.
■ Fruit is better tasting and more nutritious than processed fruit with tapioca and sugar-laden desserts.	**DISADVANTAGES**
■ Convenience after eight months when you can offer soft foods and finger foods from the meals you prepare for the family.	■ Expensive compared to homemade.
■ Ability to offer separate foods (i.e., vegetables, rice, and meat), which older babies and toddlers prefer (Combined commercial baby food has only one taste, which seldom resembles meat, vegetables, rice, spaghetti, or noodles.)	■ Short shelf life. If the "use by" date has expired, the jar must be discarded.
	■ Short fridge life. Once a jar has been opened and refrigerated, it will stay fresh for only one to two days, after which it should be discarded.
DISADVANTAGES	■ Inconvenient: If fed from a jar and baby does not finish everything, the remaining food must be thrown away, as bacteria is transferred to the jar.
■ Food not prepared in adequate, clean, and sanitary conditions is susceptible to bacteria. Infants under twelve months could get sick more easily.	■ Freezing baby food from a jar is not recommended.
■ Parents may not make food for their baby that they themselves do not like. This will limit the baby's exposure to a large variety of foods.	■ If the vacuum seal button on the lid has popped, food is unsafe and the jar has to be discarded.
■ The danger of using food that is not fresh, has spoiled, is poor quality, has a low nutritional value, or has been grown in soil high in nitrate.	■ May be hard to transition to table food: Once used to commercial baby food from baby jars, toddler may refuse to eat the same vegetables from the table.
	■ Less nutritious: Some store-bought fruit has tapioca added but no vitamin C, making it more filling but less nutritious.
	■ Combination foods and dinners generally have less nutritional value by weight than single–ingredient foods. Commercially prepared baby desserts offer little nutrition but lots of sugar.
	■ Some jarred vegetables contain unnecessary salt and additives.
	■ Taste and nutritional value are generally inferior.

PREPARING HOMEMADE BABY FOOD

Wash the dishes, wipe the dishes

Ring the bell for tea;

Three good wishes, three good kisses,

I will give to thee.

—WASH THE DISHES

You probably already have most of the things you'll need to prepare your baby's food in your kitchen. You should not have to spend a lot of money on this. If any of the equipment is too pricey, put it on your wish list if someone throws you a baby shower.

EQUIPMENT

Infant and toddler foods can be prepared with many kinds of equipment, from a simple fork, sieve, or strainer to an expensive food processor. Alternatives are food mills, baby food grinders, and blenders. If using a wire strainer, make sure it is in very good condition so there is no danger of small pieces of mesh getting into the food. Here is a list of basic equipment for making baby food.

- One of the following, for pureeing: baby food grinder, small sieve or strainer, food mill, food processor, or blender
- Small scale
- Potato masher
- Steamer basket or saucepan with steamer
- Lidded saucepans in various sizes
- Frying pans in various sizes
- Wok, optional
- Oven- and microwave-safe baking dishes
- Microwave-safe glass bowls in various sizes
- Small covered containers for leftovers
- Individual ice cube trays for freezing
- Storage bags for freezing
- Measuring spoons and cups
- Paring knife and other knives in various sizes
- Vegetable peeler
- Vegetable brush (should be dishwater safe)
- Colored plastic or tempered glass cutting boards (dishwasher safe)
- Disposable dishrags or cloths that may be laundered
- Instant-read meat thermometer
- Plastic spray bottle (a spritzer) for lightly spraying oil when frying
- Rubber spatula
- Kitchen scissors
- Timer
- Thermos bottles (For outings or babysitters, small lunch-box thermos bottles are ideal for storing soft steamed or microwaved vegetables and fruits. When your baby can tolerate more textured foods, use several small thermos jars for pasta, rice, beans, cottage cheese, yogurt, meats, and soups.)

A WORD ABOUT NONSTICK COOKWARE

It has been thought for many years that Teflon-treated cookware may be harmful, especially if the surface is scratched. New studies are even more convincing that there is reason for concern. An ingredient in Teflon coating is one of hundreds of chemicals listed as showing up in the umbilical cord of newborn babies. Although the results are not definitive, I believe it better to err on the side of caution, and therefore I do not recommend using nonstick coated pans for any cooking purposes, and particularly in the preparation of children's food.

TIPS AND GUIDELINES FOR PREPARING YOUR BABY'S FOOD

The following guidelines should be followed any time you prepare food in your kitchen, whether it is for your baby, toddler, yourself, or the family.

Wash your hands thoroughly with hot, soapy water before preparation and in between handling raw and cooked food. Wash all surfaces, boards, and utensils with hot soapy water and rinse. Wash all equipment thoroughly in hot soapy water and rinse well before using. Take apart food grinders, blenders, and processors after each use and wash thoroughly. Dry each part before putting appliances together again. Use disposable paper towels or freshly laundered cloths and dishrags or sponges. (Sponges and scrubbers can be put in the dishwasher.)

Use fresh, good-quality food that has been stored in clean containers at correct refrigerator temperatures (no higher than 40°F, or 4°C). Fresh fruits and vegetables should be used within a few days of purchase. Root vegetables can be stored for at least one week. Frozen vegetables are a great option, as well, especially for busy parents who may not have the time to clean and chop fresh veggies. And don't worry that you're trading convenience for nutrition. In fact, the nutrient content of frozen vegetables is quite comparable to fresh produce. Frozen vegetables are usually processed within hours after being picked, thus "locking in" their nutrients and making them a better option than fresh produce which might take upwards of two weeks to reach your home.

Wash, scrub, or peel all fruits and vegetables. Remove seeds and pits.

Wash fish, meats (except ground meats), and poultry before preparing. Remove skin, bones, gristle, fat, and connective tissue. Use a separate cutting board for all meats to reduce the risk of cross-contamination.

For optimum nutrition, microwave, steam, stir-fry, bake, broil, or roast food. Boiling foods allows nutrients to leech into the water, so if you do boil vegetables or fruit, use as little water as possible and save the cooking water for pureeing or soups.

Cook meat to a temperature of at least 160°F (70°C). Use an instant-read meat thermometer. Ground meat should be cooked until there is no red or pink showing.

Grind tough food, seeds, and nuts. Puree, mash, or cut food into small pieces according to age. (Follow the instructions for each month of the recipe preparation): Use breast milk, formula, juice, or water to thin food to the desired consistency.

When preparing family meals, remove the baby's portion before adding salt, sugar, or spicy seasoning.

Leftover food in the feeding dish should be discarded. Leftovers from the pan or serving dish can be put in clean, covered containers and refrigerated immediately. Refrigerated leftovers should be eaten within four days, according to the U.S. Department of Agriculture. The USDA also recommends the following time limits for preventing refrigerated leftovers from spoiling or becoming dangerous to eat.

* Hot dogs (opened package) , 1 week

* Cooked meat and meat casseroles, 3 to 4 days

* Soups and stews (vegetables or meat added), 3 to 4 days

* Cooked poultry casseroles, 3 to 4 days

* Cooked poultry pieces, plain, 3 to 4 days

* Cooked poultry pieces covered with gravy/broth, 1 to 2 days

* Chicken nuggets, 1 to 2 days

ORGANIC FOODS

WHAT DOES "ORGANIC" MEAN?

The term "organic" applies to both animal and plant foods. In 2002, the U.S. Department of Agriculture (USDA) issued national organic standards to clearly define foods that can be labeled as organic. To locate organic foods that meet the USDA standards in your favorite market, look for the word "organic" and a small sticker version of the USDA organic seal on vegetables and fruit or on the sign above the organic produce display. Labels that contain the words "natural," "free-range," and "hormone-free" do not mean organic.

The strict organic standards apply to food grown in the U.S. and foods imported from other countries. Before a product can be labeled organic, a USDA-approved certifier inspects the farm where the food is grown to make sure the farmer is in compliance with the regulations. Companies that handle or process organic food before it gets to the supermarket or restaurant must be certified as well.

The USDA's national organic standards prohibits:

- Most synthetic fertilizers and pesticides
- Sewage sludge fertilizers
- Genetic engineering
- Growth hormones
- Irradiation
- Antibiotics
- Artificial ingredients

THE ORGANIC ADVANTAGE

Because babies and toddlers are so sensitive to additives, it makes sense to feed them organic foods, even if you don't eat them yourself. In conventionally grown produce, some fruits and vegetables have been shown to have high levels of pesticide residues that are harmful, particularly to children.

Young children are developing brain function and internal organs to last a lifetime. Eating organic foods provides them with protection from exposure to some pesticides that can have harmful neurological effects, according to a study funded by the Environmental Protection Agency (EPA). Young children are more vulnerable to developmental damage from pesticide residues on foods, because of their fast growth and speedy metabolisms, and partly because of their smaller size, which means they eat more fruits and vegetables in relation to their weight than adults do. Most tests done by the EPA set the acceptable risk levels for pesticide residues for adults, not little children.

In addition, organically grown foods are also better for the health of our planet. They are cultivated using farming practices that work to preserve and protect the environment.

THE ORGANIC CHECKLIST

These fruits and vegetables have the highest and lowest levels of pesticide residues, according to the EPA and the Environmental Working Group (EWG), a research and advocacy organization.

GO ORGANIC

Organic products can now carry a "USDA Organic" seal, which guaranties that at least 95 percent of the product's ingredients have been grown without the use of insecticides, herbicides, fungicides, or chemical fertilizers. (See Organic Foods, beginning on page 70.) There is no doubt that it is safer for your baby if you use organic produce and packaged goods. Unfortunately, organic products are usually more expensive than conventional products. However, if you could use as much organic food as possible, at least until your baby is one year old (the time when her immune system is most vulnerable), it will be a real benefit. Organic foods are found in many areas of the country, in local specialty and health-food stores and in national supermarket chains.

Highest Levels of Pesticide Residues

FRUITS	VEGETABLES
■ Apples	■ Bell peppers
■ Cantaloupes	■ Celery
■ Cherries	■ Potatoes
■ Grapes (domestic and imported)	■ Green beans
■ Nectarines	■ Spinach
■ Peaches	• Winter squash
■ Pears	
■ Red raspberries	
■ Strawberries	

Lowest Levels of Pesticide Residues

FRUITS	VEGETABLES
▪ Bananas	▪ Asparagus
▪ Kiwis	▪ Avocados
▪ Mangoes	▪ Broccoli
▪ Papayas	▪ Cauliflower
▪ Pineapples	▪ Corn (sweet)
	▪ Onions
	▪ Peas (sweet)

Organic food is expensive. If you're on a tight budget, you may be torn between the desire to "do the right thing" for your baby and justifying the expense. Don't despair—there are two alternatives you can try without going all the way organic. One is growing your own fruits and vegetables without adding any harmful pesticides, and supplementing your produce with organic meats and dairy products. The other is to focus on the foods that are most heavily dosed with chemicals and buy those organically grown, rather than buying all organic.

ORGANIC MILK

Although milk is an important food source in your toddler's diet, many questions have been raised about the safety of our milk sources. How can we be confident that milk is safe for our children, and who is responsible for ensuring milk safety? These are difficult questions with long and complex answers that are beyond the scope of this book. In short, however, there are two opposite factions; those who say that the milk is safe for our children to drink, and those who believe it is not. At the center of the debate is a synthetic form of a bovine growth hormone given to cows to stimulate milk production called recombinant bovine growth hormone, or rBST. (The bovine growth hormone, called BGH or BST, is naturally produced in cattle.) The U.S. Food and Drug Administration (FDA) concluded that milk from cows that are supplemented with rBST is safe. An article from the Dairy Farmers of Oregon entitled, "Product Information on Milk and Health Facts" says that in addition to the FDA the following organizations have deemed (both) BST and rBST milk safe for human consumption: The American Medical Association,

American Dietetic Association, and the National Institutes of Health.

Environmental groups, organic consumer groups, and food safety advocacy organizations such as the Center for Food Safety, question the FDA's conclusion. Canada and the European Union countries have gone so far as to ban the use of the synthetic hormone rBGH and rBST in cows. Critics say that cows treated with rBST frequently develop significant health problems, such as udder infections. Dairy farmers treat these infections with antibiotics. The concern is that residues from these antibiotics end up in the milk we drink, which creates antibiotic resistant bacteria in humans and erodes the efficacy of the antibiotics we use to treat infections. So as consumers and parents concerned about our children's health, what can we do? The safest thing to do is to buy organic milk and organic dairy products. Alternatively, you could request that your market or grocery store buy milk that is labeled rBGH or rBST-free. Keep in mind, however, there is no mandatory federal labeling law yet, and different states have different laws and rules about labeling.

STORE-BOUGHT ORGANIC BABY FOOD

Organically grown commercial baby food is free from pesticides and other agricultural chemicals. Meats are free from added hormones, antibiotics, dyes, waxes and other additives. However, they are expensive, and do not taste as good as home-cooked organic food. Also, oftentimes in commercial baby food, all the different foods are mixed together and lack age-appropriate textures. You will be better off buying organic meats and produce to make your own baby food.

WHAT YOU CAN DO

In 1993, the National Academy of Sciences released a report on the effectiveness of removing pesticide residues in produce by washing, peeling, and cooking. The result indicates that residue levels in most produce are substantially reduced after washing, peeling, and cooking. This may not get rid of all the residues, but researchers stress that consumers--even young children--should not reduce consumption of fruits and vegetables. The best option is to eat a varied diet, wash all produce, and choose organic when possible to reduce exposure to potentially harmful chemicals.

Urge your local supermarket or produce supplier to buy fruits and vegetables grown without high-risk pesticides. This may eventually force growers and produce buyers to make available for you a wider selection of safe produce.

A recent study funded by the Environmental Protection Agency turned up surprisingly good news. When parents switched their children to organic food, the pesticide levels in their bodies quickly dropped to almost undetectable levels, and remained there until the parents switched back to conventionally grown foods. These dramatic results mean that, even if you didn't start your baby or toddler out on organic foods, switching now will quickly flush the toxins from your child's system.

Hush, baby, my dolly,

I pray you don't cry

And I'll give you some bread,

and some milk by-and-by;

Or perhaps you like custard,

or, maybe a tart,

Then to either you're welcome,

with all my heart.

—HUSH, BABY, MY DOLLY

INTRODUCING SOLID FOOD

How do you know if your baby is ready for solid food? Each baby is unique, but around six months most babies are ready to start solids (but note that the very first food offered is really semi-liquid). Here are some signs to look for to see if your baby is ready.

- Your baby consumes more than 32 ounces of breast milk or formula a day.

- The birth weight has doubled.

- Your infant can hold his neck steady and sit up with support.

- Baby shows interest in food when others are eating.

- Baby expresses a desire for food by leaning toward a spoon with an open mouth when hungry, or leaning back and turning away when full.

Here are some physiological reasons for your baby to start eating semi-solid food.

- At six months, most of the iron supply a baby is born with has been used up.

- Breast milk is not an adequate source of iron and it must be supplemented.

- Enzymes needed to digest solid food are now present.

- Infants are now able to swallow semi-solids without choking. (Babies are born with a strong sucking and extrusion reflex, which makes them instinctively push the tongue out. Until this reflex disappears, starting at around four months, solids will automatically be pushed out of the mouth.)

- Up-and-down chewing ability begins around six months.

Six months of age is generally a good time for infants to get familiar with spoon-feeding and the taste and texture of various foods. If it is postponed much longer than six months, baby may be less willing to accept a wide variety of solids. Babies need to learn how to chew and swallow, so do not give semi-solids in a bottle.

YOUR BABY'S FIRST MEAL

Rice cereal is the best first food to feed your baby, because it is a single grain, iron-fortified infant cereal, easily digested, least likely to cause an intolerance or allergic reaction, and contains important nutrients.

For your baby's first meal, mix 1 teaspoon rice cereal with 4 to 5 teaspoons warm breast milk, formula, or water or follow the directions on the box.

Fill a small, plastic-coated baby spoon with a little of the cereal and gently put it on your baby's tongue. The first few times the cereal may wind up on her little face or the bib, which is okay. Relax and enjoy this new experience; if you're relaxed, your baby will be as well. You are learning how to feed your baby, and your baby is learning how to eat. In a short time you will both have mastered it. Try one more spoon, and continue, unless she refuses, until the cereal is gone. This may seem like a tiny amount, but these initial feedings are mostly to get your baby used to new textures and taste. Most nourishment is still obtained from breast milk or formula.

The best time for the very first meal is in the morning, after a partial breast- or bottle-feeding, when your little one is not too hungry. After this new treat, offer the breast or bottle again.

Once rice cereal is well tolerated, gradually increase the amount to 3 to 4 tablespoons. Follow the directions on the box.

These can be divided into two daily feedings. Remember, never force your baby to finish food that is refused.

ADDING NEW FOODS

If your infant refuses a new food, remove it and offer it again after a few days. Babies who are coaxed or forced to eat a new food may

WHAT KIND OF CEREAL?

It is preferable to buy infant cereals fortified with iron and zinc, rather than to make your own, until your baby is at least one year old. However, if your infant is drinking an iron-fortified formula, talk to your pediatrician about a possible excess of iron.

FIRST FOODS

Good first fruits:

- Very ripe banana, soft and well mashed
- Cooked Pureed Pear (page 84)
- Cooked Pureed Apple (page 84)

Good first vegetables:

- Pureed Sweet Potato (page 85)
- Pureed Green Peas (page 86)

learn to dislike it. After retrying foods with no pressure, infants will often accept food they initially rejected.

CEREALS: After three or four days of accepting rice cereal, introduce another single-grain, iron-fortified cereal, such as barley or oatmeal. Use the same rule every time you introduce a new food: Serve it for three to four days and watch carefully for any signs of intolerance or allergy before trying another. (See "Allergies and Food Intolerance" on page 46.)

JUICE: After you have introduced the variety of cereals, try some fruit juices. Start with apple, white grape, or pear juice. At this age, it is best to use commercial baby juice. Dilute the juice half and half with water and offer it in a small cup with a covered lid and drinking spout. Start with 1 ounce and gradually work up to 4 ounces of diluted juice until the baby is eight months old. After eight months, you do not need to dilute juices, but don't serve more than 1/2 cup a day. Too much juice can spoil your baby's appetite and cause cramping and diarrhea.

FRUITS AND VEGGIES: Once your baby is comfortable with cereals, try other new foods. Start with fruits or with vegetables, or alternate between the two. Use fruits and vegetables rich in vitamin C; they should be cooked, peeled, and pureed. Use the same method introducing fruits and vegetables as you did with cereals. Start with 1 tablespoon per serving. After a day or two, if there is no sign of intolerance or allergy, add another tablespoon. Gradually increase the amount to 2 to 4 tablespoons twice daily (1/4 to 1/2 cup a day total), depending on your baby's appetite.

When first introducing vegetables, choose those that are mild tasting and rich in vitamins A and C. These vegetables will be ample to take your baby into the seventh month.

See the Introducing Solids Summary chart on page 81 for a rundown on when you can introduce specific foods and the Month-By-Month Feeding Guides (starting on page 78) for more detailed listings.

GUIDELINES FOR FEEDING SOLIDS, SIX- TO TWELVE-MONTH-OLDS

1. Never give food while your baby is lying down, crying, or laughing.

2. Always test food first for appropriate temperature.

3. Don't add salt, spices, or sweeteners to any foods or juices during the first twelve months. (An infant's taste buds are sensitive enough to enjoy the natural flavors of food without any enhancement.)

4. Don't give excessive amounts of juice. This may decrease your baby's desire for nursing or formula, which is still the most important food source.

5. Try only one new food at a time. When introducing a new food, serve it for three or four days, watching carefully for any reaction, before moving on to another new food.

6. Bananas should be very ripe. During baby's sixth and seventh months, all other fruits should be peeled, cored or pitted, cooked, and pureed. All vegetables should be peeled, cooked, and pureed during the sixth and seventh months.

7. There may be changes in your baby's bowel movements once started on solids. This is normal. A breast-fed baby will probably have more frequent stools once started on solids, while there may be no change with a bottle-fed baby. Keep in mind that most fruits, especially prunes, have a mild laxative effect, which is worth knowing if your baby is constipated.

8. If your baby opens his mouth, he may be asking for food. When the mouth is shut, food is spat out, or his head turns away, it probably means he does not like the food or he is full.

9. Never force your baby to eat. Remove the food and offer it again when he indicates he is hungry and ready to eat.

10. Allow infants to eat at their own pace.

11. If the new food is rejected, wait a few days and try again. Be patient; it may take up to ten attempts. If you don't force the food, your baby may eventually accept it without any fuss.

12. Do not dilute cereal and feed it from a bottle.

13. If using commercial baby food, do not serve it directly from the jar. This will prevent your baby's saliva from spoiling the rest of the food.

14. Avoid using teething pain relief medicine before mealtimes, as it may make chewing difficult.

PART IV

Baby's Month-by-Month Feeding Guide and Recipes

FEEDING YOUR BABY, SIX TO TWELVE MONTHS

UNTIL YOUR BABY IS A YEAR OLD, HER main nutrition will continue to come from nursing or formula. Even so, this is a time to start introducing her to new food so she can gradually get used to different flavors and textures. Some of the food will also contribute needed vitamins and minerals. See page 81 for the Introducing Solids Summary chart, detailing when you can offer specific foods to your baby.

💡 *Before you start feeding your baby, you'll want to read the chapters on Allergies and Food Intolerance (page 46) and Choking Hazards (page 50). And before you start making the recipes, read the chapter on Preparing Homemade Baby Food (page 67).*

Each monthly chapter here also includes a detailed list of foods to introduce, along with feeding instructions appropriate to the age group and recipes for making your baby's meals.

A broad selection of recipes is included, from which your baby will eventually choose his favorites. The more variety in your little one's diet, the greater the probability that his meals will contain all the nutrients he needs. In addition, if your baby is used to eating many different foods, it will be easier to find several he likes and will accept if his appetite occasionally declines or becomes irregular.

Many of the recipes are simple to make and are probably familiar to you. (Occasionally, when there is extra food left over after you prepare your baby's recipe, I give suggestions for using the leftover ingredients in an adult/family recipe.) Others may be unknown to your family, but all are nutritious and part of a balanced diet. But remember, for babies, every newly introduced food is unknown and unusual and may take some getting used to.

Here are a few notes about the recipes:

COOKING METHODS: Many of the baby recipes can be prepared in several ways: on the stovetop, baked, or in the microwave. Look for the ◎ Stovetop, ▭ Microwave, and ▣ Baking icons in the recipes for quick identification. 💡 *I recommend microwaving; it is a quick way to prepare fruit and vegetables and retains more of the vitamins.*

FATS AND OILS: When using oil, choose regular olive oil (also called *traditional* or *classical*) unless extra-virgin olive oil or other oils are suggested. The taste is more gentle. If using butter, it should be unsalted. Don't skip on the fat. At this age, fat and cholesterol are important nutrients in your baby's diet. Half of her

MICROWAVE COOKING

When you use the microwave for cooking, always use microwave-safe dishes (ideally glass). Use a glass lid or plate as a cover instead of plastic or plastic wrap, which could leach chemicals into the food. Parchment paper is also safe. ❗ **Never use metal or tinfoil in the microwave. Use an oven mitt or towel when removing dishes from the microwave oven to prevent getting burned.**

Microwave directions in these recipes are based on an 800-watt oven. Keep in mind that your cooking time may vary depending on the wattage of your oven.

calorie intake should come from fat. For more on fats in your baby's diet, see page 19.

PRODUCE: Buy fresh produce and prepare within a day to preserve the vitamins. When boiling fruit and vegetables, use very little water to preserve nutrients.

YOGURT: In the yogurt recipes, use plain yogurt. Be sure the yogurt is not sweetened with honey. Do not mistake vanilla yogurt with plain yogurt—they should not be used interchangeably in these recipes. Vanilla yogurt has a high sugar content and should only be used as a sweetener in moderation. Whole-milk yogurt is preferable.

PUREEING: Although I recommend a food processor or blender for pureeing or mashing, a food mill, baby grinder, fork, or strainer may also be used. If the puree needs thinning, use breast milk, formula, juice, or water.

LEFTOVERS: When making larger quantities of baby recipes, put aside the amount needed for the next two days and freeze the remainder (but never leftovers from the plate) in an ice cube tray. Once frozen, remove the cubes from the tray and place in a resealable plastic bag or freezer bag, which should be labeled and dated. It is safe to keep frozen, homemade baby food in the freezer for up to a month. But I would suggest using the frozen baby food within one to two weeks. Defrost cubes overnight in the refrigerator as needed. Warm in the microwave for 10 seconds. Stir well and ensure that the temperature is lukewarm throughout. The consistency and taste remains virtually unchanged.

SEASONINGS: Do not add salt, spices, sugar, or sweeteners to your baby's food at this time (six to twelve months). Instead, season with pureed fruit or fruit juice.

Introducing Solids

Use the chart below as a quick reference for when you can introduce particular foods to your baby. This information is also given in the Monthly Feeding Guides.

Introducing Solids Summary (6 to 8 Months)

	SIX MONTHS	SEVEN MONTHS	EIGHT MONTHS
Iron-Fortified Baby Cereal, cooked	Single-grain rice, barley, and oatmeal		
Juice	Juice, diluted half-and-half with water: apple, pear, and white grape	Baby juice, diluted half-and-half with water: peach, nectarine, and prune	Regular juice: apricot and carrot
Vegetables	Sweet potatoes and peas	Acorn squash, butternut squash, potatoes, yellow squash, and zucchini	Carrots, string beans, wax beans
Fruits	Apples, pears, and very ripe bananas	Nectarines, peaches, plums, and prunes	Very ripe apricots or dried (unsulfured) cooked apricots
Dairy			
Miscellaneous			Hard-cooked egg yolk, rice, rice noodles, barley Finger food: baby crackers (oat or rice), plain oat Cheerios, pieces of peeled soft fruit (fresh or cooked), ripe banana slices, soft cooked vegetable pieces, and cut cooked rice noodles

Introducing Solids Summary (9 to 11 Months)

	NINE MONTHS	TEN MONTHS	ELEVEN MONTHS
Fortified Baby Cereal, cooked		Single-grain wheat	Rice, Cream of Wheat, oatmeal, barley, multigrain cereal
Juice	Regular juice: red grape, cantaloupe, papaya nectar	Regular juice: blueberry, cherry, kiwi	Regular juice: cranberry, pineapple, raspberry
Vegetables	Broccoli, cauliflower	cabbage, parsnip, leek, red, green, orange or yellow bell pepper (all cooked), parsley, and celery (well cooked)	Brussels sprouts, turnips, rutabaga, beets, kale, (all cooked), romaine lettuce
Fruits	Avocado, cantaloupe, papaya	Kiwi, melon, cherries (halved and pitted), blueberries	Pineapple, raisins (softened or cooked), grapes, (seeded and halved), figs, raspberries
Dairy	Yogurt	Cream cheese, mascarpone, fresh or soft mozzarella, Jack, Swiss	Cottage cheese, whole-fat ricotta, cheddar, goat, Parmesan, Romano
Miscellaneous		Tofu, soy, pancakes, waffles Legumes: lentils and split peas	Polenta, couscous Legumes: black, white, or red beans, lima beans, refried beans

SIX MONTHS

Away down south where bananas grow

A grasshopper stepped on an elephant's toe.

The elephant cried with tears in his eyes,

"Pick on someone your own size."

Your six-month-old should have five feedings (totaling 28 to 32 ounces) a day of nursing or formula, which will continue to provide the principal nutrition. However, you can begin to offer your little one solid foods. First, you start with baby cereal; rice is a good choice. Try one, two, or three teaspoons, and then let your baby decide if he wants more. You can give him cereal twice a day if you want to. At this stage, you are just teaching your baby how to eat and get used to new tastes and textures. After three days, if your baby tolerates the cereal well, you can try a fruit (for three days), then a vegetable (for three days). If the baby tolerates the rice cereal, the one fruit and one vegetable, you can serve all three during one day, serving the fruit with the cereal or with the vegetable. In other words, once you know that your baby tolerates the foods, you can mix them.

Solid foods you can begin to introduce to your baby are:

- Iron-fortified baby cereal, cooked: single-grain rice, barley, or oatmeal
- **VEGETABLES:** sweet potatoes and peas
- **FRUIT:** apples, pears, and very ripe bananas
- Baby juice (diluted half-and-half with water): apple, pear, and white grape
- *Single-grain cereal* means that you should not mix different grains together (for example, rice and barley or rice and oatmeal). You want to start with a single-grain cereal because if he has a reaction to a mixed-grain cereal, you won't know which grain he is reacting to.
- All vegetables and fruits (with the exception of bananas) should be washed, peeled, cored, and cooked.
- All food should be pureed or strained. Start with a semi-liquid consistency and change to a more solid consistency as your baby's eating skills develop. To thin pureed food, use a few drops of breast milk, formula, water, or age-appropriate juice.
- Food and drink should be lukewarm (about the temperature of breast milk).
- Start with small portions, a couple of teaspoons, and let your baby decide if he wants more.
- Introduce new foods one at a time, every three days or so, and watch for reactions. (See "Allergies and Food Intolerance" on page 46 .)

RECIPES

Pureed Apple 👶

To double the quantity, use two apples and follow the same method. I would not use Granny Smith apples in this recipe, because they tend to be sour.

- 1 sweet, ripe apple (Fuji, gala, or golden delicious are all good choices.)
- ¼ to ⅓ cup (60 to 75 ml) water (if cooking on stovetop)

▭ Wash, quarter, and core, but do not peel the apple. Place the apple on a plate cut sides down. Microwave on high, uncovered, 3 to 4 minutes, until the apple is soft. Let the apple cool, then peel. Blend in a food processor 30 seconds, or until the apple is completely pureed.

◎ Wash, quarter, core, and peel the apple and cut into small pieces. Add ¼ to ⅓ cup (60 to 75 ml) water to a small saucepan and bring to a boil. Add the apple pieces to the boiling water, cover, reduce the heat, and simmer about 10 minutes, or until the apple is soft. Check occasionally to see if you need to add more water. Blend the apple and water in a food processor 1 to 2 minutes until the apple is completely pureed. If needed, add 1 to 2 tablespoons (14 to 28 ml) liquid.

YIELD: *Makes 6 heaping tablespoons (scant ½ cup)*

EACH WITH: 6.0 calories; 0.0 gm total fat; 0.0 gm saturated fat; 0.0 mg cholesterol; 0.1 mg sodium; 1.5 gm carbohydrate; 0.3 gm dietary fiber; 0.0 gm protein; 0.5 mg calcium; 0.0 mg iron; 4.3 IU vitamin A; 0.0 mg vitamin C.

Pureed Pear 👶

- 1 sweet, ripe pear (Bartlett, Anjou, Bosc, or any variety)

▭ Wash, quarter, core, and peel the pear. Place it on a plate and microwave on high 5 minutes, or until soft. Blend in a food processor 30 seconds, or until the pear is completely pureed.

◎ Wash, quarter, core, and peel the pear and cut into small pieces. Add ¼ to ⅓ cup (60 to 75 ml) water to a small saucepan and bring to a boil. Add the pear pieces to the boiling water, cover, reduce the heat, and simmer about 10 minutes, or until the pear is soft. Check occasionally to see if you need to add more water. Blend in a food processor 30 seconds, or until the pear is completely pureed.

YIELD: *Makes about 6 tablespoons*

EACH WITH: 16.0 calories; 0.0 gm total fat; 0.0 gm saturated fat; 0.0 mg cholesterol; 0.3 mg sodium; 4.3 gm carbohydrate; 0.9 gm dietary fiber; 0.1 gm protein; 2.5 mg calcium; 0.0 mg iron; 6.4 IU vitamin A; 1.2 mg vitamin C.

Pureed Sweet Potato

- 1 sweet potato (about 1/2 pound, or 225 g)

- 1/2 to 1 cup (120 to 235 ml) water, apple juice, pear juice, breast milk, or formula

- Oil (if baking)

Wash the sweet potato and prick the skin with a fork in several places. Microwave on high 8 to 10 minutes, until the potato is soft. Let the potato cool until it is easy to handle and peel. Cut the potato into chunks. Place in a food processor with 1/2 cup (120 ml) liquid and puree until completely smooth. Add up to 1/2 cup (120 ml) additional liquid if needed.

Preheat the oven to 400°F (200°C, or gas mark 6). Wash and scrub the sweet potato. Dry, rub with a little oil, and place on a baking sheet. Bake until soft, 30 to 50 minutes, depending on size.

Cool, peel, and chop into chunks. Place in a food processor with 1/2 cup (120 ml) liquid and puree until completely smooth. Add another 1/2 cup (120 ml) additional liquid if needed.

Sweet potatoes that are greased before baking peel easily. Do not wrap them in tinfoil, because they will steam and loose the sweet, syrupy flavor of a baked potato.

YIELD: *Makes 12 tablespoons or 3/5 cup*

APPROXIMATE SERVING SIZE: 2 tablespoons. **EACH WITH:** 17.1 calories; 0.0 gm total fat; 0.0 gm saturated fat; 0.0 mg cholesterol; 6.8 mg sodium; 3.9 gm carbohydrate; 0.6 gm dietary fiber; 0.4 gm protein; 7.2 mg calcium; 0.1 mg iron; 3651.4 IU vitamin A; 3.7 mg vitamin C.

Sweet Potato and Banana

- 3 teaspoons Pureed Sweet Potato (page 85)

- 3 teaspoons pureed banana

Mix together the sweet potato and banana. Serve with a little breast milk or formula on the side.

VARIATION: Use pureed apple or pureed pear instead of the banana.

YIELD: *1 baby serving*

APPROXIMATE SERVING SIZE: 2 tablespoons. **EACH WITH:** 23.8 calories; 0.1 gm total fat; 0.0 gm saturated fat; 0.0 mg cholesterol; 4.6 mg sodium; 5.8 gm carbohydrate; 0.8 gm dietary fiber; 0.4 gm protein; 5.5 mg calcium; 0.1 mg iron; 2411.3 IU vitamin A; 3.7 mg vitamin C.

SWEET POTATOES

Sweet potatoes are one of the most nutritious vegetables you can feed your baby. For the most food value, choose sweet potatoes of a deep orange color. The more traditional white flesh types are sometimes mistakenly called yams in the United States, but they are actually sweet potatoes, and the terms are used interchangeably. ⚪ A baked sweet potato contains about 10 milligrams of beta-carotene, about twice the adult RDA of vitamin A, 42 percent of the adult RDA for vitamin C, or some B vitamins (including folic acid), iron, vitamin E, magnesium, and calcium. One sweet potato has about 141 calories—about the same number as white potatoes, but with many more nutrients. Their sweet taste is usually pleasing to babies and toddlers. Don't refrigerate sweet potatoes; it alters the taste when cooked. Store sweet potatoes in a dry, dark place at 55 to 60°F (13 to 16°C) for no longer than 2 weeks. Cooked sweet potatoes can be stored in the refrigerator for up to 1 week. Sweet potato dishes freeze well.

Pureed Green Peas 👶

You may want to add breast milk or formula to mellow the taste until your baby is used to the flavor of peas.

- 1 cup (160 g) fresh or frozen peas
- ¼ cup (60 ml) water
- ¼ cup (60 ml) breast milk or formula

▭ Place the peas and water in a glass dish. Cover and microwave on high about 5 minutes, or until the peas are soft. Place the peas in a blender with the breast milk or formula and puree until smooth, about 1 minute. Adjust the amount of liquid depending on how thin you want the puree.

◎ Bring the water to a boil in a small pan. Add the peas and return to a boil. Cover, reduce the heat to low, and simmer 5 to 6 minutes, or until the peas are tender. Stir once during cooking. Place the peas and the water in a food processor. Add the breast milk or formula and puree until smooth, about 1 minute.

🔘 *Peas cooked in the microwave contain twice as much vitamin C as commercially prepared baby food strained peas.*

YIELD: *Makes 6 tablespoons*

EACH WITH: 22.4 calories; 0.1 gm total fat; 0.0 gm saturated fat; 0.0 mg cholesterol; 0.8 mg sodium; 4.2 gm carbohydrate; 1.5 gm dietary fiber; 1.4 gm protein; 7.2 mg calcium; 0.4 mg iron; 213.6 IU vitamin A; 3.8 mg vitamin C.

SEVEN MONTHS

Peter, Peter, pumpkin eater.

Had a wife and couldn't keep her;

He put her in a pumpkin shell,

And there he kept her very well.

—PETER, PETER, PUMPKIN EATER

At seven months, your baby should be having five feedings (26 to 32 ounces, or 765 to 896 ml) a day of breast milk or formula, which still provides the primary nutrition. Your little one is now developing an up-and-down chewing motion. Continue to offer the foods from the six months guide, but begin to change to a soft, mashed texture instead of pureed. After seven months, you can make these additions to your baby's diet:

- **VEGETABLES:** acorn squash, butternut squash, potatoes, yellow squash, and zucchini

- **FRUITS:** nectarines, peaches, plums, and prunes

- **BABY JUICE (DILUTED HALF-AND-HALF WITH WATER):** peach, nectarine, and prune

- Continue feeding iron-fortified cereal, eventually working the amount up to $1/4$ cup and then $1/2$ cup, which can be divided into two $1/4$ cup feedings a day. Serve with juice or fruits rich in vitamin C.

- Vegetables should be washed, peeled (seeds removed), and cooked. Exceptions are summer squashes, such as zucchini and yellow crookneck, which do not need to be peeled.

- Apples should still be washed, peeled, cored, and cooked, then mashed. Pears, if very ripe, can be washed, peeled, and cored, and then mashed well with a fork (without cooking). Fresh, ripe peaches, plums, and nectarines can also be washed, peeled, pitted, and pureed (without cooking).

- Dilute juice half-and-half with water. Give no more than $1/2$ cup diluted juice a day.

- Both food and drink should be lukewarm or at room temperature.

- Continue to introduce new foods one at a time every three days or so and watch for reactions.

Pureed Butternut Squash 👶

When first introducing this squash to your baby, mix it with a little apple puree, breast milk, or formula.

- 1 butternut squash (about 1 pound, or 455 g)
- 2 tablespoons to ½ cup (28 ml to 120) water
- Oil (if baking)
- Breast milk, formula, or apple juice (if microwaving or baking)

💡 *If peeling the squash is too time-consuming, cut it in half and microwave on high for 10 minutes, or until soft. Or bake at 400°F (200°C, or gas mark 6) 30 minutes and remove the flesh.*

⊡ Wash the squash, cut in half, then into eighths. Peel the squash and discard the seeds and strings. Cut into 1-inch (2.5-cm) cubes. Place the squash in a microwave-safe dish, add 2 tablespoons (28 ml) water, and cover. Microwave on high 10 minutes, or until soft. Puree in a food processor 30 seconds.

Alternatively, cut the squash in half. Remove the seeds and strings. Add the water. Microwave on high in a covered microwave-safe dish about 8 minutes, or until tender. Let it stand 5 to 10 minutes. Scoop out the flesh and puree in a food processor, adding a little breast milk, formula, or apple juice if needed .

◎ Wash the squash, cut in half, then into eighths. Peel the squash and discard the seeds and strings. Cut into 1-inch (2.5-cm) cubes. Place the squash in a small pan with ½ cup (120 ml) water. Cover and bring to a boil. Reduce the heat and simmer 10 minutes. Pour the squash and water into a food processor and pulse until pureed, about 30 seconds.

▦ Preheat the oven to 400°F (200°C, or gas mark 6). Cut the squash in half and scoop out the seeds and strings. Brush the cut sides with a little oil; place the squash cut sides down on a baking sheet (or tinfoil or glass baking dish). Bake 30 to 45 minutes, or until the squash is soft. Place upright and scoop out the flesh and puree in a food processor, adding a little breast milk, formula, or apple juice if needed.

YIELD: *Makes about 16 t ablespoons or 1 cup*

EACH WITH: 5.1 calories; 0.0 gm total fat; 0.0 gm saturated fat; 0.0 mg cholesterol; 0.5 mg sodium; 1.3 gm carbohydrate; 0.0 gm dietary fiber; 0.1 gm protein; 5.3 mg calcium; 0.1 mg iron; 1429.2 IU vitamin A; 1.9 mg vitamin C.

👪 **MAKE IT FOR GROWN-UPS:** Bake an additional squash until tender alongside the squash for baby. For the adults, add ½ tablespoon (7 g) butter to each half and sprinkle with 1 teaspoon brown sugar, honey, or maple syrup. If you like, add 1 teaspoon lime juice and ¼ teaspoon ground ginger. Cover and microwave on high 30 to 45 seconds.

Pureed Zucchini I 👶

- 2 small zucchini (1 pound, or 455 g)

⌨ Wash the zucchini and trim the ends. Cut into thin strips (3 x 1/4 x 1/4-inch); this will make about 4 cups (450 g). Place in a covered microwave-safe dish; microwave on high 5 minutes. Cool until the dish is comfortable to handle and pour off the liquid. Remove 1 cup (180 g) and puree in the food processor. (Use the remaining cooked zucchini in the "Make It for Grown-Ups" recipe below or Pureed Zucchini II recipe on this page, if you like.)

YIELD: *Makes about 4 tablespoons or 1/4 cup*

EACH WITH: 2.4 calories; 0.0 gm total fat; 0.0 gm saturated fat; 0.0 mg cholesterol; 0.5 mg sodium; 0.6 gm carbohydrate; 0.2 gm dietary fiber; 0.1 gm protein; 2.0 mg calcium; 0.1 mg iron; 167.5 IU vitamin A; 0.7 mg vitamin C.

Pureed Zucchini II 👶

- 1 small zucchini (1/2 pound, or 225 g)
- 1/4 cup (60 ml) water

◎ Wash and trim the ends of the zucchini. Cut in half lengthwise and slice.

Place in a small pan with the water. Cover and bring to a boil. Reduce the heat and simmer 5 minutes. Transfer the zucchini and water to a blender and puree.

YIELD: *Makes about 2/3 cup*

👪 **MAKE IT FOR GROWN-UPS:**
Combine the remaining 2 cups (360 g) zucchini with 1/4 cup (45 g) chopped tomato in a microwave-safe dish and season with salt and pepper. Cover and microwave on high 2 minutes. Stir, sprinkle with 1/4 cup (25 g) grated Parmesan cheese, and microwave 1 minute longer.

Pureed Acorn Squash 👶

If you like, bake one squash for your baby and another for yourself. (See "Make It for Grown-Ups" below.)

- 1 acorn squash (about 1¹/₂ pounds, or 680 g)
- 2 tablespoons to ¹/₄ cup (28 to 60 ml) breast milk, formula, or apple juice (optional)

▣ Preheat the oven to 400°F (200°C, or gas mark 6). Wash the squash, cut it in half, and remove the seeds and strings. Place each half cut side down in a shallow 8 x 11-inch baking dish with ¹/₄ inch water. Bake 35 minutes, or until tender. Let cool. Scoop out the flesh from the skin. Puree in the food processor with 2 tablespoons to ¹/₄ cup liquid from the pan (or breast milk, formula, or apple juice) for desired consistency.

YIELD: *Makes about 16 tablespoons or 1 cup*

EACH WITH: 7.2 calories; 0.0 gm total fat; 0.0 gm saturated fat; 0.0 mg cholesterol; 0.5 mg sodium; 1.9 gm carbohydrate; 0.6 gm dietary fiber; 0.1 gm protein; 5.6 mg calcium; 0.1 mg iron; 54.8 IU vitamin A; 1.4 mg vitamin C.

👪 **MAKE IT FOR GROWN-UPS:** Bake an additional squash alongside the squash for baby until tender. Then, place the 2 halves right side up and leave in the baking dish. Sprinkle with salt and pepper, dot with 1 tablespoon (14 g) of butter, and sprinkle with 1 tablespoon (5 g) grated Parmesan cheese. Place under preheated broiler for 1 minute.

Pureed Yellow (Crookneck) Squash 👶

- 1 small yellow squash, trimmed, cut in half lengthwise, and cut into 1/2-inch-thick slices
- 1 tablespoon (14 ml) apple juice or water (if microwaving)
- 1/3 cup (75 ml) water (if cooking on stovetop)

▭ Place the squash in a microwave-safe dish, cover, and microwave on high 3 minutes. Place the squash and the 1 tablespoon (14 ml) apple juice or water in a blender or food processor and puree or mash with a fork.

◎ Place the squash in a small pan with 1/3 cup (75 ml) water. Cover and simmer 5 minutes, or until the squash is soft. Place the squash in a blender or food processor with 1 tablespoon (14 ml) of the cooking water and puree. Add more liquid if needed.

YIELD: *Makes about 4 tablespoons or 1/4 cup*

EACH WITH: 3.0 calories; 0.0 gm total fat; 0.0 gm saturated fat; 0.0 mg cholesterol; 0.0 mg sodium; 0.6 gm carbohydrate; 0.2 gm dietary fiber; 0.1 gm protein; 3.3 mg calcium; 0.1 mg iron; 24.4 IU vitamin A; 0.8 mg vitamin C.

Oven-Baked Potato 👶 👪

- 1 baking (russet or Idaho) potato (about 1 pound, or 455 g)
- Olive oil for coating (optional)

▦ Preheat the oven to 450°F (230°C, or gas mark 8). Scrub the potato and pierce the skin two or three times with a fork. For a crispier skin, rub the potato with a light coating of olive oil. Place the potato directly on the middle oven rack. Bake 50 to 60 minutes, or until soft or a fork easily pierces the potato. When the potato is done, cut a small "X," lengthwise and crosswise across the top. Push the ends together to open it.

YIELD: *Makes 1 baked potato—1 baby serving (1 to 2 tablespoons) and 1 adult serving*

EACH WITH: 29.0 calories; 0.0 gm total fat; 0.0 gm saturated fat; 0.0 mg cholesterol; 2.4 mg sodium; 6.4 gm carbohydrate; 0.7 gm dietary fiber; 0.8 gm protein; 5.4 mg calcium; 0.3 mg iron; 3.0 IU vitamin A; 3.9 mg vitamin C.

💡 *When baking a potato in a conventional oven, don't wrap it in tinfoil, which creates moisture and steams the potato. The result is a less crispy skin and the texture of a boiled potato.*

Microwaved-Baked Potato

If your baby hesitates to eat the potato, add a little pureed sweet potato, apple, or pear.

- 1 baking (russet or Idaho) potato (about 1 pound, or 455 g)
- Breast milk or formula

Scrub the potato well. Prick the skin with a fork in several places. Microwave on high about 10 minutes, or until soft. Let sit until cool enough to handle.

Mash about 1 to 2 tablespoons potato flesh for your baby, adding a little bit of breast milk or formula.

For adults who like a more fluffy potato with a crisp skin, microwave the potato 5 to 10 minutes, depending on size. Then bake on the middle rack of a 450°F (230°C, or gas mark 8) oven an additional 10 minutes, or until the potato is soft.

Potato prepared in the microwave has 25 percent more vitamin C than commercially prepared potatoes for toddlers and twice as much vitamin C as peeled boiled potatoes.

YIELD: *Makes 1 baby serving and 1 adult serving*

EACH WITH: 23.6 calories; 0.0 gm total fat; 0.0 gm saturated fat; 0.0 mg cholesterol; 1.8 mg sodium; 5.4 gm carbohydrate; 0.5 gm dietary fiber; 0.5 gm protein; 2.5 mg calcium; 0.3 mg iron; 0.0 IU vitamin A; 3.4 mg vitamin C.

MAKE IT FOR GROWN-UPS: Add 1 tablespoon (14 g) of butter and salt and pepper to taste to the rest of the potato for your meal.

Prune Puree ♟ �adult

For older children and adults: Spread the puree on crackers, bread, bagels, pancakes, and waffles or use as a topping for yogurt, ice cream, rice pudding, or hot cereal.

- 8 pitted prunes
- $3/4$ to 1 cup (175 to 235 ml) apple, pear, or white grape juice, or water

▭ Combine the prunes and $1/2$ cup (120 ml) of the liquid in a microwave-safe dish, cover, and microwave on high 5 minutes. Transfer the prunes and liquid into a food processor. Add $1/4$ cup (60 ml) additional liquid (or more, depending on how thin you want the puree) and blend 2 minutes.

◎ Combine the prunes and $1/2$ cup (120 ml) liquid in a small pan, cover, and bring to a boil over medium high heat. Reduce the heat to low and simmer 5 minutes. Transfer the prunes and liquid into a food processor. Add $1/4$ cup (60 ml) additional liquid (or more, depending on how thin you want the puree) and blend 2 minutes.

YIELD: *Makes about 4 tablespoons or $1/4$ cup*

EACH WITH: 16.6 calories; 0.0 gm total fat; 0.0 gm saturated fat; 0.0 mg cholesterol; 0.2 mg sodium; 4.4 gm carbohydrate; 0.5 gm dietary fiber; 0.1 gm protein; 2.9 mg calcium; 0.1 mg iron; 53.0 IU vitamin A; 0.4 mg vitamin C.

PRUNES

Prunes are sometimes called dried plums. In addition to being a source of iron and fiber, they contain an exceptional amount of the vitamins E and A, antioxidants, which are reputed to help protect against heart disease and cancer, as well as to lower LDH, the "bad" cholesterol. Homemade prune puree has more than three times as much iron as the commercially prepared baby food Strained Prunes with Tapioca.

Stewed Plums 👶

If plums are too tart for your baby, mix them with a little mashed banana.

- 12 ripe, sweet, plums, halved and pitted
- 1/2 cup (120 ml) water
- Peach or white grape juice (optional)
- Ripe mashed banana (optional)
- Breast milk or formula

◎ Place the plums and water in a small saucepan over medium heat and bring to a boil. Stir, reduce the heat, cover, and simmer 15 minutes, or until tender. Drain liquid from plums. (See Tip below.) Puree the plums in a blender until smooth. Add a little peach or white grape juice for thinning, if necessary, or use some of the plum liquid. Mash in the banana if desired. Serve with a little breast milk or formula on the side.

💡 *The plum liquid can be diluted half-and-half with water and served as juice in a cup.*

YIELD: *Makes about 5 tablespoons or 1/3 cup*

EACH WITH: 5.1 calories; 0.0 gm total fat; 0.0 gm saturated fat; 0.0 mg cholesterol; 0.0 mg sodium; 1.3 gm carbohydrate; 0.2 gm dietary fiber; 0.1 gm protein; 0.7 mg calcium; 0.0 mg iron; 37.9 IU vitamin A; 1.0 mg vitamin C.

Peach Puree 👶

Use this recipe for nectarines also.

- 1 small ripe peach, halved and pitted (if microwaving)
- 4 small ripe peaches, halved and pitted (if cooking on stovetop)
- 1 cup (235 ml) water (if cooking on stovetop)

⬜ Place the peach cut sides down on a microwave-safe plate and microwave on high 1 to 2 minutes until it is soft. Cool, remove the peel, and puree in the blender.

◎ Cooking on the stove takes longer, so I make a bigger batch and store leftovers in the fridge or freezer. Blanch 4 peaches in boiling water 10 to 15 seconds. Peel, halve, remove the pits, and cut into pieces. Place the peaches and 1 cup (235 ml) water in a small pan over medium-high heat. Bring to a boil, reduce the heat, and simmer 5 to 10 minutes, or until soft. Place the peaches and 1/2 cup (120 ml) of the cooking liquid in the blender and puree. Add more liquid as needed.

YIELD: *Makes about 24 tablespoons or 1 1/2 cups*

EACH WITH: 4.4 calories; 0.0 gm total fat; 0.0 gm saturated fat; 0.0 mg cholesterol; 0.0 mg sodium; 1.1 gm carbohydrate; 0.2 gm dietary fiber; 0.1 gm protein; 0.7 mg calcium; 0.0 mg iron; 36.8 IU vitamin A; 0.7 mg vitamin C.

Peachy Plum 👶

To sweeten this, add some mashed banana or a little prune puree.

* 1 sweet, ripe plum, halved and pitted
* 1 small, ripe peach, halved and pitted
* 1 tablespoon to ¹/₂ cup (14 to 235 ml) water
* Breast milk or formula

▭ Place the peach and the plum cut sides down on a microwave-safe plate and microwave on high 1 minute. Cool, remove peels, and puree in a blender. If the puree is too thick, thin with 1 or 2 tablespoons (14 to 28 ml) water. Serve breast milk or formula on the side.

◎ Blanch the peach and plum in boiling water 10 to 15 seconds. With a slotted spoon, remove from the water, cool, peel, quarter, and pit the fruit. Combine the fruit and ¹/₂ cup (120 ml) water in a saucepan over medium-high heat and bring to a boil. Reduce the heat and simmer 5 to 10 minutes (depending on the ripeness of the fruit) until soft. Puree the fruit with ¹/₄ cup (60 ml) of the cooking liquid in a blender about 30 seconds. Add more liquid as needed. Serve with breast milk or formula on the side.

YIELD: *Makes about 8 tablespoons or ¹/₂ cup*

EACH WITH: 4.4 calories; 0.0 gm total fat; 0.0 gm saturated fat; 0.0 mg cholesterol; 0.0 mg sodium; 1.1 gm carbohydrate; 0.2 gm dietary fiber; 0.1 gm protein; 0.6 mg calcium; 0.0 mg iron; 34.7 IU vitamin A; 0.8 mg vitamin C.

Peach and Banana Whip 👶

* 1 small, ripe peach, halved and pitted
* 2 tablespoons mashed, ripe banana
* 1 tablespoon breast milk or formula

▭ Place the peach cut sides down on a microwave-safe plate and microwave on high 1 minute. When cool enough to handle, remove the skin. Puree the peach and banana in a blender. Remove and whisk in the breast milk or formula with a fork.

YIELD: *Makes about 7 tablespoons*

APPROXIMATE SERVING SIZE: 2 tablespoons. **EACH WITH:** 18.9 calories; 0.1 gm total fat; 0.0 gm saturated fat; 0.0 mg cholesterol; 0.1 mg sodium; 4.8 gm carbohydrate; 0.6 gm dietary fiber; 0.3 gm protein; 1.8 mg calcium; 0.1 mg iron; 72.5 IU vitamin A; 2.4 mg vitamin C.

EIGHT MONTHS

Every lady in this land

Has twenty nails, upon each hand

Five, and twenty on hands and feet:

All this is true, without deceit.

—FINGER AND TOES

At this age, your baby should be getting three to four feedings of breast milk or formula (24 to 32 ounces, or 710 to 946 ml) per day. You'll also be starting finger food and self-feeding. Finger food encourages chewing, manual coordination, and independence.

Your baby may have four teeth at this age. Up-and-down chewing movements and the ability to grasp and bring objects to the mouth continue to develop. Now is the time to introduce finger foods. Even though the desire and ability of your baby to self-feed may be hampered by lack of coordination, be patient and encourage independence. This is an age of self-discovery and exploration that you'll want to encourage—even though your baby may want to play with the food, feel it, squish it, smell it, taste it, spit it out, or eat it. This can be a messy process, and it may be a trying time for parents. Just keep face cloths handy and put a plastic cloth underneath the high chair.

Offer soft, chunky food to encourage your baby to chew and swallow in a more mature way. It is fine to continue serving mashed and pureed food, as well. You will be doing most of the spoon-feeding. Encourage your little one's independence and try to sense how much you should help. This is a good age for your baby to join you at the dining table in a high chair.

After eight months, you can make these additions to your baby's diet:

- **VEGETABLES:** carrots, string beans, and wax beans

- **FRUITS:** very ripe apricots or dried (unsulfured) cooked apricots

- **MISCELLANEOUS:** hard-cooked egg yolk, rice, rice noodles, and barley

- **FINGER FOOD:** baby crackers (oat or rice), plain oat Cheerios, pieces of peeled soft fruit (fresh or cooked), ripe banana slices, soft cooked vegetable pieces, and cut cooked rice noodles

- **JUICE:** apricot and carrot

- Leftover cooked egg whites can be used in tuna or egg salad. Cooked egg whites may be frozen for later use in baking or other cooked dishes for family and toddlers a year and older.

- Serve 1/4 cup iron-fortified cereal twice a day.

- Offer 2 tablespoons of vegetables rich in vitamin C and A twice a day. (Vegetables should be washed, peeled, seeds removed, and cooked.)

- Offer 2 tablespoons of fruit rich in vitamins C and A twice a day. The texture can now be thicker and chunkier. (Wash, peel, core, and remove seeds or pits of very ripe fruit. Mash or cut into thin, small pieces and serve as finger food.)

- Serve 1/2 cup juice rich in vitamins C and A once daily. Juices do not have to be diluted.

- All liquids at mealtime should be offered in a two-handled sippy cup. The one without a valve works best, but you may want to try others.

- Do not add salt, sugar, honey, or seasoning.

- Do not force-feed.

- Never leave your child unattended when eating or drinking.

- Continue to introduce one new food at a time, every three days.

Apricot Puree ⚉

- 1/2 cup (65 g) unsulfured dried apricots
- 1 cup (120 ml) water

◎ Bring the dried apricots and water to a boil in a small saucepan over medium heat. Cover, reduce heat, and simmer 30 minutes. When the apricots are soft, puree them with the cooking water in a blender until smooth.

▭▤ Combine the apricots and water in a microwave-safe dish, cover, and microwave on high 5 minutes. Transfer the apricots and liquid into a food processor and blend 2 minutes.

YIELD: *Makes about 8 tablespoons or 1/2 cup*

EACH WITH: 4.6 calories; 0.0 gm total fat; 0.0 gm saturated fat; 0.0 mg cholesterol; 0.1 mg sodium; 1.1 gm carbohydrate; 0.2 gm dietary fiber; 0.1 gm protein; 1.3 mg calcium; 0.0 mg iron; 186.6 IU vitamin A; 1.0 mg vitamin C.

Pureed or Mashed Carrots ⚉

Ready-to-eat baby carrots are available in grocery stores and markets. Be sure they don't have any preservatives. Always rinse ready-to-eat carrots.

- 4 baby carrots (not the very smallest ones)
- 1 tablespoon to 1/4 cup (14 ml to 60 ml) water
- Apple juice, breast milk, or formula (optional)

▭▤ Cut the carrots lengthwise, then in half, and place in a small glass bowl with 1 tablespoon (14 ml) water. Cover and microwave on high 2 minutes. Puree in a food processor or mash, adding apple juice, breast milk, or formula if more liquid is needed.

◎ Wash and chop or slice the carrots and place in a saucepan with 1/4 cup (60 ml) water. Bring to a boil, cover, reduce the heat, and simmer 10 minutes, or until carrots are soft. Puree in a food processor or mash, using apple juice, breast milk, or formula if more liquid is needed.

YIELD: *Makes 2 to 4 tablespoons*

APPROXIMATE SERVING SIZE: 1 tablespoons. **EACH WITH:** 3.4 calories; 0.0 gm total fat; 0.0 gm saturated fat; 0.0 mg cholesterol; 5.6 mg sodium; 0.8 gm carbohydrate; 0.3 gm dietary fiber; 0.1 gm protein; 2.9 mg calcium; 0.0 mg iron; 1668.6 IU vitamin A; 0.3 mg vitamin C.

Pureed Carrots with Pears 👶

* 4 baby carrots
* ¼ pear, peeled, cored, and chopped
* 3 tablespoons (45 ml) water
* Apple juice, breast milk, or formula (optional)

▭ Cut the carrots lengthwise, then in half, and place in a small glass bowl with the pear and water. Cover and microwave on high 2 minutes. Puree in a food processor or mash, adding apple juice, breast milk, or formula if more liquid is needed.

YIELD: *Makes about 4 to 6 tablespoons*

EACH WITH: 4.7 calories; 0.0 gm total fat; 0.0 gm saturated fat; 0.0 mg cholesterol; 2.9 mg sodium; 1.2 gm carbohydrate; 0.3 gm dietary fiber; 0.1 gm protein; 1.9 mg calcium; 0.0 mg iron; 835.5 IU vitamin A; 0.4 mg vitamin C.

Pureed Carrots with Apples 👶

* 4 baby carrots
* ¼ apple, peeled, cored, and chopped
* 2 tablespoons (28 ml) water
* Apple juice, breast milk, or formula (optional)

▭ Cut the carrots lengthwise, then in half, and place in a small glass bowl with the apple and water. Cover and microwave on high 2 minutes. Puree in a food processor or mash, adding apple juice, breast milk, or formula if more liquid is needed.

YIELD: *Makes 4 to 6 tablespoons*

EACH WITH: 4.7 calories; 0.0 gm total fat; 0.0 gm saturated fat; 0.0 mg cholesterol; 2.9 mg sodium; 1.2 gm carbohydrate; 0.3 gm dietary fiber; 0.1 gm protein; 1.7 mg calcium; 0.0 mg iron; 836.4 IU vitamin A; 0.2 mg vitamin C.

💡 FINGER FOOD

Baby carrots can also be cut in thin strips (julienne) and microwaved, steamed, or simmered until very soft and used as finger food.

Carrots with Sweet Potato 👶

- 4 baby carrots
- 1/4 cup (50 g) cubed, peeled, and cooked sweet potato
- 3 tablespoons (45 ml) water
- Apple juice, breast milk, or formula (optional)

⬛ Cut the carrots lengthwise, then in half, and place in a small glass bowl with the sweet potato and water. Cover and microwave on high 2 minutes. Puree in a food processor or mash, using apple juice, breast milk, or formula if more liquid is needed.

YIELD: *Makes about 6 tablespoons*

EACH WITH: 7.3 calories; 0.0 gm total fat; 0.0 gm saturated fat; 0.0 mg cholesterol; 5.1 mg sodium; 1.7 gm carbohydrate; 0.4 gm dietary fiber; 0.2 gm protein; 3.8 mg calcium; 0.1 mg iron; 2035.4 IU vitamin A; 1.4 mg vitamin C.

Carrots with Apricots 👶

- 1/2 cup (55 g) shredded carrots (about 4 baby carrots)
- 1/4 cup (35 g) finely diced dried apricots
- 1/2 to 1 cup (120 to 235 ml) water

⬛ Place the carrots, apricots, and 1/2 cup (120 ml) water in a 2-cup microwave-safe bowl and microwave on high 5 minutes. Puree in a food processor until smooth. Add more water if needed.

◎ Bring the carrots, apricots, and 1 cup (235 ml) water to a boil in a small saucepan over medium heat. Cover, reduce heat, and simmer 5 to 10 minutes. Puree in a food processor until smooth. Add more water
if needed.

YIELD: *Makes about 8 tablespoons or 1/2 cup*

EACH WITH: 4.2 calories; 0.0 gm total fat; 0.0 gm saturated fat; 0.0 mg cholesterol; 2.9 mg sodium; 1.0 gm carbohydrate; 0.2 gm dietary fiber; 0.1 gm protein; 2.1 mg calcium; 0.0 mg iron; 933.6 IU vitamin A; 0.7 mg vitamin C.

Sweet Potato Fries

These beat regular french fries in both taste and nutrition; fast food joints, watch out! They make wonderful baby finger food, if the adults don't eat them first.

- 1 large sweet potato, peeled
- 1 to 2 tablespoons (14 to 28 ml) olive oil

Preheat the oven to 400°F (200°C, or gas mark 6). Cut the sweet potato in half, then into 1/4-inch-thick slices, and again into 1/4-inch sticks. Put in a large bowl, add the oil, and toss until coated with oil. Place on a baking sheet. (Alternatively, arrange sweet potato sticks in a single layer on a baking sheet and spray with olive oil.) Bake on the middle rack 10 minutes. Turn the potatoes and bake 10 minutes more.

YIELD: *1 baby serving AND 1 adult serving*

APPROXIMATE SERVING SIZE: 1 fry slice. **EACH WITH:** 29.3 calories; 1.7 gm total fat; 0.2 gm saturated fat; 0.0 mg cholesterol; 5.1 mg sodium; 3.3 gm carbohydrate; 0.5 gm dietary fiber; 0.3 gm protein; 5.1 mg calcium; 0.1 mg iron; 2970.9 IU vitamin A; 2.4 mg vitamin C.

> **MAKE IT FOR GROWN-UPS:** Before baking, sprinkle (kosher) salt on two-thirds of the potatoes, leaving one-third of the potatoes unsalted for the baby. When baked, cool and pick out the unsalted fries for baby. The rest are yours. This recipe also works well with regular potatoes sprinkled with Parmesan cheese instead of salt.

Carrot-Potato Puree

- 1 cup (130 g) chopped carrots
- 3 small potatoes, peeled and cubed
- 1 cup (235 ml) water
- 1 tablespoon (14 g) butter
- 1/4 cup (60 ml) breast milk or formula (optional)

Place the carrots and potatoes in a small saucepan with the water. Cover and bring to a boil. Reduce the heat and simmer 25 minutes, until the vegetables are soft. Drain. Whisk in the butter. Take out baby's portion, 1 to 2 tablespoons, and mash with the breast milk or formula (or use 1/4 cup, or 60 ml of the cooking water).

YIELD: *1 baby serving AND 1 adult serving*

EACH WITH: 6.7 calories; 0.4 gm total fat; 0.2 gm saturated fat; 1.0 mg cholesterol; 3.0 mg sodium; 0.8 gm carbohydrate; 0.2 gm dietary fiber; 0.1 gm protein; 1.7 mg calcium; 0.0 mg iron; 845.4 IU vitamin A; 0.4 mg vitamin C.

> **MAKE IT FOR GROWN-UPS:** Add milk, salt, and pepper (according to taste) to the remaining carrot-potato mixture and coarsely mash.

Buttered Green Beans

This recipe may also be used for yellow wax or purple beans.

- 6 green beans, washed, trimmed, and cut into thin strips (French style) (about 1/4 cup, or 25 g)
- 1 teaspoon unsalted butter

Bring a small pot with 1/2 cup (120 ml) of water to a boil and add the beans. Cook 5 minutes. Pour the beans, butter, and water into the blender and puree.

FOR FINGER FOOD: Drain the beans and toss with the butter.

YIELD: *Makes 2 1/2 tablespoons or 1 baby serving finger food*

EACH WITH: 7.0 calories; 0.5 gm total fat; 0.3 gm saturated fat; 1.3 mg cholesterol; 0.1 mg sodium; 0.6 gm carbohydrate; 0.3 gm dietary fiber; 0.2 gm protein; 3.6 mg calcium; 0.1 mg iron; 69.5 IU vitamin A; 0.8 mg vitamin C.

Baby Rice

- 1/4 cup (50 g) short-grain white, brown, or basmati rice
- 1/2 cup (120 ml) water
- 1/4 cup (60 ml) breast milk or formula

Wash the rice well under running water. Drain and place in a small saucepan. Cover the rice with the water and bring to a boil. Stir, cover, and reduce heat to the lowest setting. Steam (simmer) 20 minutes. Place the cooked rice in a blender with the breast milk or formula and blend 45 seconds.

Larger amounts of rice may be made and frozen in small batches. Instead of breast milk or formula, you can use 1/4 cup (60 ml) water for 2/3 cup (110 g) cooked rice for blending.

YIELD: *Makes about 11 tablespoons or 2/3 cup*

EACH WITH: 14.6 calories; 0.0 gm total fat; 0.0 gm saturated fat; 0.0 mg cholesterol; 0.0 mg sodium; 3.2 gm carbohydrate; 0.0 gm dietary fiber; 0.3 gm protein; 0.1 mg calcium; 0.2 mg iron; 0.0 IU vitamin A; 0.0 mg vitamin C.

Rice and Apricot Pudding 👶

- ¹/₂ cup (80 g) cooked Baby Rice (page 102)
- ¹/₄ cup (50 g) Apricot Puree (page 98)
- ¹/₄ cup (60 ml) breast milk or formula

Mix the rice and apricot puree with the breast milk or formula. If a creamier consistency is desired, add more liquid.

VARIATIONS: Replace the apricot with ¹/₄ cup Prune Puree (page 93), mashed banana, Pureed Apple (page 84), Pureed Pear (page 84), Peach Puree (94), or Pureed Sweet Potato (page 85).

YIELD: *Makes about 11 tablespoons or ²/₃ cup*

EACH WITH: 11.7 calories; 0.0 gm total fat; 0.0 gm saturated fat; 0.0 mg cholesterol; 0.0 mg sodium; 2.6 gm carbohydrate; 0.1 gm dietary fiber; 0.2 gm protein; 0.5 mg calcium; 0.1 mg iron; 66.2 IU vitamin A; 0.3 mg vitamin C.

Fruit Compote 👶

- ¹/₄ cup (40 g) pitted prunes
- ¹/₄ cup (35 g) unsulfured dried apricots
- 1 apple, peeled, cored, and diced
- 1 pear, peeled, cored, and diced
- 2 cups (475 ml) water
- Breast milk or formula

◎ Place the prunes, apricots, apple, pear, and water in a small saucepan. Bring to a boil, reduce the heat, and simmer 20 to 30 minutes, until the fruit is soft and most of the water is absorbed. Stir occasionally to prevent sticking and add more water if needed. Mash and serve warm with breast milk or formula.

YIELD: *Makes ²/₃ to 1 cup or about 16 tablespoons*

EACH WITH: 8.4 calories; 0.0 gm total fat; 0.0 gm saturated fat; 0.0 mg cholesterol; 0.1 mg sodium; 2.2 gm carbohydrate; 0.3 gm dietary fiber; 0.1 gm protein; 1.4 mg calcium; 0.0 mg iron; 64.6 IU vitamin A; 0.5 mg vitamin C.

NINE MONTHS

The man in the moon

Came down too soon

To inquire the way to Norwich;

The man in the south

He burnt his mouth

With eating cold plum porridge.

— THE MAN IN THE MOON

- Continue to give breast milk or formula three to four times a day (22 to 32 ounces).

After nine months, you can make these additions to your baby's diet.

- **VEGETABLES:** broccoli and cauliflower

- **FRUITS:** avocado, cantaloupe, and papaya

- **JUICE:** red grape, cantaloupe, and papaya nectar

- **DAIRY:** yogurt

- Continue daily feeding of $1/2$ cup iron-fortified cereal, but change to a thicker consistency. Serve with fruit or fruit juice rich in vitamin C.

- Serve $1/3$ cup cooked and mashed vegetables per day or cut up for finger food. Use vegetables rich in vitamins A and C. (See "Vitamins" on page 25.)

- Offer $1/3$ cup peeled, cored, or seeded ripe fruit per day, mashed or as finger food.

- Offer 1 well-cooked egg yolk, 2 to 4 times a week. Start with 1 table-spoonful at a time, adding more if your baby indicates he is still hungry and wants more.

REFUSING FOOD

When your child exhibits a strong dislike for a certain food, accept it without any fuss. Foods with the same nutritional values can be substituted, although it may take several other kinds to compensate for the nutrients of a rejected food. Don't offer the refused food again for some months; you may find your infant's tastes have changed, and the refused food may later be accepted. Do not verbally reinforce your child's dislike of a food. Psychologically, this may cause him to resist trying it again at a later time.

Variety is important. Problems often arise if family members are fussy eaters, as the rejection of many foods may be modeled to the child.

When introducing a new food, start with a very tiny portion. Your baby may initially look at it, feel it, or just smell it. This is part of learning to accept it. Some children reject all foods of a certain texture, so it may help to combine a soft food with a crisp or chewy food. The color and attractiveness of food influence appetites as well. Mix the colors of vegetables to make them more appealing; for instance, combine small pieces of cauliflower, broccoli, and yellow squash to stimulate an unenthusiastic palate.

EGGS

Eggs provide protein, vitamin A, some B vitamins, calcium, phosphorus, iron, and zinc. For many years health officials recommended reducing eggs in the average diet. Today they say that unless a person has a high cholesterol problem, three or four eggs a week are not harmful. New studies indicate that dietary cholesterol is affected more by saturated fat than the cholesterol from eggs.

By their eighth month, babies may be given well-cooked, mashed hard-cooked egg yolks mixed with other age-appropriate foods. One-year-olds may be given whole eggs, provided that there is no history of egg allergies in the family. (See "Allergies and Food Intolerance" on page 46.)

Potato with Hard-Cooked Egg Yolk 🍼

This is an alternative to plain hard-cooked egg yolks. A baked or microwaved potato may be substituted for boiled.

* 1 small unpeeled potato, well-washed and boiled
* 1 to 2 tablespoons (14 to 28 ml) breast milk or formula
* 1 hard-cooked egg yolk, mashed
* 1 teaspoon butter (optional)

Peel the potato and mash with a fork. Add the breast milk or formula, egg yolk, and butter, if desired, and mix well.

YIELD: *Makes 1 baby serving*

EACH WITH: 21.8 calories; 0.6 gm total fat; 0.2 gm saturated fat; 23.6 mg cholesterol; 7.5 mg sodium; 3.1 gm carbohydrate; 0.3 gm dietary fiber; 1.0 gm protein; 3.5 mg calcium; 0.1 mg iron; 33.0 IU vitamin A; 2.0 mg vitamin C.

Green Beans with Carrot and Apple 🍼

* 1 tablespoon (6 g) cut green beans
* 1 tablespoon (8 g) thinly sliced carrot
* 1 tablespoon to ¼ cup (14 to 60 ml) water
* ¼ apple, peeled, cored, and cubed
* 1 to 2 tablespoons (14 to 28 ml) breast milk, formula, or apple juice

⬛ Combine the green beans, carrot, and 1 tablespoon (14 ml) water in a small glass bowl. Cover and microwave on high 2 minutes. Add the apple and continue cooking 30 seconds. Mash with the breast milk, formula, or apple juice or puree in blender.

◎ Place the green beans, carrot, ¼ cup (60 ml) water, and apple in a small pan. Cover and bring to a boil. Reduce the heat and simmer 5 minutes. Mash with the cooking liquid and the breast milk, formula, or apple juice or puree in blender.

YIELD: *Makes 1 baby serving*

EACH WITH: 4.0 calories; 0.0 gm total fat; 0.0 gm saturated fat; 0.0 mg cholesterol; 1.9 mg sodium; 1.0 gm carbohydrate; 0.3 gm dietary fiber; 0.1 gm protein; 2.3 mg calcium; 0.0 mg iron; 575.8 IU vitamin A; 0.4 mg vitamin C.

Broccoli ♟

Using breast milk or formula to mash the broccoli will mellow the taste and make it more pleasing for your baby.

* 1 broccoli floret
* 1 to 2 tablespoons (14 to 28 ml) breast milk, formula, or carrot juice
* 1 tablespoon (14 ml) water (if microwaving)

◎ Place the broccoli in a steamer basket in a saucepan with a little water; cover and steam over medium-high heat 5 minutes. Mash the broccoli with the breast milk, formula, or carrot juice.

▭ Place the broccoli in a small microwave-safe bowl with 1 tablespoon (14 ml) water. Cover and microwave on high 1 to 2 minutes, until soft. Mash with the breast milk, formula, or carrot juice.

YIELD: *Makes 1 baby serving*

EACH WITH: 1.7 calories; 0.0 gm total fat; 0.0 gm saturated fat; 0.0 mg cholesterol; 2.0 mg sodium; 0.4 gm carbohydrate; 0.2 gm dietary fiber; 0.1 gm protein; 2.0 mg calcium; 0.0 mg iron; 95.9 IU vitamin A; 3.2 mg vitamin C.

Cauliflower ♟

* 1 (2-inch) cauliflower floret
* 1 tablespoon (14 ml) breast milk, formula, or carrot juice
* 1 tablespoon (14 ml) water (if microwaving)

◎ Place the cauliflower in a steamer basket in a saucepan with a little water; cover and steam over medium-high heat 5 minutes. Mash the cauliflower using the breast milk, formula, or carrot juice.

▭ Place the cauliflower in a small microwave-safe bowl with 1 tablespoon (14 ml) water. Cover and microwave on high 1 to 2 minutes, or until soft. Mash with the breast milk, formula, or carrot juice.

YIELD: *Makes 1 baby serving*

EACH WITH: 0.9 calories; 0.0 gm total fat; 0.0 gm saturated fat; 0.0 mg cholesterol; 0.6 mg sodium; 0.2 gm carbohydrate; 0.1 gm dietary fiber; 0.1 gm protein; 0.6 mg calcium; 0.0 mg iron; 0.5 IU vitamin A; 1.7 mg vitamin C.

Cauliflower and Carrot ⚇

- 1 (2-inch) cauliflower floret
- 1 baby carrot, shredded
- ¼ cup (60 ml) water
- 1 teaspoon butter

▭ Combine the cauliflower, carrot, and water in a small glass bowl. Cover and microwave on high 3 minutes. Puree or mash with the butter, or serve as finger food.

YIELD: *Makes 1 baby serving*

EACH WITH: 5.0 calories; 0.3 gm total fat; 0.2 gm saturated fat; 0.8 mg cholesterol; 3.1 mg sodium; 0.5 gm carbohydrate; 0.2 gm dietary fiber; 0.1 gm protein; 1.9 mg calcium; 0.0 mg iron; 844.4 IU vitamin A; 1.0 mg vitamin C.

Vegetable Custard ⚇

This recipe is perfect for using leftover pureed vegetables in the freezer or fridge.

- Oil or butter for greasing the custard cup
- 1 egg yolk
- ¼ cup (60 ml) breast milk or formula
- ¼ cup pureed cooked vegetables (carrots, page 98; broccoli, page 107; cauliflower; or cauliflower and carrots, on this page)

▦ Preheat the oven to 350°F (180°C, or gas mark 4). Oil or butter a 6-ounce custard cup. In a small bowl beat the egg yolk well with a fork. Mix in the breast milk or formula and pureed vegetable. Pour into the custard cup. Place in a water bath and bake, uncovered, 20 to 30 minutes, or until a knife inserted comes out clean. See "Water Baths for Custards" on page 109) Cool thoroughly.

YIELD: *Makes 1 baby serving*

EACH WITH: 12.3 calories; 0.9 gm total fat; 0.3 gm saturated fat; 42.0 mg cholesterol; 3.9 mg sodium; 0.4 gm carbohydrate; 0.1 gm dietary fiber; 0.6 gm protein; 5.6 mg calcium; 0.1 mg iron; 719.9 IU vitamin A; 0.1 mg vitamin C.

Baked Rice Cup with Apple and Egg Yolks 👶

- ½ cup (80 g) cooked rice
- ½ cup (75 g) peeled, cored, and grated apple
- 2 tablespoons (28 ml) breast milk or formula
- 2 egg yolks
- 1 teaspoon olive oil

🔲 Preheat the oven to 350°F (180°C, or gas mark 4). Oil or butter two 6-ounce custard cups. Mix the rice, apple, breast milk or formula, egg yolks, and oil. Divide the mixture between the two prepared cups. Place in a water bath and bake, uncovered, 20 to 30 minutes, or until a knife inserted comes out clean. (Follow "Water Baths for Custards" on this page.) Cool thoroughly and serve. Or cover with plastic wrap and refrigerate for up to 2 days.

YIELD: *Makes 2 baby servings*

EACH WITH: 17.7 calories; 0.8 gm total fat; 0.2 gm saturated fat; 23.3 mg cholesterol; 1.0 mg sodium; 2.2 gm carbohydrate; 0.1 gm dietary fiber; 0.4 gm protein; 2.7 mg calcium; 0.1 mg iron; 29.1 IU vitamin A; 0.0 mg vitamin C.

VARIATIONS: Use other fruits, such as mashed pears, papaya, plums, or peaches. Use only a ¼ cup if substituting purees, such as Apricot Puree (page 98) and Prune Puree (page 93).

WATER BATHS FOR CUSTARDS

Here are basic instructions for baking custards in a water bath (also called a bain-marie):

1. Preheat the oven to 350°F (180°C, or gas mark 4).

2. You can use ramekins, custard cups, or other oven-proof cups in sizes from 6 to 8 ounces.

3. Oil the custard cups and fill with the recipe.

4. Place the filled cups in an 8 x 8-inch baking dish.

5. Fill the dish halfway with hot water.

6. Bake uncovered for 20 to 30 minutes, until the custard is set and a knife inserted comes out clean.

7. Remove carefully, so you won't burn yourself.

8. Let the custard stand for at least 5 minutes.

9. Unmold by sliding a knife around the edge of the custard cup and invert the custard on a plate or into a bowl.

Fruit Custard

- 2 egg yolks
- 1/2 cup (120 g) pureed fruit (banana, plums, pears, peaches, or combination of any two)
- 1/4 cup (60 ml) breast milk or formula

Preheat the oven to 350°F (180°C, or gas mark 4). Oil or butter two 6-ounce custard cups. Beat the egg yolks well in a small bowl. Add the pureed fruit and breast milk or formula and beat until smooth. Divide the mixture between the 2 prepared cups. Place in a water bath and bake, uncovered, 20 to 30 minutes, until a knife inserted comes out clean. (See "Water Baths for Custards" on page 109.) Cool thoroughly and serve. Or cover with plastic wrap and refrigerate for up to 2 days.

YIELD: *Makes 2 baby servings*

EACH WITH: 21.0 calories; 0.9 gm total fat; 0.3 gm saturated fat; 42.0 mg cholesterol; 1.7 mg sodium; 2.7 gm carbohydrate; 0.3 gm dietary fiber; 0.7 gm protein; 4.9 mg calcium; 0.1 mg iron; 56.2 IU vitamin A; 1.0 mg vitamin C.

Apple Omelet

- 1 teaspoon oil or butter for frying
- 1/4 cup (40 g) apple, peeled, cored, and grated
- 2 egg yolks
- 1 tablespoon (14 ml) water, formula, or breast milk

Heat the oil in a small frying pan over low heat. Add the apple and cook for 1 minute. In a small bowl, whisk the egg yolks with the water, formula, or breast milk and pour over the apples. Cook, turning once, until the egg is well set. Cool and cut into small strips or pieces and serve as finger food.

YIELD: *Makes 1 baby serving*

EACH WITH: 22.2 calories; 1.5 gm total fat; 0.5 gm saturated fat; 69.9 mg cholesterol; 2.8 mg sodium; 1.2 gm carbohydrate; 0.2 gm dietary fiber; 0.9 gm protein; 7.7 mg calcium; 0.2 mg iron; 84.5 IU vitamin A; 0.0 mg vitamin C.

VARIATIONS: Replace the apple with 1/4 cup mashed papaya, plums, banana, or grated or mashed pears.

Fried Rice with Egg Yolk

- 2 tablespoons (20 g) cooked rice
- 1 egg yolk
- 1 teaspoon oil or butter

Mix the rice and egg yolk in a cup. Heat the oil in a small frying pan over medium heat. Add the rice mixture and mold into a small pancake with a spatula. Cook well on one side, turn, and continue to cook until well done. Cool and cut into pieces and serve as finger food.

YIELD: *Makes 1 baby serving*

EACH WITH: 28.3 calories; 1.5 gm total fat; 0.5 gm saturated fat; 69.9 mg cholesterol; 2.7 mg sodium; 2.4 gm carbohydrate; 0.0 gm dietary fiber; 1.1 gm protein; 7.4 mg calcium; 0.3 mg iron; 81.7 IU vitamin A; 0.0 mg vitamin C.

EGG SAFETY

Fresh eggs may contain salmonella bacteria that can cause an intestinal infection. Healthy adults usually recover in less than a week, but the infection can be very dangerous for infants and toddlers. Eggs should be cooked until both yolk and white are firm. Scrambled eggs, casseroles, and other dishes containing eggs should be cooked to 160°F (70°C). Use a food thermometer to check the temperature.

Serve cooked egg dishes immediately after cooking or refrigerate at once for serving later. Use the dish within three to four days, or freeze for longer storage.

Warm Banana-Yogurt Pudding

- 1 teaspoon butter
- 2 to 4 tablespoons mashed banana
- 1 to 2 tablespoons (14 to 28 ml) vanilla yogurt

Melt the butter in a frying pan over low heat. Mash the banana well and mix in the vanilla yogurt. Add the banana mixture to the pan, stir well, and fry until heated through. Cool and serve.

YIELD: *Makes 1 baby serving*

EACH WITH: 20.6 calories; 1.1 gm total fat; 0.7 gm saturated fat; 2.9 mg cholesterol; 5.2 mg sodium; 2.5 gm carbohydrate; 0.2 gm dietary fiber; 0.5 gm protein; 13.7 mg calcium; 0.0 mg iron; 36.9 IU vitamin A; 0.6 mg vitamin C.

AVOCADOS

Avocado is an ideal baby food. Its flavor is mild, its texture smooth, and it is high in the fat (mostly healthy monounsaturated fat) and calories your baby needs at this age. ⭘ It also contains iron, vitamin A, folate, and vitamin B6—but no cholesterol.

To easily peel and pit an avocado, cut it in half and twist to separate the two halves. Slip a tablespoon between the pit and avocado to remove the pit. Then slip the spoon between the skin and the avocado to loosen it. If you like, cut the flesh into slices or cubes before you take it out of the skin.

Avocado, Cantaloupe, and Yogurt ![baby] ![family]

The remaining avocado can be used for an adult tortilla lunch, with the rest of the cantaloupe for desert.

- 1 slice (1/2 inch) ripe peeled avocado
- 1 slice (1/4 inch) ripe seeded cantaloupe
- 2 tablespoons (28 ml) vanilla yogurt

Cut the avocado and cantaloupe into small pieces or mash lightly and serve with the yogurt.

YIELD: *Makes 1 baby serving*

EACH WITH: 15.5 calories; 1.0 gm total fat; 0.2 gm saturated fat; 0.3 mg cholesterol; 4.8 mg sodium; 1.5 gm carbohydrate; 0.4 gm dietary fiber; 0.4 gm protein; 11.4 mg calcium; 0.0 mg iron; 77.0 IU vitamin A; 1.3 mg vitamin C.

![family] **MAKE IT FOR GROWN-UPS:** To make two easy tortillas, divide the remaining avocado (about 3/4 of an avocado) between 2 tortillas. Add 1 tablespoon (16 g) salsa and 1 tablespoon (10 g) crumbled feta cheese to each tortilla.

YIELD: *2 servings*

EACH WITH: 198.6 calories; 12.7 gm total fat; 2.9 gm saturated fat; 8.3 mg cholesterol; 277.7 mg sodium; 19.5 gm carbohydrate; 6.0 gm dietary fiber; 4.4 gm protein; 102.9 mg calcium; 0.8 mg iron; 232.1 IU vitamin A; 7.2 mg vitamin C.

Avocado and Mashed Banana 👶

Combine the banana and avocado for a new flavor combination. If this is not pleasing to your baby, alternate feeding a teaspoon avocado and a teaspoon banana.

- 2 tablespoons (30 g) mashed avocado
- ¼ ripe mashed banana

In a bowl, mix together the avocado and banana.

VARIATION: Use 2 tablespoons (30 g) apricot puree instead of banana. Serve with 1 to 2 tablespoons (14 to 28 ml) plain or vanilla yogurt.

YIELD: *Makes 1 baby serving*

EACH WITH: 17.6 calories; 1.1 gm total fat; 0.2 gm saturated fat; 0.0 mg cholesterol; 0.6 mg sodium; 2.1 gm carbohydrate; 0.7 gm dietary fiber; 0.2 gm protein; 1.3 mg calcium; 0.1 mg iron; 14.6 IU vitamin A; 1.2 mg vitamin C.

Avocado and Peach with Papaya Nectar 👶

- 1 slice (½ inch) ripe peeled avocado, cut into small pieces or mashed
- ¼ small, ripe peach, peeled and cut into small pieces or mashed
- 1 tablespoon (14 ml) papaya nectar

Place the avocado and peach in a small cup and mash lightly. Pour the papaya nectar over the fruit and mix.

YIELD: *Makes 1 baby serving*

EACH WITH: 12.2 calories; 0.9 gm total fat; 0.1 gm saturated fat; 0.0 mg cholesterol; 0.6 mg sodium; 1.2 gm carbohydrate; 0.4 gm dietary fiber; 0.1 gm protein; 1.2 mg calcium; 0.1 mg iron; 26.7 IU vitamin A; 0.7 mg vitamin C.

YOGURT CHEESE

One of my family's favorite health-ful indulgences is yogurt cheese—plain yogurt that has been drained of its whey so its texture resembles cream cheese.

To make yogurt cheese, line a colander with several layers of clean cheesecloth (or use a yogurt drainer, a small sieve with muslin liner). Fill the colander with pas-teurized whole-milk yogurt. Place the colander in a container that will catch the whey, leaving at least 1¹/₂ inches for the liquid to drain off. Cover and refrigerate 8 to 12 hours.

Use the cheese as a substitute for sour cream or cream cheese. And don't throw out the whey! It can be added to soups, stews, or smoothies.

Carrot-Papaya Yogurt 👶

The flesh of the papaya is golden-yellow, juicy, and silky smooth, with a sweet and mellow flavor. It is an excellent source of vitamins A and C and potassium. There are also small amounts of calcium, iron, thi-amin, riboflavin, and niacin. It contains a protein-digesting enzyme that is used as a remedy for indigestion.

- ¹/₄ to ¹/₂ cup (60 to 120 ml) water
- ¹/₂ cup (55 g) shredded carrots (about 4 baby carrots)
- ¹/₄ cup (35 g) peeled, seeded, finely diced ripe papaya
- 1 tablespoon (15 g) plain or vanilla yogurt

▥ Place ¹/₄ cup (60 ml) water and carrots in a microwave-safe glass bowl. Cover and cook on high 4 minutes. Transfer to a food processor and add the papaya; process 45 seconds. Remove the puree from the food processor. Use 1 tablespoon of the puree and blend with 1 tablespoon yogurt. The remaining puree can be stored in the refrigerator for up to 2 days.

◎ Combine ¹/₂ cup (120 ml) water and the carrots in a small pan over medium-high heat. Cover and bring to a boil. Transfer to a food processor and add the papaya; process 45 seconds. Remove the puree from the food processor and blend 1 tablespoon yogurt with 1 tablespoon of the carrot-papaya puree.

VARIATIONS: Substitute ¹/₄ cup (40 g) peeled, pitted, ripe fresh apricots or ¹/₄ cup (40 g) very ripe peeled, pitted plums for the papaya.

YIELD: *Makes a bout 8 tablespoons or ¹/₂ cup*

EACH WITH: 3.8 calories; 0.0 gm total fat; 0.0 gm saturated fat; 0.1 mg choles-terol; 2.7 mg sodium; 0.8 gm carbohydrate; 0.2 gm dietary fiber; 0.1 gm protein; 4.0 mg calcium; 0.0 mg iron; 565.0 IU vitamin A; 2.9 mg vitamin C.

TEN MONTHS

Good night,

   Sleep tight,

      Don't let the bedbugs bite.

—SLEEP TIGHT

Continue breast milk or formula, three to four feedings a day (20 to 32 ounces).

Changes may occur intermittently in your child's eating pattern. Most of us don't enjoy eating if we have no appetite, especially if forced to eat. It takes keen observation and good intuition to recognize when your baby is hungry and needs to eat, as opposed to waiting until he is very hungry before feeding him. "Starving a child to eat" will not promote good eating habits.

Children are normally rhythmic in their habits, so satisfying their hunger should be in tune with that rhythm. Meals should be served at the same time each day whenever possible. Although this may conflict with adult schedules initially, babies eventually seem to adapt to the rest of the family's mealtimes, probably because they enjoy the social interaction.

Fatigue is often a major factor in loss of appetite. An exhausted child's appetite is seldom restored until he has had a nap or a good night's sleep.

Your baby's diet will now start to resemble the rest of the family's. He will eat three to four small meals a day and continue to make progress in self-feeding, but he may not be able to use a spoon independently until after his first birthday. Until then, fill the spoon and help him guide it to his mouth. Talk to your baby while feeding, and tell him the name and the colors of the food.

After ten months, you can make these additions to your baby's diet:

▪ **BABY CEREAL, COOKED:** iron-fortified wheat cereal

- **VEGETABLES:** cabbage, parsnip, leek, and red, green, orange or yellow bell pepper (all cooked) and parsley and celery (well cooked)

- **FRUIT:** fresh, ripe kiwi, melons, cherries (halved and pitted), and blueberries

- **JUICE:** blueberry, cherry, and kiwi

- **DAIRY:** cream cheese, mascarpone cheese, fresh or soft mozzarella, Jack cheese, and Swiss cheese

- **GRAINS:** whole-wheat breads, crackers, and pasta

- **LEGUMES:** lentils and split peas

- **MISCELLANEOUS:** tofu, soy, pancakes, and waffles

- Always strap your baby in a high chair while he is eating and watch your baby the whole time he is eating and drinking. As babies grow, they develop an amazing ability to wiggle out of high chairs.

- The intake from one meal to the next may vary dramatically. Over the course of a day, your baby will eat what he needs. Make sure he can choose from a variety of wholesome foods.

- Continue feeding $1/2$ cup iron-fortified rice, barley, or oatmeal cereal. You can now also add wheat cereal if there is no allergy to wheat in the family. Serve a vitamin C–rich food with the cereal for better iron absorption.

- Encourage your baby to drink from a cup.

- Offer up to $1/3$ cup fruit and $1/3$ cup peeled soft-cooked vegetables rich in vitamins C, or B, and A. (See "Vitamins" on page 25.)

- 1 to 4 tablespoons legumes: split peas or lentils.

- 1 to 4 tablespoons rice or noodles.

Typical Daily Menu for a Ten-Month-Old

MEAL	FOODS
Breakfast	$1/4$ to $1/2$ cup iron-fortified whole wheat cereal
	1 slice mashed kiwi
	2 tablespoons lightly mashed blueberries
	and breast milk or formula
Snack	$1/4$ cup oat Cheerios (finger food),
	and breast milk or formula
Lunch	Vegetables with Tofu (sweet potato, carrots, tofu page 127),
	2 small rice crackers, and breast milk or formula
Snack	Mascarpone, Yogurt, and Apricot (page 122),
	and breast milk or formula
Dinner	Lentils, Potato, and Cheese (page 119),
	Red Bell Pepper and Green Beans (page 126),
	and water from a cup if thirsty
Before Bedtime	Breast milk or formula

This sample covers the minimum daily requirements for a ten- or eleven-month old.

- 20 to 32 ounces (570 to 946 ml) breast milk or formula

- 4 servings grains (half from whole grain): $1/2$ cup (50 g) whole-wheat cereal, $1/4$ cup (25 g) oat Cheerios, and 2 rice crackers

- 3 servings vegetables: sweet potato and carrot, green beans, plus red bell pepper

- 2 to 3 servings fruit: 1 slice kiwi, blueberries, apricot

- 2 servings protein: tofu, lentils (with cheese)

Scrambled Egg Yolk with Cheese 🍼

- Oil or butter for frying
- 1 egg yolk
- 1 tablespoon (14 ml) breast milk, formula, or water
- 1 tablespoon (8 g) grated Swiss cheese

◎ Heat the oil in a small frying pan over medium heat. In a bowl, whisk together the egg yolk; breast milk, formula, or water; and cheese. Pour into the frying pan and cook, stirring, until cooked through completely.

YIELD: *Makes 1 baby serving*

EACH WITH: 40.2 calories; 3.2 gm total fat; 1.4 gm saturated fat; 108.0 mg cholesterol; 10.6 mg sodium; 0.5 gm carbohydrate; 0.0 gm dietary fiber; 2.3 gm protein; 37.7 mg calcium; 0.2 mg iron; 150.6 IU vitamin A; 0.0 mg vitamin C.

Lentils 🍼

Carrots, celery, and potatoes may also be cooked together with the lentils and mashed. Leftover lentils can be frozen in small batches.

- 1/4 cup (50 g) brown lentils, washed well
- 2 1/2 cups (595 ml) water
- Butter (optional)

◎ Place the lentils and water in a saucepan and bring to a boil over medium-high heat. Cover, reduce heat, and simmer 45 minutes. Check occasionally to add more water if needed. When the lentils are soft, mash with a fork. Add some butter if desired.

YIELD: *Makes almost 1 cup, or 16 tablespoons*

EACH WITH: 14.4 calories; 0.0 gm total fat; 0.0 gm saturated fat; 0.0 mg cholesterol; 0.2 mg sodium; 2.5 gm carbohydrate; 1.0 gm dietary fiber; 1.1 gm protein; 2.4 mg calcium; 0.4 mg iron; 1.0 IU vitamin A; 0.2 mg vitamin C.

VARIATIONS: Serve with cooked carrots, celery, rice, or potatoes; or bananas, avocados, or pureed apricots.

Lentils and Banana Mash 👶

- 2 tablespoons cooked Lentils (page 119)
- 2 tablespoons (30 g) mashed ripe banana

Mash the lentils and banana together. Warm gently over low heat, if desired.

YIELD: *Makes 1 baby serving*

EACH WITH: 13.4 calories; 0.0 gm total fat; 0.0 gm saturated fat; 0.0 mg cholesterol; 0.2 mg sodium; 2.8 gm carbohydrate; 0.7 gm dietary fiber; 0.6 gm protein; 1.5 mg calcium; 0.2 mg iron; 5.0 IU vitamin A; 0.7 mg vitamin C.

Lentils, Potato, and Cheese 👶

- 2 tablespoons cooked Lentils (page 118), mashed
- 1 small potato, cooked and mashed
- 1 tablespoon (8 g) grated Swiss cheese

▭ Mix the lentils and potato. Place in a microwave-safe dish and sprinkle with the cheese. Microwave on medium until warmed through, less than 60 seconds. Cool, stir, and check food temperature before serving.

YIELD: *Makes 1 to 2 baby servings*

EACH WITH: 10.1 calories; 0.1 gm total fat; 0.1 gm saturated fat; 0.4 mg cholesterol; 1.2 mg sodium; 1.9 gm carbohydrate; 0.3 gm dietary fiber; 0.4 gm protein; 4.3 mg calcium; 0.1 mg iron; 3.9 IU vitamin A; 0.6 mg vitamin C.

Lentil Roast 👶

This dish is also tasty with just lentils, sweet potato, and carrots mashed together with butter. Precooked lentils, carrots, and sweet potato will make this a quick and easy dish. If made from scratch, use the microwaved Pureed Sweet Potato (page 85) and Pureed Carrots (page 98).

- Oil or butter to grease a small ovenproof dish
- ¼ cup cooked Lentils (page 118)
- 1 sweet potato, peeled, cooked, and mashed
- 3 baby carrots, cooked and mashed
- 1 tablespoon (14 ml) butter
- 2 egg yolks, beaten
- ¼ cup apple juice

▣ Preheat the oven to 350°F (180°C, or gas mark 4). Grease a small ovenproof dish. Mix together the lentils, potato, carrots, and butter. In a bowl, whisk the egg yolks and apple juice and blend with the lentil mix. Pour into the dish, cover, and bake in a water bath 30 to 45 minutes,. (See "Water Baths for Custards" on page 109.) Let cool before serving. Divide any leftovers into small portions and freeze.

YIELD: *Makes 1 cup*

EACH WITH: 22.5 calories; 1.4 gm total fat; 0.7 gm saturated fat; 30.0 mg cholesterol; 3.5 mg sodium; 1.8 gm carbohydrate; 0.4 gm dietary fiber; 0.7 gm protein; 5.6 mg calcium; 0.2 mg iron; 1140.7 IU vitamin A; 0.8 mg vitamin C.

Lentil Stew 👶

- ¼ cup (50 g) brown lentils, washed well
- 1½ cups (355 ml) water
- 1 small potato, peeled and cubed
- 4 baby carrots, sliced
- 1 small stalk celery, sliced
- 1 tablespoon (14 g) butter

◎ Place the lentils and water in a saucepan and bring to a boil over medium-high heat. Cover, reduce heat, and simmer 30 minutes. Add the potato, carrots, and celery. Add more water if needed. Cook for 15 minutes longer, or until the vegetables are soft. Add the butter and mash with a fork. Divide the leftovers into small portions and freeze.

YIELD: *Makes 16 tablespoons or about 1 cup*

EACH WITH: 9.1 calories; 0.3 gm total fat; 0.2 gm saturated fat; 0.8 mg cholesterol; 2.7 mg sodium; 1.3 gm carbohydrate; 0.3 gm dietary fiber; 0.3 gm protein; 2.0 mg calcium; 0.1 mg iron; 223.4 IU vitamin A; 0.4 mg vitamin C.

Split Pea Stew 👶

- ¼ cup (50 g) dried split green peas, rinsed
- 2 cups (475 ml) water
- 1 small potato, peeled and cut into small cubes
- 1 small carrot, peeled and cut into small pieces
- Butter (optional)

◎ In a medium saucepan, combine the split peas, water, potato, and carrot over medium heat. Cover and slowly bring to a boil. Reduce the heat and simmer 45 minutes, stirring from time to time, until the peas and vegetables are soft. Check occasionally to see if more water is needed. When done, mash with the butter, if desired. Divide any leftover stew into small portions and freeze.

YIELD: *Makes 16 tablespoons or about 1 cup*

EACH WITH: 9.6 calories; 0.0 gm total fat; 0.0 gm saturated fat; 0.0 mg cholesterol; 1.4 mg sodium; 2.0 gm carbohydrate; 0.5 gm dietary fiber; 0.4 gm protein; 1.5 mg calcium; 0.1 mg iron; 316.9 IU vitamin A; 0.5 mg vitamin C.

Sweet Potato-Tofu Custard

This is a healthy, tasty dish that would satisfy anyone's sweet tooth.

- Oil or butter for greasing two 6-ounce custard cups
- 1 medium sweet potato (about ¹/₂ pound, or 225 g)
- ¹/₄ cup (60 g) soft tofu
- ¹/₄ cup (60 ml) apple, pear, or white grape juice
- 1 egg yolk
- 2 teaspoons olive oil

Preheat the oven to 350°F (180°C, or gas mark 4). Oil or butter two small custard cups. Prick the sweet potato with a fork. Place on a baking sheet and bake in oven for 45 minutes, or until potato is soft. (Or microwave on high 8 to 10 minutes, until soft.) Cool the potato, then peel. Transfer the sweet potato flesh to a blender; add the tofu, juice, egg yolk, and oil and process 30 to 45 seconds. Divide the mixture between the two prepared custard cups. Bake in a water bath. (See "Water Baths for Custards" on page 109.) Cool and serve with a dot of butter, if the custard seems a little dry. The extra soufflé can be saved in the refrigerator for up to 2 days.

YIELD: *Makes 2 baby servings*

EACH WITH: 17.3 calories; 0.6 gm total fat; 0.1 gm saturated fat; 8.1 mg cholesterol; 4.0 mg sodium; 2.6 gm carbohydrate; 0.3 gm dietary fiber; 0.4 gm protein; 7.1 mg calcium; 0.1 mg iron; 1995.3 IU vitamin A; 2.6 mg vitamin C.

MAKE IT FOR GROWN-UPS: Here's how to make a Sweet Potato Soufflé for two. Bake an extra sweet potato when making your baby's custard. Follow directions for the baby custard but substitute orange juice for the apple juice and add a pinch each of salt, cinnamon, nutmeg, and ginger. Then whip the leftover egg white until it peaks and fold into the custard mix. Divide between two oiled custard cups. Bake in a water bath 20 to 30 minutes. (See "Water Baths for Custards" on page 109.) Test with a knife. When the knife blade comes out clean, the custard is done.

YIELD: *1 serving*

EACH WITH: 745.1 calories; 19.8 gm total fat; 3.5 gm saturated fat; 214.7 mg cholesterol; 508.5 mg sodium; 125.1 gm carbohydrate; 16.6 gm dietary fiber; 20.2 gm protein; 296.2 mg calcium; 6.3 mg iron; 103703.6 IU vitamin A; 115.2 mg vitamin C.

Mascarpone, Yogurt, and Apricot ♟

Mascarpone is a soft, Italian sweet cheese that is very pleasing to babies. If it is difficult to find, use regular cream cheese.

* 1 tablespoon (15 g) mascarpone (or cream cheese)
* 1 tablespoon (14 ml) plain or vanilla yogurt
* 1 tablespoon Apricot Puree (page 98)

Mix the mascarpone and yogurt well with a fork and top with the apricot puree.

VARIATIONS: Instead of the apricot puree, try ¼ mashed banana, ¼ ripe mashed peach, or 1 tablespoon Prune Puree (page 93).

YIELD: *Makes 1 baby serving*

EACH WITH: 30.0 calories; 2.8 gm total fat; 1.8 gm saturated fat; 9.0 mg cholesterol; 25.0 mg sodium; 0.5 gm carbohydrate; 0.0 gm dietary fiber; 0.8 gm protein; 15.1 mg calcium; 0.1 mg iron; 105.2 IU vitamin A; 0.0 mg vitamin C.

Tofu and Apricot Puree ♟

This puree can be served with cooked rice or with Baby Rice (page 102).

* ¼ cup (2 ounces, or 55 g) silken tofu
* ¼ cup (60 g) apricot puree

Place the tofu and apricot puree in a blender and process until smooth.

YIELD: *Makes 2 baby servings*

EACH WITH: 5.4 calories; 0.2 gm total fat; 0.0 gm saturated fat; 0.0 mg cholesterol; 0.3 mg sodium; 0.6 gm carbohydrate; 0.1 gm dietary fiber; 0.4 gm protein; 14.2 mg calcium; 0.2 mg iron; 102.6 IU vitamin A; 0.5 mg vitamin C.

Steamed Cauliflower with Grated Cheese

- 2 or 3 cauliflower florets
- 1 tablespoon (14 ml) water
- 1 tablespoon (8 g) grated Swiss cheese

Place the cauliflower in a small glass bowl with the water. Cover and microwave on high 1 to 2 minutes, or until soft. Transfer to a plate and cut into small pieces or mash lightly and sprinkle with the cheese.

Place the cauliflower in a steamer basket with a little water and steam 5 minutes, or until soft. Transfer to a plate and cut into small pieces or mash lightly and sprinkle with the cheese.

YIELD: *Makes 1 baby serving*

EACH WITH: 7.9 calories; 0.3 gm total fat; 0.2 gm saturated fat; 0.8 mg cholesterol; 4.7 mg sodium; 0.9 gm carbohydrate; 0.5 gm dietary fiber; 0.6 gm protein; 9.9 mg calcium; 0.1 mg iron; 9.4 IU vitamin A; 9.0 mg vitamin C.

Tofu, Cheese, and Scrambled Egg Yolks

- 2 tablespoons (30 g) silken tofu
- 2 egg yolks
- 1 tablespoon (14 ml) water
- 1/2 teaspoon butter
- 2 tablespoons (15 g) grated Swiss cheese

Place the tofu, egg yolks, and water in a blender and process 3 seconds. Melt the butter in a small frying pan over medium heat. Pour the tofu-egg mix into the frying pan. Stir in the cheese and scramble until the mixture is cooked through.

YIELD: *Makes 1 baby serving*

EACH WITH: 31.6 calories; 2.6 gm total fat; 1.2 gm saturated fat; 72.8 mg cholesterol; 7.3 mg sodium; 0.4 gm carbohydrate; 0.0 gm dietary fiber; 1.7 gm protein; 34.2 mg calcium; 0.3 mg iron; 112.5 IU vitamin A; 0.0 mg vitamin C.

Bubble and Squeak (Modified) 👶 👨‍👩‍👧

🕐 *However, cabbage is high in calcium, vitamin C, or and folate. Buy the smallest cabbage you can find, about 1 pound (455 g); a head of cabbage goes a long way. Remaining cabbage can be used in Fish Taco (page 221), Cabbage and Apple (this page), coleslaw, stir-fries, and soups.*

* 1 medium potato, peeled and diced
* 1 cup (90 g) finely grated cabbage
* 1 leek, well cleaned and finely chopped
* ³/₄ cup (175 ml) water
* 2 tablespoons (28 g) butter
* Salt (for the adult portion)
* Pepper (for the adult portion)

◎ Place the potato, cabbage, leek, and water in a medium saucepan over medium-high heat. Bring to a boil, reduce the heat, cover, and simmer about 20 minutes; add water if needed. When the potato and cabbage are soft and the water is almost absorbed, add the butter and mash. Cool a small portion (1 to 2 tablespoons) for your baby. Add salt and pepper to the adult portion.

YIELD: *Makes 1 baby serving AND 1 adult serving*

EACH WITH: 7.4 calories; 0.4 gm total fat; 0.3 gm saturated fat; 1.1 mg cholesterol; 0.6 mg sodium; 0.9 gm carbohydrate; 0.1 gm dietary fiber; 0.1 gm protein; 1.5 mg calcium; 0.0 mg iron; 16.2 IU vitamin A; 0.6 mg vitamin C.

Cabbage and Apple 👶

* 1 cup (90 g) finely shredded cabbage
* 1 apple, peeled, cored, and cut into wedges
* ¹/₃ cup (75 ml) water
* 1 tablespoon (14 g) butter (optional)

◎ Place the cabbage, apple, and water in a small saucepan over medium heat. Slowly bring to a simmer, cover, and cook about 5 minutes, until the cabbage and apple are soft. Add more water, if needed. Lightly mash and add butter if desired.

YIELD: *Makes 1 to 2 baby servings*

EACH WITH: 3.5 calories; 0.0 gm total fat; 0.0 gm saturated fat; 0.0 mg cholesterol; 0.2 mg sodium; 0.9 gm carbohydrate; 0.2 gm dietary fiber; 0.0 gm protein; 1.0 mg calcium; 0.0 mg iron; 5.4 IU vitamin A; 0.5 mg vitamin C.

Creamy Potato, Parsnip, and Carrot Mash

- 2 potatoes, peeled and cubed
- 2 parsnips, peeled, and diced
- 2 carrots, peeled and diced
- 1 cup (235 ml) water
- 2 tablespoons (28 g) butter
- 2 tablespoons (28 ml) milk
- 1 tablespoon (12 g) sour cream
- Salt (for the adult portion)
- Pepper (for the adult portion)
- 1/4 cup (15 g) parsley, finely chopped

Place the potatoes, parsnips, carrots, and water in a medium saucepan over medium-high heat and bring to a boil. Reduce the heat, cover, and simmer 30 minutes. Check occasionally and add water if needed. When the vegetables are soft and the water has been mostly absorbed, add the butter, milk, and sour cream.

Mash until all the lumps are gone, then whisk until the vegetables are light and fluffy. Season the adult portion with salt and pepper. Sprinkle both the baby and adult portions with the parsley.

YIELD: *Makes 1 baby serving (1 to 2 tablespoons) AND 1 or 2 adult side-dish servings*

EACH WITH: 9.7 calories; 0.3 gm total fat; 0.2 gm saturated fat; 0.8 mg cholesterol; 1.5 mg sodium; 1.6 gm carbohydrate; 0.2 gm dietary fiber; 0.1 gm protein; 2.8 mg calcium; 0.0 mg iron; 203.1 IU vitamin A; 0.9 mg vitamin C.

Creamy Green Beans

- 1/4 pound (115 g) fresh green beans, trimmed and snapped in half
- 2 tablespoons (28 ml) water
- 1 tablespoon (14 ml) plain yogurt
- 1 tablespoon (15 g) cream cheese

Place the green beans in a microwave-safe dish with the water. Cover and microwave on high 3 minutes. When cool, cut the beans into small pieces. In a bowl, mix the yogurt and cream cheese together and add the beans.

YIELD: *Makes 2 baby servings*

EACH WITH: 5.8 calories; 0.3 gm total fat; 0.2 gm saturated fat; 1.0 mg cholesterol; 2.8 mg sodium; 0.6 gm carbohydrate; 0.2 gm dietary fiber; 0.2 gm protein; 4.7 mg calcium; 0.1 mg iron; 60.3 IU vitamin A; 0.7 mg vitamin C.

ROASTING RED BELL PEPPERS

All bell peppers are good sources of vitamin C, or but red bell peppers have twice as much vitamin C as green peppers. Roasted and pureed red peppers go well with baked fish or steamed vegetables. For your baby, adding a little breast milk or formula can mellow the pureed roasted peppers. Here's how to roast them.

1. Preheat the oven to 400°F (200°C, or gas mark 6).

2. Wash the peppers, wrap in tinfoil, and place on a baking sheet. Bake for 1 hour.

3. Carefully remove the tinfoil with the peppers; they will be very hot. Let cool until the foil can be safely opened.

4. Peel the peppers and remove the strings and seeds. Cut peppers into strips or puree in a blender or food processor.

Here's a quick alternative way to roast the peppers.

1. Preheat the broiler.

2. Wash the peppers and cut in half (do not remove stems and seeds).

3. Place peppers cut sides down on a baking sheet covered with a piece of tinfoil, 3 inches below the broiler. Broil until the halves are blackened.

4. Carefully remove and place in a sealed plastic bag for 15 minutes.

5. Remove the skin, stems, and seeds and cut into $1^1/_2$-inch strips or puree.

Red Bell Pepper and Green Beans

- 5 green beans, cut into thin strips
- $1/_4$ small red bell pepper, seeded and cut into thin strips

 Place the beans and pepper in a steamer basket and steam until soft.

Cool and serve as finger food.

VARIATIONS: Combine 2 tablespoons cooked green peas with the red pepper strips. Your baby may also enjoy eating Roasted Red Bell Pepper (left), peeled and cut into thin strips. Serve with a slice of avocado cut into small pieces.

YIELD: *Makes 1 baby serving*

EACH WITH: 2.6 calories; 0.0 gm total fat; 0.0 gm saturated fat; 0.0 mg cholesterol; 0.1 mg sodium; 0.6 gm carbohydrate; 0.2 gm dietary fiber; 0.1 gm protein; 2.0 mg calcium; 0.0 mg iron; 172.9 IU vitamin A; 9.2 mg vitamin C.

Apple "Cream"

- $^1/_4$ cup (60 g) mascarpone (mild Italian cheese), cream cheese, or yogurt cheese (See "Yogurt Cheese" on page 114.)
- 2 tablespoons (28 ml) frozen apple juice concentrate

Place the cheese and juice concentrate into blender and whip until creamy.

YIELD: *Makes about $^1/_4$ cup or 4 tablespoons*

EACH WITH: 43.5 calories; 3.4 gm total fat; 2.1 gm saturated fat; 10.6 mg cholesterol; 30.1 mg sodium; 2.7 gm carbohydrate; 0.0 gm dietary fiber; 0.8 gm protein; 8.9 mg calcium; 0.2 mg iron; 130.1 IU vitamin A; 0.1 mg vitamin C.

Vegetables with Tofu

- $^1/_4$ cup (35 g) cubed peeled sweet potato
- 2 small carrots, peeled and sliced
- 1 cup (235 ml) water
- 1 tablespoon (14 g) butter
- Breast milk, formula, apple juice, or cooking water, as needed for mashing
- $^1/_4$ cup (2 ounces, or 55 g) silken tofu, cut into small pieces

Place the sweet potato, carrots, and water in a medium saucepan over medium-high heat and bring to a boil. Reduce the heat, cover, and simmer 20 to 30 minutes, or until tender. Mash with the butter and breast milk, formula, apple juice, or cooking water. Toss the tofu with the vegetables.

YIELD: *Makes 2 baby servings*

EACH WITH: 15.0 calories; 1.0 gm total fat; 0.6 gm saturated fat; 2.3 mg cholesterol; 2.9 mg sodium; 1.3 gm carbohydrate; 0.2 gm dietary fiber; 0.3 gm protein; 10.8 mg calcium; 0.2 mg iron; 1280.2 IU vitamin A; 0.9 mg vitamin C.

ELEVEN MONTHS

High diddle, diddle

The Cat and the Fiddle,

The Cow jump'd over the Moon;

The little Dog laugh'd

To see such Craft,

And the Dish ran away with the Spoon.

—HEY DIDDLE, DIDDLE

Your baby may be taking 16 to 24 ounces of breast milk or formula. As she approaches her first birthday, most of her nutrition should be coming from solids.

By now, your little one has been exposed to a variety of foods, and you probably have a good idea of what she likes and dislikes. Continue to offer a broad selection of new age-appropriate foods.

After eleven months, you can make these additions to your baby's diet.

- **BABY CEREAL COOKED:** iron-fortified rice, Cream of Wheat, oatmeal, barley, and multigrain cereal

- **VEGETABLES:** brussels sprouts, turnips, rutabaga, beets, kale (all cooked), and romaine lettuce

- **FRUIT:** pineapple, raisins (softened or cooked), grapes (seeded and halved), figs, and raspberries

- **JUICE:** cranberry, pineapple, and raspberry

- **DAIRY:** cottage cheese, whole-fat ricotta, cheddar, goat cheese, Parmesan, and Romano

- **LEGUMES:** black, white, or red beans, lima beans, and refried beans

- **MISCELLANEOUS:** polenta and couscous

- Offer 2 to 4 servings of iron-fortified cereal, whole-grain breads, muffins, crackers, rice, (preferably brown), cooked grains, or pasta. Each serving should be about $1/4$ of an adult serving, that is: $1/4$ piece of bread, $1/4$ small muffin, $1/4$ cup cooked or cold cereal, or $1/4$ cup cooked rice or pasta.

- Give 3 servings of 1 to 2 tablespoons each of fruits and vegetables. Vary the fruits and vegetables introduced during the past five months, so your baby will get all the necessary vitamins. (See "Vitamins" on page 25 and "Minerals" on page 31.)

- In addition to breast milk or formula, serve yogurt, cottage cheese, cream cheese, mascarpone, and ricotta (2 to 4 tablespoons), or other cheeses ($1/2$ to $3/4$ ounces).

- Give 2 servings (2 ounces total) of protein equivalents, such as egg yolk, tofu, beans, and legumes. (See "Protein" on page 11.)

Typical Daily Menu for an Eleven-Month-Old

MEAL	FOODS
Breakfast	$1/4$ cup Cream of Wheat, 2 tablespoons raspberries, 1 small slice (2 tablespoons) mashed cantaloupe, and breast milk or formula
Snack	Beet, Avocado, and Pear Medley (page 136), and breast milk or formula
Lunch	$1/4$ cup Polenta with Mascarpone (page 137), and water from a cup if thirsty
Snack	$1/4$ piece of toast with butter and raisin puree, and breast milk or formula
Dinner	$1/4$ cup Elbow Macaroni with Peas and Parmesan (page 138), and water from a cup if thirsty
Before Bedtime	Breast milk or formula

White Beans 👶 👪

Dried beans should be soaked prior to cooking. Soak 1 cup beans in 6 cups water overnight.

- 1 cup (215 g) dried small white beans, soaked
- 6 cups (1410 ml) water
- 2 bay leaves
- Salt (for the adults)

◎ Drain and rinse the soaked beans. Combine the beans, water, and bay leaves in a 4-quart saucepan over medium heat. Bring to a boil and skim off foam. Cover, reduce heat, and simmer 1½ hours, or until tender. Stir occasionally during cooking and add more water if needed. Discard the bay leaves and drain the beans, reserving some cooking liquid for mashing the beans (or use breast milk or formula for your baby's portion). Serve your baby 1 to 2 tablespoons. Serve the leftover beans to the rest of the family or divide the beans into small portions and freeze.

YIELD: *Makes 3 cups*

EACH WITH: 15.9 calories; 0.1 gm total fat; 0.0 gm saturated fat; 0.0 mg cholesterol; 0.2 mg sodium; 2.9 gm carbohydrate; 1.2 gm dietary fiber; 1.0 gm protein; 8.2 mg calcium; 0.3 mg iron; 0.0 IU vitamin A; 0.0 mg vitamin C.

Broccoli and White Beans 👶

- 2 tablespoons (25 g) cooked white beans (homemade or canned)
- 1 small broccoli floret, steamed
- 1 teaspoon butter or oil

◎ Gently warm the beans in a small saucepan over low heat, adding some of the cooking liquid from the beans, if necessary. Add the broccoli and butter or oil and mash with a fork.

VARIATIONS: Try mashing the beans with 2 tablespoons cooked and mashed carrots, potatoes, sweet potatoes, zucchini, other squash, or avocados.

YIELD: *Makes 1 baby serving*

EACH WITH: 7.2 calories; 0.3 gm total fat; 0.2 gm saturated fat; 0.6 mg cholesterol; 3.6 mg sodium; 1.0 gm carbohydrate; 0.4 gm dietary fiber; 0.3 gm protein; 4.6 mg calcium; 0.1 mg iron; 179.5 IU vitamin A; 5.7 mg vitamin C.

BEAN EQUIVALENTS

1 cup dried beans uncooked =
3 cups cooked =
two 15-ounce cans of beans (drained)

1 pound dried beans =
2 cups dried beans =
6 cups cooked beans =
four 15-ounce cans of beans, drained

Black Beans 👪

Dried beans should be soaked prior to cooking. Soak 1 1/2 cups beans in 7 cups water overnight.

- 1 1/2 cups (290 g) dried black beans, soaked
- 8 cups (1880 ml) water
- 2 bay leaves
- Salt (for adults)

◎ Drain and rinse the soaked beans. Combine the beans, water, and bay leaves in a 4-quart saucepan over medium heat. Bring to a boil and skim off foam. Cover, reduce heat, and simmer 2 hours, or until soft. Stir occasionally during cooking and add more water if needed. When the beans are done, remove the bay leaves and drain. Save some of the cooking liquid for mashing the beans (or use breast milk or formula for your baby's portion). Serve your baby 1 to 2 tablespoons. Serve some for the rest of the family or divide leftover beans into small portions and freeze.

YIELD: *Makes 4 1/2 cups*

EACH WITH: 14.2 calories; 0.1 gm total fat; 0.0 gm saturated fat; 0.0 mg cholesterol; 0.1 mg sodium; 2.5 gm carbohydrate; 0.9 gm dietary fiber; 1.0 gm protein; 2.9 mg calcium; 0.2 mg iron; 0.6 IU vitamin A; 0.0 mg vitamin C.

Black Beans and Rice 👶

Serve with 1 tablespoon Pureed Sweet Potatoes (page 85)

- 1 tablespoon (10 g) cooked rice
- 1 tablespoon (10 g) cooked black beans (home-made or canned)
- Breast milk or formula
- 1 teaspoon plain yogurt
- 1 tablespoon (7 g) grated cheddar cheese

▭ Gently warm the rice and beans in a small covered microwave-safe dish about 10 to 20 seconds. Add the breast milk, formula, or cooking liquid if needed and mash with a fork. Top the beans and rice with the yogurt and cheese.

YIELD: *Makes 1 baby serving*

EACH WITH: 19.5 calories; 0.9 gm total fat; 0.5 gm saturated fat; 2.7 mg cholesterol; 15.5 mg sodium; 1.9 gm carbohydrate; 0.3 gm dietary fiber; 1.1 gm protein; 20.3 mg calcium; 0.1 mg iron; 25.5 IU vitamin A; 0.0 mg vitamin C.

Peruvian Bean Puree 👶

- 1 tablespoon (14 g) butter
- 1 small leek, white part only, washed and finely sliced
- 1/4 cup (60 g) canned lima beans with about 1 tablespoon (14 ml) liquid
- 1 tablespoon finely chopped parsley

◎ Melt the butter in a small frying pan over medium heat. Add the leek and sauté about 3 to 5 minutes, or until tender. Stir in the lima beans and liquid and heat through. Transfer to a small bowl and mash. (For a smoother consistency, puree in blender 20 seconds.) Garnish with the parsley.

YIELD: *Makes 1 baby serving*

EACH WITH: 6.5 calories; 0.5 gm total fat; 0.3 gm saturated fat; 1.2 mg cholesterol; 3.8 mg sodium; 0.6 gm carbohydrate; 0.1 gm dietary fiber; 0.1 gm protein; 2.2 mg calcium; 0.1 mg iron; 31.1 IU vitamin A; 0.5 mg vitamin C.

Cottage Cheese with Scrambled Egg Yolk 👶

Serve with a small piece of buttered whole-wheat toast and 1/2 kiwi fruit, sliced

- 1 tablespoon (15 g) cottage cheese
- 1 egg yolk
- 1 teaspoon olive oil

◎ Mix the cottage cheese and egg yolk in a small cup and beat well with a fork. Heat the oil in a frying pan over medium heat. Add the egg-cheese mixture and scramble until the egg is well cooked.

YIELD: *Makes 1 baby serving*

EACH WITH: 34.6 calories; 2.6 gm total fat; 1.0 gm saturated fat; 105.9 mg cholesterol; 32.6 mg sodium; 0.5 gm carbohydrate; 0.0 gm dietary fiber; 2.2 gm protein; 15.2 mg calcium; 0.2 mg iron; 134.0 IU vitamin A; 0.0 mg vitamin C.

Refried Beans with Cheddar Cheese

Serve with mashed avocado.

- 2 tablespoons (30 g) canned full-fat refried beans
- 1 tablespoon (7 g) grated cheddar cheese
- 1/2 teaspoon olive oil
- 2 teaspoons yogurt cheese (see "Yogurt Cheese" on page 114) or sour cream

In a small frying pan over medium heat, combine the beans, cheddar cheese, and oil. Cook, until the mixture is warm and the cheese is melted. Top with the yogurt cheese

YIELD: *Makes 1 baby serving*

EACH WITH: 23.9 calories; 1.7 gm total fat; 0.7 gm saturated fat; 3.4 mg cholesterol; 35.9 mg sodium; 1.4 gm carbohydrate; 0.4 gm dietary fiber; 0.9 gm protein; 17.9 mg calcium; 0.1 mg iron; 30.7 IU vitamin A; 0.5 mg vitamin C.

> **MAKE IT FOR GROWN-UPS:** For a quick adult meal, use the remaining canned refried beans to make Tostada (page 161).

Raisin Puree I

This very sweet puree is made with dark, seedless raisins.

- 1/4 cup (40 g) dark, seedless raisins
- 1/4 cup (60 ml) water

Place the raisins and water in a 1-cup microwave-safe measuring cup. Microwave on high until hot, about 40 seconds. Transfer to a blender and puree 30 to 60 seconds, until smooth.

YIELD: *Makes 1/4 cup or 4 tablespoons*

EACH WITH: 30.8 calories; 0.0 gm total fat; 0.0 gm saturated fat; 0.0 mg cholesterol; 1.1 mg sodium; 8.2 gm carbohydrate; 0.4 gm dietary fiber; 0.3 gm protein; 5.2 mg calcium; 0.2 mg iron; 0.0 IU vitamin A; 0.2 mg vitamin C.

Raisin Puree II

This puree is made with golden, seedless raisins and is mellow and less sweet. The iron content is the same in both kinds of raisins.

- 1/4 cup (40 g) golden, seedless raisins
- 3 tablespoons (45 ml) hot water

Place the raisins and water in a blender. Puree 1 minute, until smooth. (You may need to scrape the raisins down with a spatula.)

YIELD: *Makes 1/4 cup or 4 tablespoons*

EACH WITH: 31.1 calories; 0.0 gm total fat; 0.0 gm saturated fat; 0.0 mg cholesterol; 1.2 mg sodium; 8.2 gm carbohydrate; 0.4 gm dietary fiber; 0.3 gm protein; 5.5 mg calcium; 0.2 mg iron; 0.0 IU vitamin A; 0.3 mg vitamin C.

RAISINS

Raisins are a good source of iron and therefore make a nutritious snack for babies and toddlers. However, dried raisins can cause choking; they also stick to teeth and can cause cavities. Avoid these problems by soaking raisins in hot water until they become plump and soft, and then cut up or puree. Pureed raisins can be spread on crackers, bread, waffles, and pancakes or served with yogurt or cream cheese. Raisin puree can also be added to milk shakes or smoothies. Raisins can also be cooked with foods such as rice, oatmeal cereals, or in bread pudding.

Raisin Smoothie

- 2 tablespoons Raisin Puree (page 133)
- ¹/₂ banana
- 1 cup (235 ml) milk

Place the raisin puree, banana, and milk in a blender and process until smooth.

YIELD: *Makes 1 generous cup*

EACH WITH: 17.8 calories; 0.0 gm total fat; 0.0 gm saturated fat; 0.0 mg cholesterol; 0.5 mg sodium; 4.6 gm carbohydrate; 0.3 gm dietary fiber; 0.2 gm protein; 2.1 mg calcium; 0.1 mg iron; 5.4 IU vitamin A; 0.8 mg vitamin C.

Carrot, Apple, and Raisins

- 1 tablespoon (14 ml) vegetable oil
- 1 cup (125 g) sliced carrots
- ¹/₂ apple, peeled, cored, and finely chopped
- ¹/₄ cup (40 g) raisins
- ¹/₂ cup (120 ml) water

Heat the oil in a medium saucepan over low heat. Add the carrots and sauté 5 minutes. Add the apple, raisins, and water; cover, and simmer 10 minutes, or until the carrots are soft.

YIELD: *Makes 1 baby serving AND 1 adult serving*

EACH WITH: 11.0 calories; 0.5 gm total fat; 0.0 gm saturated fat; 0.0 mg cholesterol; 1.7 mg sodium; 1.7 gm carbohydrate; 0.2 gm dietary fiber; 0.1 gm protein; 1.7 mg calcium; 0.0 mg iron; 464.0 IU vitamin A; 0.1 mg vitamin C.

Cooked Beets 👶

This is not a recipe; it just cooks 4 small beets to be used different ways in the following recipes.

• 4 small beets, trimmed and scrubbed

▣ Preheat the oven to 350°F (180°C, or gas mark 4). Wrap the beets in foil and place on a cookie sheet. Bake 60 to 90 minutes, or until the beets are soft. Cool and slip off the peel.

◎ Fill a medium saucepan with 2 to 3 inches water; place a steamer with the beets in the pan. Cover the pan and bring the water to a boil. Reduce the heat and simmer 35 to 40 minutes, or until the beets are soft (test with a knife or fork). Cool and slip off the peel.

▭ Place the beets in a microwave-safe bowl with a small amount of water. Cover and microwave on high 15 to 20 minutes, or until the beets are soft. Cool and slip off the peel.

YIELD: *4 beets*

BEETS

Beets, a good source of folic acid, are naturally sweet and pleasing to babies. Baking or roasting beets brings out their sweetness and flavor.

Note that dark purple beets can be messy; don't be alarmed if the diapers turn red! There are other varieties available, yellow or white, and they taste even sweeter than the red ones.

Your baby may enjoy beets plain, or lightly mashed with butter. Plain yogurt or sour cream is also delicious with beets.

Beet greens are the most nutritious part of the beet plant, and they are high in potassium, beta-carotene, and folic acid. The tops can be cooked and prepared like other greens.

Beet, Avocado, and Pear Medley 👶

The colors in this dish make it appealing to babies.

- ¹/₄ cup (55 g) Cooked Beets (page 135), peeled and mashed
- ¹/₄ cup (60 g) mashed avocado
- ¹/₄ ripe pear, peeled, cored, and sliced

Place the mashed beet on one side of a baby bowl and the mashed avocado on the other. Top with thin slices of ripe pear.

YIELD: *Makes 1 baby serving*

EACH WITH: 25.4 calories; 1.1 gm total fat; 0.2 gm saturated fat; 0.0 mg cholesterol; 3.2 mg sodium; 4.1 gm carbohydrate; 1.2 gm dietary fiber; 0.3 gm protein; 3.3 mg calcium; 0.1 mg iron; 16.4 IU vitamin A; 1.6 mg vitamin C.

👪 **MAKE IT FOR GROWN-UPS:** Use the rest of the beets (and pear) in a Warm Beet Salad with Pears and Blue Cheese for the adults.

Toss 3 small cooked and peeled beets cut into 1-inch cubes with 1 ripe pear plus the ³/₄ left over from your baby's dish, cored and sliced with ¹/₄ cup chopped walnuts and a splash of olive oil. Add ¹/₄ cup crumbled blue cheese and freshly ground black pepper to taste. This may be served over salad greens.

YIELD: *2 servings*

EACH WITH: 359.0 calories; 22.6 gm total fat; 5.0 gm saturated fat; 12.7 mg cholesterol; 352.5 mg sodium; 36.8 gm carbohydrate; 8.2 gm dietary fiber; 8.0 gm protein; 134.9 mg calcium; 1.9 mg iron; 229.8 IU vitamin A; 10.7 mg vitamin C.

Polenta with Mascarpone 👶

This is a mild and sweet dish that babies will love. Made in the microwave, it has a soft consistency. Soon, when your baby is a year old, you may be changing from breast milk or formula to whole milk. This recipe is a nice introduction to milk.

- ½ cup milk
- 1 tablespoon (7 g) white cornmeal
- 1 tablespoon (15 g) mascarpone cheese

⌨ Place the milk and cornmeal in a 4-cup microwave-safe bowl. Microwave on high 2 minutes. Stir and microwave 2 minutes longer, or until the cornmeal has a soft pudding consistency. Stir with a fork and whip in the cheese. Let cool slightly before serving to your baby.

YIELD: *Makes about ¾ cup*

EACH WITH: 15.5 calories; 0.9 gm total fat; 0.5 gm saturated fat; 2.8 mg cholesterol; 9.2 mg sodium; 1.3 gm carbohydrate; 0.1 gm dietary fiber; 0.6 gm protein; 15.0 mg calcium; 0.1 mg iron; 33.8 IU vitamin A; 0.0 mg vitamin C.

POLENTA

Polenta is made from cornmeal, has a soft texture, a bland flavor, and makes wonderful comfort food for babies. Served with flavorful sauces, vegetables, or cheese, it is also a satisfying and delicious food for adults.

Ready-made polenta is now available in most grocery stores. Packed in water in a 24-ounce tube, it comes ready to slice, heat, and serve. Microwaving keeps it very moist. When sautéed in a skillet, it becomes crisp on the outside.

Melon Cup with Raspberries and Kiwi 👶

- 1 thick (2 x 2-inch) slice cantaloupe
- 5 raspberries, rinsed
- 5 small pieces kiwi fruit

With a spoon, scoop out enough of the cantaloupe slice to make a cup for the berries and kiwi fruit. Chop the scooped-out cantaloupe into small pieces and mix with the raspberries and kiwi. Spoon the fruits into the cantaloupe cup.

YIELD: *Makes 1 baby serving*

EACH WITH: 7.5 calories; 0.1 gm total fat; 0.0 gm saturated fat; 0.0 mg cholesterol; 0.8 mg sodium; 1.8 gm carbohydrate; 0.5 gm dietary fiber; 0.2 gm protein; 3.7 mg calcium; 0.1 mg iron; 113.5 IU vitamin A; 8.7 mg vitamin C.

Pineapple-Banana-Blueberry Salad 🍼

This is a healthy and refreshing dessert.

- 5 small (1 x 1-inch) pieces of pineapple, cut into very small pieces and lightly mashed
- 2 tablespoons (30 g) lightly mashed banana
- 2 tablespoons (20 g) lightly crushed blueberries

Place the pineapple, banana, and blueberries in a small bowl and feed with a small spoon.

💡 *If your baby is teething, lightly freeze the fruit before serving and serve as finger food. It will soothe sore gums.*

YIELD: *Makes 1 to 2 baby servings*

EACH WITH: 6.6 calories; 0.0 gm total fat; 0.0 gm saturated fat; 0.0 mg cholesterol; 0.1 mg sodium; 1.7 gm carbohydrate; 0.1 gm dietary fiber; 0.1 gm protein; 1.1 mg calcium; 0.0 mg iron; 6.2 IU vitamin A; 1.5 mg vitamin C.

Elbow Macaroni with Peas and Parmesan 🍼 👪

This is a finger food favorite for babies.

- 1 cup (105 g) uncooked elbow macaroni
- 1 cup (160 g) fresh or frozen peas
- 1 to 2 tablespoons (14 to 28 g) butter or olive oil
- ¼ cup (25 g) grated Parmesan or Pecorino Romano cheese

◎ Bring 2 quarts of water to a boil in a large pan. Add the macaroni and cook 8 minutes. Add the peas and continue cooking about 5 more minutes, until the macaroni is al dente (firm to the bite) and the peas are tender. Drain the pasta thoroughly and transfer to a small bowl. Add the butter or oil and cheese and stir until the butter is melted and the cheese is well mixed. Serve your baby 2 tablespoons.

YIELD: *Makes 1 baby serving AND 1 adult serving*

EACH WITH: 15.8 calories; 0.7 gm total fat; 0.4 gm saturated fat; 1.7 mg cholesterol; 9.7 mg sodium; 1.8 gm carbohydrate; 0.3 gm dietary fiber; 0.6 gm protein; 8.6 mg calcium; 0.1 mg iron; 53.9 IU vitamin A; 0.6 mg vitamin C.

Fusilli with Zucchini and Carrot Ribbons ♟ 👫

Kids love pasta, and pasta and vegetables go well together. The combinations are endless, and you can experiment with different types and sizes of pasta and a variety of vegetables to discover your baby's favorite.

- 1 cup (105 g) whole-wheat fusilli (corkscrew) pasta
- 2 tablespoons (28 ml) olive oil
- 2 small zucchini, trimmed
- 2 medium carrots, peeled
- ¼ cup (25 g) grated Parmesan or Pecorino Romano cheese
- ¼ cup (15 g) chopped fresh parsley
- Salt (for the adults)
- Pepper (for the adults)

◎ Bring 2 quarts water to a boil in large pan. Add the pasta and cook, stirring occasionally, 12 minutes, or until tender. Drain and transfer to a serving bowl. Stir in 1 tablespoon (14 ml) of the olive oil.

Meanwhile, peel the zucchini and discard the peel. Continue peeling thin ribbons from the zucchini until you come to the core with seeds. Discard the core. In the same way, peel the carrots into thin ribbons.

Heat the remaining 1 tablespoon (14 ml) oil in a frying pan over medium heat. Add the zucchini and carrot ribbons and sauté 2 minutes. Add the vegetables to the pasta along with the cheese and parsley; stir well. Serve your baby 2 tablespoons.

YIELD: *Makes 1 baby serving AND 1 adult serving*

EACH WITH: 16.4 calories; 0.7 gm total fat; 0.2 gm saturated fat; 3.3 mg cholesterol; 13.2 mg sodium; 2.1 gm carbohydrate; 0.1 gm dietary fiber; 0.6 gm protein; 6.6 mg calcium; 0.1 mg iron; 341.0 IU vitamin A; 0.6 mg vitamin C

PART V

Toddler's Month-By-Month Feeding Guide and Recipes

FEEDING YOUR BABY, ONE TO TWO YEARS

Now that your baby is a year old, she can start sharing meals with the family—and so the recipe format changes a bit here. In addition to the toddler recipes, I have added snack suggestions and breakfast, lunch, and dinner recipes that the family will enjoy as well. You can continue to use your little one's favorites from the baby recipes; just offer larger servings.

Each monthly chapter in this guide includes a typical daily menu for your toddler, along with developmental milestones, and finally, recipes for making your baby's meals.

Here are a few things to keep in mind now that your baby is one year old:

MEALS PER DAY Since a toddler's stomach is small, serve three small meals—breakfast, lunch, and dinner—and two or three small snacks during the day. Vary the food groups through the day. If your child refuses mashed sweet potato for lunch, try serving Sweet Potato Fries (page 101) the next day as a snack. If he does not want to eat beans, try hummus and bean paté spread on crackers.

🚫 **All the toddler recipes here can be given anytime between 12 and 24 months.**

ALLERGIES When your baby turns a year old, the danger of food intolerance or allergy usually decreases, but continue to watch for rash or diarrhea after introducing a new food. (See Allergies and Food Intolerance, page 46).

MILK Some mothers may choose to continue with breast-feeding. For those who don't breast feed, I suggest serving $1/2$ cup whole milk with some meals. However, you can decide how much milk to serve with each meal or snack, as long as your toddler gets at least 2 cups whole milk each day. Continue to serve whole-milk cheese and yogurt. Small children are very active and fats should still count for half of their calories. (See Fats, page 19.)

Did you know that toddlers burn about 40 calories a day for every inch in height? That's 1160 calories a day for a 29-inch-tall 18-month-old. That's one of the reasons calorie-dense fats are so important in their diet.

NEW FOODS TO TRY

If there is no history of allergies in your family (see page 48), you can start to give your toddler the following:

- whole eggs
- tomatoes
- citrus fruits
- mangoes
- spinach
- strawberries
- honey nut butters
- salt, spices, and herbs—but I would use them sparingly and in small amounts since many things are still brand new to your toddler.

CEREAL Your toddler should continue to eat cooked, iron-fortified cereals. In addition, instead of baby cereal, you can now serve Cream of Wheat, oatmeal, rice, barley, Malt-O-Meal, and grits.

VEGETABLES Hopefully, your toddler will continue to enjoy all the varied vegetables he was given as a baby. For the toddler who refuses to eat vegetables, some parents mix cooked, pureed carrots into tomato sauce and steamed pureed spinach into the pesto sauce. You might find that this works well for the child who loves pasta, but not carrots and spinach. If you have a juicer, make carrot juice and mix it with other juice, or make carrot puree and use it in smoothies. And don't be afraid to offer your toddler foods seasoned with fresh herbs: Basil and parsley are full of vitamins and minerals.

DESSERTS *1, 2, 3, Cook for Me* does not have recipes for cakes and cookies. The desserts I recommend are mainly fresh fruits, berries, sherbets, and fruit sorbets. Remember that although these desserts are also sweets, they provide valuable vitamins. If your baby enjoys fruits as sweets, the fruit may well become a lifelong preference over candy, chocolate, cakes, or cookies. Buy the best quality fruits you can find, as the flavor and sweetness will affect their appeal to your child.

Pat-a-cake, pat-a-cake

Baker's Man

That I will Master,

As fast as I can;

Pat it and prick it,

And mark it with a B,

Put it in the oven

For Baby and me.

—PAT-A-CAKE

TWELVE MONTHS

Now that your baby is one year old, the texture of the foods you offer should be chunky or well chopped into small pieces. Your baby's self-feeding will continue to improve, and she should be able to take all liquids from a cup. Do not be overly concerned if there is a sharp drop in appetite around the first birthday. This is quite common and could last until around 18 months of age.

Typical Daily Menu for a Twelve-Month-Old

Use whole milk and whole-milk dairy products.

MEAL	FOODS
Breakfast	$1/4$ cup Cream of Wheat (page 144) with a dab of butter, 2 or 3 fresh (or slightly frozen) strawberries, and $1/2$ cup (120 ml) milk
Snack	$1/2$ cup Fig-Banana-Kiwi Shake (page 146)
Lunch	Avocado ($1/4$) and Hard-Cooked Egg ($1/2$) Sandwich ($1/2$ slice rye) (page 148), and $1/4$ cup (60 ml) milk
Snack	3 small pieces fresh Mozzarella and 1 cherry tomato (cut into small pieces) (page 146), and $1/4$ cup (60 ml) milk
Dinner	Chicken (1 ounce) with Rice ($1/4$ cup) and Broccoli (page 150), and $1/2$ cup (120 ml) milk

Remember that your toddler may not eat all that you offer him, or he may want more of one kind of food, less of another and completely refuse some. That is OK. What I have suggested is just a guideline. If you continue to offer him a varied menu, over a week he will most likely have gotten all the nourishment he needs. Don't force or entreat him to eat when he signals he has had enough.

ONE-YEAR CHECKUP WITH THE PEDIATRICIAN

When your baby turns into a toddler at age one, she will probably have more or less tripled her birth weight, stand about 29 inches tall, and have six or eight teeth.

An annual assessment of a child's weight and height gives important indicators of normal growth, as does measuring the head circumference. The most rapid and critical period of human brain growth begins at conception and continues into the second year. Brain cells increase in number until the child is twelve to fifteen months of age, and increase thereafter in mass and size. Although growth slows, babies become stronger and more coordinated.

BREAKFAST

Cream of Wheat 🧒

Start with 1 tablespoon, then add more if wanted, with a dab of butter and a little milk. You can add fresh sliced strawberries, raspberries, blueberries, or frozen berries partially thawed. They are comforting for your baby during teething. Frozen strawberries are very high in vitamin C. Serve with whole milk.

- ⅓ cup (75 ml) whole milk
- 1 tablespoon Cream of Wheat
- 1 teaspoon butter

◉ Bring the milk to a boil in a pan, stirring constantly. Slowly stir in the Cream of Wheat. Cook, stirring constantly, until desired consistency is reached, 1 minute or more. Cool and serve with a dot of butter and a little milk.

YIELD: *Makes 1 toddler serving*

EACH WITH: 15.1 calories; 1.1 gm total fat; 0.7 gm saturated fat; 3.0 mg cholesterol; 7.1 mg sodium; 0.9 gm carbohydrate; 0.0 gm dietary fiber; 0.5 gm protein; 16.7 mg calcium; 0.1 mg iron; 33.5 IU vitamin A; 0.0 mg vitamin C.

Toad in the Hole 🧒

Serve with ½ glass of orange juice. To cut a circle, use a small glass. For special occasions, cookie cutters with a heart for Valentine's Day, a cloverleaf for St. Patrick's Day, a rabbit for Easter, etc., are fun.

- Oil, for spraying
- 1 teaspoon soft butter
- 1 slice whole-wheat bread
- 1 egg

◉ Lightly spray a pan with olive oil and heat over medium heat. Spread the butter on the bread and cut out a circle with a drinking glass or round cookie cutter. Put the bread slice in the pan, butter side up, and break the egg into the hole. Place the cut out circle, butter side up, in the pan. Cook until the white of the egg begins to firm, 1 to 1½ minutes. Carefully turn the bread with the egg and the cut-out circle over to the buttered side and cook until the egg is cooked through, 30 to 45 seconds longer. Serve on a plate, with the circle on the side. It can be spread with a little jam.

YIELD: *Makes 1 toddler serving*

EACH WITH: 195.2 calories; 12.1 gm total fat; 4.7 gm saturated fat; 220.4 mg cholesterol; 241.9 mg sodium; 13.3 gm carbohydrate; 1.9 gm dietary fiber; 9.0 gm protein; 48.4 mg calcium; 1.8 mg iron; 454.3 IU vitamin A; 0.0 mg vitamin C.

Cereal, Applesauce, and Milk 👶

- 1 tablespoon (7 g) nut-like cereal nuggets (such as Grape-Nuts)
- 1 tablespoon (15 g) applesauce
- 1/4 cup (60 ml) whole milk

Combine the cereal, applesauce, and milk in a small bowl. Let it stand for 2 to 3 minutes to soften. Add more milk if desired.

YIELD: *Makes 1 toddler serving*

EACH WITH: 73.1 calories; 2.1 gm total fat; 1.2 gm saturated fat; 6.1 mg cholesterol; 67.6 mg sodium; 11.4 gm carbohydrate; 0.8 gm dietary fiber; 2.7 gm protein; 71.9 mg calcium; 2.0 mg iron; 154.4 IU vitamin A; 0.3 mg vitamin C.

Yogurt Cone Sundae 👶

Serve with 1/4 cup (60 ml) whole milk.

- 1/4 cup (60 g) plain whole-milk yogurt
- 1 whole-wheat ice-cream cup
- 1/3 banana, lightly mashed
- 1/4 cup (40 g) fresh blueberries, lightly mashed

Place the yogurt in the ice-cream cup and top with the banana and blueberries.

YIELD: *Makes 1 toddler serving*

EACH WITH: 132.9 calories; 2.6 gm total fat; 1.4 gm saturated fat; 8.0 mg cholesterol; 60.9 mg sodium; 25.4 gm carbohydrate; 2.1 gm dietary fiber; 3.6 gm protein; 82.6 mg calcium; 0.7 mg iron; 105.1 IU vitamin A; 7.2 mg vitamin C.

Dried Figs in Milk 👶

This is a nice way to introduce whole milk to your toddler.

- 3 large or 6 small dried figs, hard stem removed
- 1/2 cup (120 ml) whole milk

Cut the figs in half and place them in a glass dish with the milk. Cover and refrigerate overnight. The next day, drain the figs, reserving the milk. Serve your toddler the milk with breakfast or lunch. Cut 1 or 2 of the figs into small pieces and serve as finger food or chop up all the figs and serve them with yogurt cheese as a dessert. (See "Yogurt Cheese" on page 114.)

YIELD: *Makes 1 toddler serving*

APPROXIMATE SERVING SIZE: 0.25 cup. **EACH WITH:** 29.9 calories; 0.6 gm total fat; 0.3 gm saturated fat; 1.7 mg cholesterol; 7.0 mg sodium; 5.9 gm carbohydrate; 0.8 gm dietary fiber; 0.7 gm protein; 28.5 mg calcium; 0.1 mg iron; 55.1 IU vitamin A; 0.5 mg vitamin C.

DRIED FIGS

Dried figs are a good source of iron, and they contain vitamin A, folate, calcium, zinc, and fiber. The iron in the figs is better absorbed when eaten with a vitamin C–rich food, so serve papaya, kiwi, cantaloupe, raspberries, guava, or honeydew melon with this recipe.

SNACKS

Fig-Banana-Kiwi Shake ⬤

- 1 fig, cut into small pieces
- 1/4 banana
- 1/2 peeled kiwi
- 1/2 cup (120 ml) whole milk

Combine the fig, banana, kiwi, and milk in the blender and process until smooth.

YIELD: *Makes 1 toddler serving*

APPROXIMATE SERVING SIZE: 0.25 cup. **EACH WITH:** 34.7 calories; 1.0 gm total fat; 0.5 gm saturated fat; 2.7 mg cholesterol; 11.0 mg sodium; 6.0 gm carbohydrate; 0.7 gm dietary fiber; 1.1 gm protein; 36.9 mg calcium; 0.1 mg iron; 53.8 IU vitamin A; 8.4 mg vitamin C.

Fresh Mozzarella and Tomato ⬤ ⬤

Fresh mozzarella is soft, silky, creamy, and it tastes delicious with ripe tomatoes. Serve with a slice of sweet ripe melon, if you like.

- One 1-inch-thick slice fresh Mozzarella cheese
- 1 cherry tomato, sliced
- Fresh basil leaves (optional)

Cut the mozzarella slice into 3 pieces. Place the mozzarella on a plate with the cut-up tomato. If you have fresh basil, cut a few leaves into pieces and place in between the mozzarella and tomatoes.

YIELD: *Makes 1 toddler serving*

EACH WITH: 88.8 calories; 6.4 gm total fat; 3.7 gm saturated fat; 22.4 mg cholesterol; 179.6 mg sodium; 1.4 gm carbohydrate; 0.2 gm dietary fiber; 6.4 gm protein; 144.3 mg calcium; 0.2 mg iron; 297.9 IU vitamin A; 4.4 mg vitamin C.

⬤ **MAKE IT FOR GROWN-UPS:** For an adult version of your toddler's snack, cut up 1 large tomato and cut the mozzarella into slices. In a fan pattern, layer a slice of fresh mozzarella, a basil leaf, and a slice of tomato; repeat. Drizzle lightly with extra-virgin olive oil and add some fresh, ground pepper. Serve with slices of prosciutto and melon. If you like, wrap prosciutto slices around the melon slices.

Cream Cheese–Pineapple Finger Sandwich

- 1 tablespoon (15 g) cream cheese
- 1 tablespoon (15 g) pureed fresh pineapple
- $1/2$ slice oatmeal bread

Whip the cream cheese with a fork. Mix in the pineapple puree and spread on the bread.

Fold the bread over and cut into $1/2$-inch wide pieces.

YIELD: *Makes 1 toddler serving*

EACH WITH: 91.3 calories; 5.7 gm total fat; 3.3 gm saturated fat; 16.0 mg cholesterol; 123.9 mg sodium; 8.1 gm carbohydrate; 0.5 gm dietary fiber; 2.3 gm protein; 21.8 mg calcium; 0.6 mg iron; 202.4 IU vitamin A; 1.6 mg vitamin C.

LUNCH

Chicken Soup with Alphabet Pasta

This soup is quick and easy to make. You can use raw, frozen, or cooked vegetables. If you have leftover beans, add them to the soup. I often add some chicken-vegetable pot stickers to the soup and cut them into small pieces before serving them. This dish was a hit with my family. Serve with whole-wheat bread, $1/2$ cup of milk, and a small piece of peeled and cored pineapple.

- 1 can (14-ounces, or 425 ml) chicken broth or 2 cups (475 ml) homemade
- 3 tablespoons (25 g) alphabet pasta (or star, tubettini, or other small pasta)
- $1/2$ cup (50 g) mixed fresh or frozen vegetables, carrots, corn, peas or green beans, cut into small pieces
- $1/4$ cup (40 g) potatoes, peeled, washed, and cut into small pieces
- $1/3$ cup (45 g) shredded cooked chicken

Bring the chicken broth to a boil in a medium saucepan. Add the pasta, vegetables, and potatoes. Cover, reduce the heat to low, and cook 5 minutes, or until the vegetables are tender. Add the chicken. Heat gently and stir.

YIELD: *Makes 2 servings*

APPROXIMATE SERVING SIZE: 0.25 cup. **EACH WITH:** 25.0 calories; 0.7 gm total fat; 0.2 gm saturated fat; 4.1 mg cholesterol; 233.8 mg sodium; 1.7 gm carbohydrate; 0.2 gm dietary fiber; 2.8 gm protein; 4.0 mg calcium; 0.2 mg iron; 164.3 IU vitamin A; 0.2 mg vitamin C.

Stelline with Cottage Cheese

Serve with 1/4 cup (60 ml) carrot juice.

- 3 tablespoons (25 g) stelline (stars) or other small pasta
- 1 1/2 cups (355 ml) water
- 1 tablespoon (14 g) butter
- 1/4 cup (55 g) small-curd cottage cheese
- 3 tablespoons (30 g) cooked fresh or frozen green peas

In a small pan, combine the stelline with the water over medium-high heat and bring to a boil. Cook about 5 minutes, or until the pasta is soft. Drain. Add the butter, cottage cheese, and peas and mix well before serving.

YIELD: *Makes about 1/2 cup, or 2 toddler servings*

EACH WITH: 20.4 calories; 1.3 gm total fat; 0.8 gm saturated fat; 4.4 mg cholesterol; 21.1 mg sodium; 1.2 gm carbohydrate; 0.2 gm dietary fiber; 0.9 gm protein; 4.4 mg calcium; 0.1 mg iron; 63.0 IU vitamin A; 0.4 mg vitamin C.

Avocado and Hard-Cooked Egg Sandwich

Serve lightly frozen or fresh blueberries as finger food for dessert.

- 1 to 2 teaspoons mayonnaise
- 1/2 slice rye bread, crust removed, cut in half
- 1 slice ripe, peeled, and pitted avocado, lightly mashed
- 2 slices hard-cooked egg, lightly mashed

Spread the mayonnaise on both slices of the bread. Add the mashed avocado and egg to one slice and top with the other slice. Press firmly and cut the sandwich into small pieces.

YIELD: *Makes 1 toddler serving*

EACH WITH: 107.5 calories; 6.0 gm total fat; 1.1 gm saturated fat; 54.9 mg cholesterol; 174.2 mg sodium; 10.6 gm carbohydrate; 1.7 gm dietary fiber; 3.2 gm protein; 20.4 mg calcium; 0.7 mg iron; 106.6 IU vitamin A; 1.0 mg vitamin C.

> **MAKE IT FOR GROWN-UPS:** Use the remaining avocado and hard-boiled egg to make an adult sandwich, adding a slice of tomato.

Hummus 👫

For a finger sandwich for your toddler, cut two small triangles of pita bread and spread hummus on one triangle, then cover with the other triangle. You can also spread a little bit of hummus on crackers or use it as a dip for fresh, thin pieces of vegetables like carrots, broccoli, cauliflower, or red, green, yellow, or orange peppers for your toddler. (Steam or lightly microwave the vegetables until soft.)

- 1 can (15 ounces, or 430 g) garbanzo beans, drained
- 1/4 cup (60 ml) fresh lemon juice
- 3 tablespoons (45 g) tahini
- 2 to 4 garlic cloves, crushed (depending on taste)
- 2 tablespoons (28 ml) olive oil
- 1/2 teaspoon salt (optional)

Place the beans, lemon juice, tahini, garlic, oil, and salt if using in a food processor. Process the mixture until smooth. Stop the processor and scrape down the mixture with a spatula, if needed. Remove, cover, and refrigerate.

YIELD: *Makes about 1 cup*

EACH WITH: 27.2 calories; 1.3 gm total fat; 0.2 gm saturated fat; 0.0 mg cholesterol; 37.2 mg sodium; 3.1 gm carbohydrate; 0.6 gm dietary fiber; 0.7 gm protein; 7.5 mg calcium; 0.2 mg iron; 0.8 IU vitamin A; 1.2 mg vitamin C.

TAHINI

Tahini is roasted and toasted sesame seeds that have been ground to a paste. You can find it in larger supermarkets and in health food stores.

DINNER

Toddler's Shepherd's Pie 👶

Serve with mashed peas and half a pitted plum for dessert.

- 1/4 cup (80 g) cooked ground turkey
- 1/4 cup (50 g) cooked mashed potatoes
- 2 tablespoons (15 g) grated cheddar cheese

Preheat the oven to 350°F (180°C, or gas mark 4). Lightly oil an oven-safe 6-ounce custard cup. Place the turkey in the cup, cover with the potatoes, and sprinkle with the cheese. Bake 10 to 15 minutes, until the cheese is melted.

Lightly oil a microwave-safe custard cup. Place the turkey in the cup, cover with the potatoes, and sprinkle with the cheese. Microwave on high 30 to 60 seconds, until the cheese has melted and the pie is heated through.

YIELD: *Makes 1 toddler serving*

EACH WITH: 38.9 calories; 2.8 gm total fat; 0.8 gm saturated fat; 9.5 mg cholesterol; 31.1 mg sodium; 0.8 gm carbohydrate; 0.1 gm dietary fiber; 2.4 gm protein; 12.2 mg calcium; 0.2 mg iron; 19.1 IU vitamin A; 0.3 mg vitamin C.

POULTRY SAFETY

When buying fresh chicken or turkey, the package should feel cold to the touch and have a sell-by date of several days beyond the purchase date. Make the grocery market your last stop before going home. Once home, immediately place chicken in a refrigerator that maintains 40°F (4°C) temperature. Use the poultry within 1 or 2 days or freeze at 0°F (-18°C). Whole chicken and ground chicken and turkey can be frozen up to one month, if well wrapped.

Follow instructions on the package on how to handle the chicken during preparation. For safety, tenderness, and doneness, cook a whole chicken to 180°F (82°C). Use a food thermometer and insert it into the thigh.

When making poultry dishes using ground chicken or turkey, be sure the meat is thoroughly cooked, with no red or pink showing. A meat thermometer should register at 170°F (77°C).

COOKING GROUND POULTRY

Here's how to safely cook ground poultry.

- 1 teaspoon olive oil
- $^{1}/_{4}$ pound (115 g) ground turkey or chicken
- $^{1}/_{4}$ cup (60 ml) chicken broth or water

Heat the oil in a small skillet over medium heat. Add the turkey or chicken and cook, breaking it up with a wooden spoon. Add the broth or water to prevent sticking if needed. Cook, stirring, until cooked through and no redmeat remains. Meat thermometer should read 170°F (77°C).

Chicken with Rice and Broccoli 🧑‍🍳

If in season, serve fresh raspberries for desert. Otherwise, serve a piece of a soft, sweet pear.

- 1 chicken tender
- 1 cup (235 ml) chicken broth
- 1 broccoli floret
- 1 to 2 tablespoons (10 to 20 g) cooked rice

◎ In a pan over low heat, simmer the chicken in the broth 20 minutes. Steam (or microwave) the broccoli until cooked through. Chop the chicken and broccoli into small pieces. Serve with the rice.

YIELD: *Makes 1 toddler serving*

EACH WITH: 5.4 calories; 0.1 gm total fat; 0.0 gm saturated fat; 1.3 mg cholesterol; 29.4 mg sodium; 0.4 gm carbohydrate; 0.1 gm dietary fiber; 0.7 gm protein; 1.7 mg calcium; 0.1 mg iron; 61.4 IU vitamin A; 2.0 mg vitamin C.

👨‍👩‍👧 **MAKE IT FOR GROWN-UPS:** For an adult lunch, serve the hummus in a pita pocket with chopped cucumbers and chopped tomatoes.

Lentils and Rice with Tomato Sauce and Yogurt

If you have some lentils already cooked (see page 119), a bit of leftover rice and tomato sauce (homemade or store-bought), you can put together this complete and tasty meal for your toddler in a couple of minutes. Serve with 1/4 cup (60 ml) milk and 1/3 banana for dessert.

- 1 tablespoon (12 g) cooked lentils
- 1 tablespoon (10 g) cooked rice
- 1 to 2 tablespoons (15 to 30 g) Tomato Sauce (page 174) or store-bought tomato sauce
- 1 tablespoon (15 g) plain whole-milk yogurt

Combine the lentils, rice, and tomato sauce in a small cup; microwave on high 30 seconds. Stir in the yogurt. Stir well and test to see if the temperature is right before you feed your toddler.

YIELD: *Makes 1 toddler serving*

EACH WITH: 11.1 calories; 0.1 gm total fat; 0.1 gm saturated fat; 0.5 mg cholesterol; 2.2 mg sodium; 1.9 gm carbohydrate; 0.3 gm dietary fiber; 0.5 gm protein; 5.8 mg calcium; 0.2 mg iron; 17.3 IU vitamin A; 0.6 mg vitamin C.

THIRTEEN MONTHS

Oh, do you know the Muffin Man

The Muffin Man, the Muffin Man,

Oh, do you know the Muffin man,

Who lives in Drury Lane?

—MUFFIN MAN

Toddlers at thirteen months need some freedom to experiment in order to assert their independence. For a toddler to master new skills, parents need to approve of his trials and errors in learning. The toddler should be allowed to work with the spoon and the food or use his fingers to try and feed himself. However, when he starts to throw the food or smear it on the chair or in his hair, it is time to take it away.

Setting limits at this age is very important to a child's well-being, and necessary in establishing good eating habits. However, I know that limits are not always easy to enforce, especially if you are anxious that your child is not eating enough. To painlessly set limits about eating issues, once a child has made it clear that he is not going to eat, remove the food and take him out of the high chair. Later, when he indicates that he is hungry, either offer him the food that was removed or give him a healthy snack. Remember that we are all vulnerable to manipulation, and children are remarkably astute at using this advantage. It is important to be consistent, without being authoritarian, inflexible, punitive, or angry. All children need limits, but limits given with love.

Typical Daily Meals for a Thirteen-Month-Old

Continue serving whole milk and whole-milk dairy products.

MEAL	FOODS
Breakfast	1/4 cup hot Oatmeal and Fruit (page 155), and 1/2 cup (120 ml) milk
Snack	1/2 cup S-S-S-Smoothie (page 156), (yogurt, banana, papaya, and white grape juice)
Lunch	1/4 cup White Bean Soup with Pasta (page 157), 1/4 slice buttered whole-wheat bread, and 1/2 cup (120 ml) milk
Snack	1 to 2 tablespoons Yogurt–Goat Cheese Dip (page 156), with 2 pieces each of steamed or microwaved julienned carrot and green beans, a small cauliflower floret, and 1/2 cup (120 ml) milk
Dinner	1 small Meat Cake (page 160), with 1 tablespoon Buttered Grated Carrots (page 159), 1/4 cup rice, and 1/2 cup (120 ml) milk

BREAKFAST

Scrambled Egg and Turkey Breakfast Link 👧

Serve with one Blueberry Muffin (page 194) or one-fourth of a store-bought muffin, extra blueberries, if available, and ¹/₂ cup (120 ml) milk.

- ¹/₂ teaspoon olive oil
- 1 egg
- ¹/₂ precooked turkey or vegetable sausage link

◎ ▭ Heat the oil in a small skillet over low heat. Lightly beat the egg; pour into the pan. Cook, stirring occasionally, until the egg is well cooked. Microwave the sausage link on medium until warmed through, 30 to 45 seconds. (Check to make sure it is not too hot before serving your toddler.)

YIELD: *Makes 1 toddler serving*

EACH WITH: 269.6 calories; 9.3 gm total fat; 2.3 gm saturated fat; 86.6 mg cholesterol; 530.8 mg sodium; 35.4 gm carbohydrate; 1.8 gm dietary fiber; 10.6 gm protein; 57.3 mg calcium; 1.8 mg iron; 134.0 IU vitamin A; 0.8 mg vitamin C.

Grape-Nut Parfait 👧

- 2 tablespoons (15 g) fresh raspberries
- 2 tablespoons yogurt cheese (See "Yogurt Cheese" on page 114.)
- 2 tablespoons (15 g) nut-like cereal nuggets (such as Grape-Nuts)

In a plastic baby cup, layer 1 tablespoon raspberries, 1 tablespoon yogurt cheese, 1 tablespoon cereal; repeat with remaining ingredients.

YIELD: *Makes 1 to 2 toddler servings*

EACH WITH: 8.8 calories; 0.2 gm total fat; 0.1 gm saturated fat; 0.7 mg cholesterol; 9.7 mg sodium; 1.5 gm carbohydrate; 0.3 gm dietary fiber; 0.3 gm protein; 7.2 mg calcium; 0.4 mg iron; 21.5 IU vitamin A; 0.7 mg vitamin C.

Blueberry Bread Pudding

If you have extra blueberry muffins left, this recipe makes a lovely Sunday breakfast. Whip orange juice in the blender briefly and serve alongside the bread pudding.

* 1 cup (80 g) crumbled blueberry muffins
* 1 egg
* 1/2 cup (120 ml) whole milk
* 2 teaspoons butter
* 1 tablespoon (15 g) brown sugar
* 1/3 cup (50 g) frozen blueberries

Preheat the oven to 350°F (180°C, or gas mark 4). Butter a 2-cup ovenproof ramekin. Place the muffin in the prepared ramekin. In a small bowl, beat the egg and milk together and pour over the muffin. Dot with the butter and sprinkle with the brown sugar. Top with the blueberries. Bake 40 minutes. Cool slightly before serving. Remove 2 to 4 tablespoons bread pudding to serve to a toddler before dividing the remainder into 2 adult servings.

YIELD: *Makes 1 toddler serving AND 2 adult servings*

EACH WITH: 32.1 calories; 1.2 gm total fat; 0.4 gm saturated fat; 10.9 mg cholesterol; 42.8 mg sodium; 4.5 gm carbohydrate; 0.3 gm dietary fiber; 0.8 gm protein; 11.2 mg calcium; 0.2 mg iron; 31.4 IU vitamin A; 0.1 mg vitamin C.

Oatmeal and Fruit

* 1 cup (235 ml) water
* 1/2 apple, cored, peeled, and finely chopped
* 1/2 pear, cored, peeled, and finely chopped
* 1/2 cup (80 g) seedless raisins
* 1/2 cup (40 g) old-fashioned rolled oats
* 1/2 cup (120 ml) water or whole milk (optional)

Combine the water, apple, pear, and raisins in a small pan and bring to a boil over medium-high heat. Reduce the heat and simmer fruit 2 minutes. Add the oats and simmer, stirring occasionally, 5 minutes longer. For thinner oatmeal, add an additional 1/2 cup water or milk.

YIELD: *Makes about 1 cup; about 4 toddler servings*

EACH WITH: 20.3 calories; 0.2 gm total fat; 0.0 gm saturated fat; 0.0 mg cholesterol; 0.4 mg sodium; 4.5 gm carbohydrate; 0.5 gm dietary fiber; 0.5 gm protein; 3.0 mg calcium; 0.2 mg iron; 2.0 IU vitamin A; 0.2 mg vitamin C.

VARIATION: To increase the iron content, replace the fresh fruit with 1/3 cup (55 g) mixed dried and chopped apricots, prunes, and raisins.

SNACKS

Bagel and Cream Cheese 🧒

Serve with ¹/₂ cup whole milk.

- ¹/₄ bagel
- 1 teaspoon plain cream cheese
- 3 strawberries, sliced

Toast the bagel and cover with the cream cheese. Serve with the strawberries.

YIELD: *Makes 1 toddler serving*

EACH WITH: 173.8 calories; 6.2 gm total fat; 3.4 gm saturated fat; 17.5 mg cholesterol; 203.6 mg sodium; 22.4 gm carbohydrate; 1.3 gm dietary fiber; 7.3 gm protein; 152.2 mg calcium; 0.6 mg iron; 193.8 IU vitamin A; 21.2 mg vitamin C.

Yogurt–Goat Cheese Dip 👨‍👩‍👧

This dip can be refrigerated for up to a week. Thinned with a little milk, it also makes a good salad dressing.

- ¹/₄ cup (60 g) plain whole-milk yogurt
- ¹/₄ cup (60 g) mild goat cheese

Mix the yogurt and cheese in a food processor until blended. Chill before serving.

YIELD: *Makes 2 cups*

EACH WITH: 30.5 calories; 2.4 gm total fat; 1.6 gm saturated fat; 6.6 mg cholesterol; 40.1 mg sodium; 0.5 gm carbohydrate; 0.0 gm dietary fiber; 1.8 gm protein; 30.4 mg calcium; 0.1 mg iron; 111.5 IU vitamin A; 0.0 mg vitamin C.

S-S-S-Smoothie 🧒

This is a toddler recipe that the family can also enjoy.

- ¹/₂ cup (90 g) papaya, peeled, chopped, and seeded
- ¹/₂ banana
- ¹/₄ cup (60 g) plain whole-milk yogurt
- 1 cup (235 ml) white grape juice
- 2 tablespoons (28 ml) lemon juice
- 1 tablespoon (14 ml) frozen orange juice concentrate
- 4 cracked ice cubes

Combine the papaya, banana, yogurt, grape juice, lemon juice, frozen orange juice concentrate, and ice cubes in a blender and blend on high 1 minute.

YIELD: *Makes about ¹/₂ cup*

APPROXIMATE SERVING SIZE: 0.25 cup. **EACH WITH:** 34.9 calories; 0.3 gm total fat; 0.2 gm saturated fat; 0.9 mg cholesterol; 4.5 mg sodium; 8.0 gm carbohydrate; 0.4 gm dietary fiber; 0.6 gm protein; 14.1 mg calcium; 0.1 mg iron; 108.8 IU vitamin A; 9.9 mg vitamin C.

VEGETABLE DIPPERS

Serve the Yogurt–Goat Cheese Dip with any of the following microwaved or steamed vegetables (washed, peeled, and cut into small pieces or julienne): carrots, yams, zucchini, squash, cauliflower, broccoli, asparagus, green beans, and sweet potato.

LUNCH

White Bean Soup with Pasta 👪

This mild tasting soup, favored by toddlers, is best made from scratch. Serve your toddler 1/4 cup soup with 1/4 slice whole-grain bread and half a pitted plum. If you don't have time for cooking dried beans, use canned beans. Use two 15-ounce cans small white beans, drained, and 6 cups water or four (14-ounce) cans nonfat chicken broth.

* 1 cup (215 g) dried small white beans (soaked overnight in 6 cups [1410 ml] water)
* 6 cups (1410 ml) water (for cooking)
* 2 bay leaves
* 2 tablespoons (28 ml) olive oil
* 1 large onion, chopped
* 3 large tomatoes, blanched, peeled, and chopped (See Tip below.)
* 1/2 cup (30 g) fresh parsley, chopped
* 1 large clove garlic, finely chopped
* 1 tablespoon (18 g) kosher salt or 1 teaspoon regular salt
* 1 cup (105 g) small whole-wheat pasta (elbow macaroni, small shells, or tubettini), cooked until just tender

💡 *To blanch tomatoes, drop in boiling water 30 seconds, drain, and rinse with cold water. This makes it easier to peel them.*

◎ Soak the beans in 6 cups of water overnight. The next day, drain and rinse the beans and place in a 4-quart saucepan with 6 cups water and the bay leaves. Bring to a boil over medium heat, skim off the foam, cover, reduce the heat, and simmer 1 1/2 hours, or until the beans are tender. Discard the bay leaves.

Heat the oil in a frying pan over medium heat; add the onion and cook, stirring occasionally, 10 minutes. Add the tomatoes, parsley, and garlic and cook 3 to 4 minutes.

Cook the pasta according to directions on package. Drain and add to the soup.

When the beans are tender, remove 1 1/2 cups beans and 1 cup cooking liquid and puree in a blender (or mash with a potato masher). Return the pureed beans to the saucepan; add the sautéed vegetables and cooked pasta. Season with the salt. Serve your toddler 1/4 to 1/2 cup.

YIELD: *Makes 6 servings*

EACH WITH: 6.2 calories; 0.1 gm total fat; 0.0 gm saturated fat; 0.0 mg cholesterol; 31.6 mg sodium; 1.0 gm carbohydrate; 0.3 gm dietary fiber; 0.3 gm protein; 2.4 mg calcium; 0.1 mg iron; 26.5 IU vitamin A; 0.9 mg vitamin C.

Carrot and Avocado with Lime Dressing 🍽

- 1 cup (120 g) washed and grated carrots
- 1 ripe avocado, peeled, pitted, and cubed
- 3 tablespoons (12 g) finely chopped parsley, cilantro, or mint

Place carrots, avocado, and parsley in a bowl and gently mix with Lime Dressing (see below).

YIELD: *Makes 2 servings*

EACH WITH: 316.7 calories; 28.5 gm total fat; 4.0 gm saturated fat; 0.0 mg cholesterol; 55.5 mg sodium; 17.4 gm carbohydrate; 8.9 gm dietary fiber; 2.9 gm protein; 45.0 mg calcium; 1.3 mg iron; 8340.8 IU vitamin A; 27.2 mg vitamin C.

Lime Dressing 🍽

- Juice of 1 lime
- 1 teaspoon balsamic vinegar
- 2 tablespoons (28 ml) olive oil
- 1 teaspoon ginger, peeled and finely chopped, optional

Place lime juice, vinegar, olive oil, and ginger in a small, clean, lidded jar and mix well.

YIELD: *Makes about 1/4 cup*

EACH WITH: 255.1 calories; 27.1 gm total fat; 3.7 gm saturated fat; 0.0 mg cholesterol; 2.2 mg sodium; 4.8 gm carbohydrate; 0.4 gm dietary fiber; 0.3 gm protein; 8.0 mg calcium; 0.4 mg iron; 21.6 IU vitamin A; 11.5 mg vitamin C.

Cottage Cheese and Noodle Casserole 👪

Serve with sliced tomatoes with olive oil and sprinkles of oregano and fresh blueberries for dessert.

- 3 cups (705 ml) water
- 1/2 cup (34 g) broad noodles
- 1 egg
- 1 cup (225 g) cottage cheese
- 2 tablespoons (28 g) butter, melted
- 3 tablespoons (20 g) bread crumbs

▣ Preheat the oven to 375°F (190°C, or gas mark 5). Grease a small baking dish. Bring the water to a boil in a medium saucepan. Add the noodles and cook about 10 minutes, or until the noodles are soft. Drain. In a small bowl, whisk the egg; mix in the cottage cheese. In a small bowl, combine the butter and 2 tablespoons of the bread crumbs.

Place half the noodles in the bottom of the pre-pared baking dish. Pour in the cottage cheese mix-ture and spread evenly. Layer the rest of the noodles on top; top with the buttered crumbs. Sprinkle the remaining 1 tablespoon bread crumbs on top. Place the dish on a baking sheet and bake for 30 minutes. Serve your toddler 1/4 cup. Cool your toddler's portion and cut the noodles into small pieces before serving.

YIELD: *Makes 1 toddler serving AND 1 adult serving*

EACH WITH: 21.6 calories; 1.4 gm total fat; 0.8 gm saturated fat; 10.4 mg cholesterol; 39.9 mg sodium; 1.0 gm carbohydrate; 0.0 gm dietary fiber; 1.3 gm protein; 7.3 mg calcium; 0.1 mg iron; 45.3 IU vitamin A; 0.0 mg vitamin C.

Sliced Tomatoes with Oregano 👶 👪

* 1 large tomato, cut into ¹/₂-inch-thick slices
* 1 tablespoon (14 ml) olive oil
* 1 tablespoon (3 g) chopped fresh oregano
* Salt (for the adult portion)
* Ground pepper (for the adult portion)

Sprinkle the tomato with the oil and oregano. Season the adult serving to taste with salt and pepper. Serve your toddler about 1 or 2 slices of the tomato. Your toddler may prefer the tomato cut up into small pieces.

YIELD: *Makes 1 toddler serving AND 1 adult serving*

EACH WITH: 10.9 calories; 0.9 gm total fat; 0.1 gm saturated fat; 0.0 mg cholesterol; 73.8 mg sodium; 0.7 gm carbohydrate; 0.3 gm dietary fiber; 0.1 gm protein; 5.9 mg calcium; 0.2 mg iron; 94.2 IU vitamin A; 3.1 mg vitamin C.

DINNER
Buttered Grated Carrots 👶 👪

* 1 teaspoon olive oil
* 1 cup (110 g) grated carrots
* 2 tablespoons (28 ml) water
* 1 clove garlic, peeled and crushed
* Pinch kosher salt
* 1 teaspoon butter

◎ Heat the oil in a frying pan over medium heat. Add the carrots, water, garlic, and salt. Cook 5 minutes, stirring often. Dot with the butter.

YIELD: *Makes 1 toddler serving AND 1 adult serving*

EACH WITH: 11.6 calories; 1.1 gm total fat; 0.3 gm saturated fat; 0.6 mg cholesterol; 12.6 mg sodium; 0.5 gm carbohydrate; 0.2 gm dietary fiber; 0.1 gm protein; 1.9 mg calcium; 0.0 mg iron; 846.0 IU vitamin A; 0.2 mg vitamin C.

Broiled Banana 👶

* ¹/₂ firm ripe banana, peeled and cut length-wise
* 1 teaspoon butter, melted
* 1 teaspoon lime or lemon juice
* 1 teaspoon brown sugar

▦ Preheat the broiler. Place the banana in a shallow heatproof dish. Drizzle with the butter, lime or lemon juice, and brown sugar. Broil 30 seconds.

YIELD: *Makes 2 toddler servings*

EACH WITH: 51.2 calories; 2.0 gm total fat; 1.2 gm saturated fat; 5.1 mg cholesterol; 1.3 mg sodium; 8.9 gm carbohydrate; 0.8 gm dietary fiber; 0.4 gm protein; 4.5 mg calcium; 0.1 mg iron; 81.8 IU vitamin A; 4.9 mg vitamin C.

LAMB AND BEEF SAFETY

It is important that meat is cooked until well done. Raw and under-cooked ground meats are danger-ous because they may contain harmful bacteria. To ensure that all bacteria are destroyed, cook meat loaf, meatballs, casseroles, and hamburgers to165°F (74°C). Use a food thermometer to check that this safe, internal temperature has been reached.

For safety, always thaw frozen ground meat in the refrigerator and cook it within one or two days. For safe handling, read the instructions on the package.

COOKING GROUND BEEF AND LAMB

Lightly coat a frying pan with olive oil and heat over medium heat. Add ground lamb or ground beef and a little water or unsalted chicken broth. Break the meat into small pieces with a wooden or plastic spoon. Cover pan and cook meat over medium heat until thoroughly cooked and a meat thermometer registers 165°F (74°C).

Meat Cakes ⚉

Serve with boiled, mashed, or baked potatoes and Buttered Grated Carrots (page 159). For dessert, serve a piece of peeled watermelon with the seeds removed. The meat cakes can be refrigerated, covered, for 2 to 3 days. Or freeze them, individually wrapped with plastic wrap, for up to 2 months.

- 1 egg
- 2 tablespoons (28 ml) whole milk
- ½ pound (225 g) ground beef
- 2 tablespoons (15 g) bread crumbs
- 1 to 2 teaspoons olive oil

◎ Whisk the egg and milk together in a small cup. In a medium bowl, mix the ground beef with the bread crumbs. Add the egg mixture and mix to combine. With your hands, form the meat into 4 small cakes.

Heat the oil in a frying pan over medium heat. Add the cakes, and cook, turning often, until the cakes are cooked through and a meat thermometer inserted sideways into the patties registers 165°F (74°C).

YIELD: *Makes about 4 small meat cakes*

EACH WITH: 144.0 calories; 6.7 gm total fat; 2.4 gm saturated fat; 96.7 mg cholesterol; 85.5 mg sodium; 2.9 gm carbohydrate; 0.2 gm dietary fiber; 16.9 gm protein; 26.4 mg calcium; 2.0 mg iron; 68.5 IU vitamin A; 0.0 mg vitamin C.

Tostada

This is quick and tasty. For dessert, serve Broiled Banana (page 159). If your toddler is not able to chew the tortilla, serve the refried beans, shredded lettuce, chopped avocado, tomatoes, and shredded cheese in a little bowl or non-sugar ice cream cup.

- 1 can (16 ounces, or 455 g) refried beans
- 4 flour tortillas
- 1 cup (55 g) shredded lettuce
- 1 cup (180 g) diced tomato
- 1 cup (115 g) shredded cheddar or Monterey Jack cheese
- 1 avocado, peeled, pitted, and sliced
- 6 black olives, sliced (for the adults)
- ½ small onion, peeled and chopped (for the adults)
- 1 cup (260 g) store-bought salsa (for the adults)
- Light sour cream
- 1 non-sugar ice cream cup

Place the refried beans in a microwave-safe dish. Microwave on high 2 minutes and stir; if needed, heat 1 to 2 minutes more. Quickly heat the tortillas in a hot, dry frying pan over medium-high heat, turning once.

Place each warmed tortilla on a plate. Spread the beans on the tortillas. Top with lettuce, tomatoes, cheese, and avocado and olives, onion, salsa, and sour cream if desired. For your toddler, fill a non-sugar ice cream cup with 1 tablespoon beans, 1 tablespoon each of lettuce, tomato, and avocado and add cheese and sour cream as desired.

YIELD: *Makes 1 toddler serving AND 4 adult servings*

EACH WITH: 16.0 calories; 1.1 gm total fat; 0.4 gm saturated fat; 2.2 mg cholesterol; 23.4 mg sodium; 1.0 gm carbohydrate; 0.4 gm dietary fiber; 0.7 gm protein; 14.8 mg calcium; 0.1 mg iron; 80.8 IU vitamin A; 1.3 mg vitamin C.

Tuna Fish Casserole

This is a quick, tasty, and easy meal. Serve with Carrot and Avocado with Lime Dressing (page 158).

For dessert offer a fresh, ripe peach, sliced.

- 6 cups (1410 ml) water
- 2 cups (110 g) whole-wheat farfalle pasta (also called bow ties or butterfly pasta)
- 1 can (10³/₄ ounces, or 305 g) cream of mushroom soup (low salt), undiluted
- 2 cans (6 ounces, or 170 g each) chunk light tuna in water
- ¹/₂ cup (80 g) fresh or frozen peas
- ¹/₂ cup (120 ml) whole milk

In a large saucepan, bring the water to a boil. Add the pasta and boil 15 minutes, stirring occasionally. Drain and pour the pasta into a 2-quart microwave-safe lidded casserole dish.

Stir in the soup and mix well. Stir in the tuna, peas, and milk. Cover and microwave on high 7 minutes, stirring halfway through, until the casserole is thoroughly heated.

YIELD: *Makes 4 adult servings AND 1 toddler serving*

EACH WITH: 116.5 calories; 1.4 gm total fat; 0.5 gm saturated fat; 13.2 mg cholesterol; 131.1 mg sodium; 13.1 gm carbohydrate; 1.1 gm dietary fiber; 12.1 gm protein; 27.6 mg calcium; 1.0 mg iron; 107.8 IU vitamin A; 1.3 mg vitamin C..

FOURTEEN MONTHS

Little Miss Muffet

    Sat on a tuffet,

Eating her curds and whey;

    There came a big spider,

Who sat down beside her

    And frightened Miss Muffet away.

—LITTLE MISS MUFFET

DECREASED APPETITE

You will likely see variations in your toddler's appetite between one and two years of age, especially a decreased appetite. This is normal. Changes in the body, changes in daily routine, and teething are some of the reasons a child's appetite may decrease. Parents often worry unduly about this, but remember that children are extremely sensitive to negative (as well as positive) emotions and will react to your anxiety. If no fuss is made over these periods of poor eating, the problem will, in all likelihood, resolve itself.

🛈 **However, if your child appears listless, loses weight, or continues to reject food, you should consult your pediatrician.** A healthy child will eat when he is hungry. If food is refused, remove it after a few minutes. Don't offer alternative foods, coax, play, or use tricks to make him eat.

Typical Daily Meals for a Fourteen-Month-Old

Continue to use whole milk and whole-milk dairy products.

MEAL	FOODS
Breakfast	$^1/_3$ cup Muesli with Yogurt (page 166), and 4 slices of banana, and $^1/_2$ cup (120 ml) milk
Snack	Rainbow Silken Tofu (with green peas, cherries and blueberries) (page 167), and $^1/_4$ cup (60 ml) milk
Lunch	$^1/_4$ cup Split Pea Soup (page 169) with $^1/_4$ slice buttered whole-wheat bread, and $^1/_2$ cup (120 ml) milk
Snack	1 Pretzel Dipped in Peanut Butter (page 167), and $^1/_2$ cup (120 ml) milk
Dinner	Chicken, Noodles, and Carrots (page 172) and $^1/_4$ cup (60 ml) milk.

BREAKFAST

Little Red Ridinghood's Grits

Serve with ¹/₂ cup (120 ml) Whipped Warm Milk with Almond Butter (right).

- ³/₄ cup (175 ml) water
- 3 tablespoons (30 g) hominy quick grits
- ¹/₄ cup (65 g) frozen sweetened sliced strawberries, thawed
- 1 teaspoon butter (optional)
- Whole milk (optional)

Bring the water to a boil in a small saucepan. Slowly stir in the grits and strawberries. Cover the pan and reduce the heat to low. Cook 5 to 6 minutes, stirring occasionally. Serve topped with a dot of butter and a little milk, if desired.

YIELD: *Makes 1 toddler serving*

EACH WITH: 408.2 calories; 1.4 gm total fat; 0.3 gm saturated fat; 0.0 mg cholesterol; 3.9 mg sodium; 95.7 gm carbohydrate; 6.0 gm dietary fiber; 8.9 gm protein; 11.0 mg calcium; 3.9 mg iron; 15.3 IU vitamin A; 26.4 mg vitamin C.

Whipped Warm Milk with Almond Butter

- ¹/₂ cup (120 ml) whole milk
- 1 teaspoon almond butter (available in health food stores and some supermarkets)

Combine the milk and almond butter in a microwave-safe container and microwave on high 30 to 60 seconds, until warmed. Stir and pour into a blender. Blend until the milk and almond butter are well blended. Pour into a cup and test to ensure the milk is not too hot for your toddler.

VARIATION: Instead of almond butter, use 1 teaspoon cashew or peanut butter.

YIELD: *Makes 1 toddler serving*

EACH WITH: 106.9 calories; 7.1 gm total fat; 2.6 gm saturated fat; 12.2 mg cholesterol; 49.4 mg sodium; 6.6 gm carbohydrate; 0.2 gm dietary fiber; 4.7 gm protein; 152.2 mg calcium; 0.2 mg iron; 124.4 IU vitamin A; 0.0 mg vitamin C.

Green Eggs and Ham

🧒

Serve with 1/2 cup (120 ml) freshly squeezed orange juice and 1/4 of a buttermilk biscuit spread with Honey Butter (page 179). Many markets have good, frozen biscuit dough that is quick and easy to bake. Read the label to make sure the dough is made with butter, not partially hydrogenated oil. Or if you have the time, make your own; see Buttermilk Biscuits (page 269).

- 1 egg
- 1/4 slice ham
- 1 slice avocado, lightly mashed

◎ Lightly spray a frying pan with oil and place over low heat. Break the egg into the pan, cover, and cook 3 1/2 minutes, for firmly set yolk and egg white. When the egg is almost done, remove the lid, add the ham, and gently heat, turning the ham once. Cut the egg and ham into small pieces on a plate with the avocado.

YIELD: *Makes 1 toddler serving*

EACH WITH: 127.9 calories; 9.9 gm total fat; 2.5 gm saturated fat; 214.2 mg cholesterol; 186.3 mg sodium; 1.9 gm carbohydrate; 1.1 gm dietary fiber; 7.7 gm protein; 30.7 mg calcium; 1.1 mg iron; 356.5 IU vitamin A; 1.5 mg vitamin C.

Muesli with Yogurt 🧒

Muesli is a cold granola-like cereal, originally from Switzerland, that is rich in essential vitamins, minerals, and enzymes. For your toddler, buy muesli without pieces of nuts or dry fruit and add fresh fruit or berries instead.

- 1/4 cup (20 g) muesli cereal
- 1/4 banana, sliced
- 1 tablespoon (15 g) plain whole-milk yogurt
- 1/2 teaspoon honey

Place the cereal in a small bowl and cover with the banana. In a bowl, mix together the honey and yogurt and spoon it on top of the cereal.

YIELD: *Makes 1 toddler serving*

EACH WITH: 10.6 calories; 0.2 gm total fat; 0.1 gm saturated fat; 0.2 mg cholesterol; 5.6 mg sodium; 2.3 gm carbohydrate; 0.2 gm dietary fiber; 0.2 gm protein; 3.1 mg calcium; 0.1 mg iron; 12.1 IU vitamin A; 0.3 mg vitamin C.

SNACKS

Rainbow Silken Tofu

Blueberries have one of the highest antioxidant levels of all fruits and vegetables. Blueberries and cherries may be fresh or frozen.

- 2 tablespoons (30 g) small pieces silken tofu
- 1 tablespoon (10 g) cooked green peas, lightly crushed
- 2 cherries, pitted and quartered
- 1 tablespoon (10 g) blueberries

Place the tofu, peas, cherries, and blueberries on a plate (in a pretty pattern, if you like) and serve as finger food.

YIELD: *Makes 1 toddler serving*

EACH WITH: 39.7 calories; 0.8 gm total fat; 0.1 gm saturated fat; 0.0 mg cholesterol; 10.6 mg sodium; 5.7 gm carbohydrate; 1.1 gm dietary fiber; 2.7 gm protein; 14.1 mg calcium; 0.5 mg iron; 93.7 IU vitamin A; 3.3 mg vitamin C.

Pretzel Dipped in Peanut Butter

- 1/4 piece unsalted pretzel
- 2 teaspoons smooth natural peanut butter

Spread a little peanut butter on the cut end of the pretzel, adding more as your toddler licks or bites it off.

VARIATION: Replace the peanut butter with sesame, almond, or cashew butter, or melted cheese.

YIELD: *Makes 1 toddler serving*

EACH WITH: 177.9 calories; 11.2 gm total fat; 2.3 gm saturated fat; 0.5 mg cholesterol; 221.2 mg sodium; 14.9 gm carbohydrate; 1.5 gm dietary fiber; 6.6 gm protein; 12.7 mg calcium; 1.0 mg iron; 0.0 IU vitamin A; 0.0 mg vitamin C.

Blueberry Milk Shake 🧒

- ½ cup (120 ml) whole milk
- ½ cup (80 g) fresh or frozen sweetened blueberries
- ¼ banana

Combine milk, blueberries, and banana in the blender and process until smooth.

YIELD: *Makes 2 toddler servings*

APPROXIMATE SERVING SIZE: 0.25 cup. **EACH WITH:** 25.5 calories; 0.8 gm total fat; 0.4 gm saturated fat; 2.2 mg cholesterol; 9.0 mg sodium; 4.1 gm carbohydrate; 0.5 gm dietary fiber; 0.9 gm protein; 26.0 mg calcium; 0.1 mg iron; 33.1 IU vitamin A; 1.7 mg vitamin C.

Yum-Yum Cheese Roll 🧒

- 1 tablespoon (15 g) Apricot Puree (page 98)
- 1 slice Edam or Havarti cheese

Spread the apricot puree on the cheese slice and roll tightly. Cut into 3 pieces.

VARIATIONS: Use Prune Puree (page 93) or Pureed Sweet Potato (page 85) instead of Apricot Puree. To make the puree thicker, use very little liquid.

YIELD: *Makes 1 toddler serving*

EACH WITH: 106.3 calories; 7.9 gm total fat; 5.0 gm saturated fat; 25.3 mg cholesterol; 274.2 mg sodium; 1.6 gm carbohydrate; 0.2 gm dietary fiber; 7.2 gm protein; 208.9 mg calcium; 0.2 mg iron; 432.9 IU vitamin A; 1.0 mg vitamin C.

LUNCH

Split Pea Soup 👥

Serve with $1/4$ slice of whole-wheat or rye bread and a small piece of ripe peach, washed, halved, and pitted, for dessert.

* 1 cup (200 g) dried green split peas, soaked in 4 cups (940 ml) water overnight
* 6 cups (1410 ml) water
* 1 bay leaf
* 2 tablespoons (28 ml) olive oil
* I small onion, chopped
* 2 cloves garlic, minced
* 1 teaspoon chopped fresh thyme or $1/2$ teaspoon dried thyme
* $1/2$ cup (60 g) sliced carrots
* $1/2$ cup (50 g) sliced celery
* 1 tablespoon (18 g) kosher salt or 1 teaspoon regular salt

◎ Rinse the peas and place in a large pot with the water and bay leaf. Bring to a boil, skim off the foam, reduce the heat to low, and simmer 45 minutes, stirring occasionally.

Meanwhile, heat the oil in a frying pan over medium heat. Add the onion, garlic, and thyme and sauté 5 minutes. Add the carrots and celery and sauté 5 minutes more. When the peas have simmered for 45 minutes, add the sautéed vegetables and salt. Stir and simmer 10 to 15 minutes more, until the peas and carrots are soft. If soup seems too thick, add more water.

Remove bay leaf before serving. Serve your toddler about $1/4$ cup.

YIELD: *Makes 4 to 6 adult servings AND 1 toddler serving*

APPROXIMATE SERVING SIZE: 0.25 cup. **EACH WITH:** 16.4 calories; 0.8 gm total fat; 0.1 gm saturated fat; 0.0 mg cholesterol; 71.3 mg sodium; 1.8 gm carbohydrate; 0.6 gm dietary fiber; 0.6 gm protein; 4.9 mg calcium; 0.1 mg iron; 209.2 IU vitamin A; 0.5 mg vitamin C.

Little Miss Muffet's Lunch

- 1 to 2 tablespoons (15 to 30 g) small-curd whole-milk cottage cheese
- 3 mandarin orange segments (canned), finely chopped, with 1 tablespoon (14 ml) mandarin juice
- ½ kiwi fruit, peeled, sliced, and cut into small pieces
- 2 or 3 fresh or frozen sweetened raspberries

Place the cottage cheese in a small bowl and top with the orange and juice, kiwi, and raspberries.

YIELD: *Makes 1 toddler serving*

EACH WITH: 7.4 calories; 0.2 gm total fat; 0.1 gm saturated fat; 0.5 mg cholesterol; 14.5 mg sodium; 1.0 gm carbohydrate; 0.2 gm dietary fiber; 0.5 gm protein; 3.9 mg calcium; 0.0 mg iron; 47.5 IU vitamin A; 4.1 mg vitamin C.

> **MAKE IT FOR GROWN-UPS:** This makes a nice snack for adults: Use low-fat cottage cheese and make a larger serving.

Black Bean Hummus

Serve the hummus on crackers, with pita bread, or as a dip for chips or vegetables.

- ½ cup (80 g) cooked black beans, homemade (page 131) or canned, drained
- ½ cup (120 g) canned lima beans, drained
- 2 tablespoons (28 ml) olive oil
- 1 tablespoon (15 g) tahini (sesame seed paste)
- 3 cloves garlic, chopped
- 2 teaspoons lemon juice
- ¼ teaspoon ground cumin
- Salt
- Pepper
- 1 tablespoon chopped fresh cilantro

Place the black beans, lima beans, oil, tahini, garlic, lemon juice, and cumin in a food processor; process until well blended. Season to taste with salt and pepper. Cover and place in refrigerator. When ready to serve, garnish with the cilantro. Serve your toddler 1 or 2 tablespoons.

YIELD: *Makes about 1 cup*

EACH WITH: 26.7 calories; 1.6 gm total fat; 0.2 gm saturated fat; 0.0 mg cholesterol; 1.2 mg sodium; 2.4 gm carbohydrate; 0.6 gm dietary fiber; 0.8 gm protein; 5.5 mg calcium; 0.2 mg iron; 15.8 IU vitamin A; 1.0 mg vitamin C.

Feathery Light Potato Patties with Cheese 👫

Serve these savory patties with applesauce and steamed asparagus. They also make a nice side dish for fish or chicken.

- 1 large (³/₄ to 1 pound, or 340 to 455 g) baked potato (page 91)
- ¹/₂ cup (120 g) mild goat cheese, crumbled
- 1 egg
- 1 tablespoon (14 ml) lemon juice
- 1 tablespoon chopped fresh dill
- ¹/₂ teaspoon salt (optional)
- ¹/₂ to 1 cup (25 to 50 g) panko (Japanese bread crumbs)
- 1 tablespoon (14 ml) olive oil
- 1 tablespoon (14 g) butter

◎ Cool the baked potato slightly; with a spoon, scrape out all of the potato flesh from the skin and place in a medium bowl. Add the cheese and mix with a fork. In a cup, whisk the egg well with a fork and add the lemon juice, dill, and salt if using. Add to the potato and cheese and mix thoroughly. Form into 6 patties.

Place the panko on a plate and dredge the patties, covering both sides with the crumbs. Heat the oil and butter in a frying pan over medium heat. Place the patties in the pan and fry each side about 5 minutes until nicely browned. Keep turning the patties if needed to prevent burning.

YIELD: *Makes 6 patties*

APPROXIMATE SERVING SIZE: 0.25 patty. **EACH WITH:** 42.1 calories; 1.9 gm total fat; 1.1 gm saturated fat; 12.7 mg cholesterol; 49.2 mg sodium; 4.5 gm carbohydrate; 0.4 gm dietary fiber; 1.9 gm protein; 22.0 mg calcium; 0.4 mg iron; 85.8 IU vitamin A; 1.5 mg vitamin C.

DINNER

Chicken, Noodles, and Carrots 👶

Refrigerate leftovers in a covered container for 2 to 3 days.

- 4 cups (940 ml) water
- ¼ cup (10 g) egg noodles
- 3 chicken tenders or one small skinless, boneless chicken breast
- Unsalted chicken broth or water
- 2 baby carrots, cut into thin sticks

◎ Bring the water to a boil in a large pan. Add the noodles and cook according to the direction on package, or until soft. Drain, rinse, and cool.

Meanwhile, place the chicken in a small saucepan and add enough broth or water to cover. Bring to a boil, reduce the heat, and simmer about 10 minutes, or until the chicken is cooked through. Add the carrot to the chicken after 5 minutes and cook until they are soft.

Cool the chicken slightly and shred into bite-size pieces. Serve the noodles, chicken, and carrots as finger food.

YIELD: *Makes 3 toddler servings*

EACH WITH: 62.4 calories; 1.1 gm total fat; 0.3 gm saturated fat; 22.9 mg cholesterol; 150.6 mg sodium; 4.0 gm carbohydrate; 0.3 gm dietary fiber; 8.5 gm protein; 7.9 mg calcium; 0.4 mg iron; 1125.7 IU vitamin A; 0.2 mg vitamin C.

ABC (Apricot-Banana-Cream) Dessert 👶

- ¼ banana
- 2 apricots, halved, peeled, pitted, and lightly mashed, or Apricot Puree (page 98)
- 1 tablespoon (3 g) whipped cream

Mash the banana in a small dish and top with the apricots and whipped cream.

YIELD: *Makes 1 toddler serving*

EACH WITH: 11.2 calories; 0.6 gm total fat; 0.4 gm saturated fat; 2.1 mg cholesterol; 0.7 mg sodium; 1.5 gm carbohydrate; 0.2 gm dietary fiber; 0.2 gm protein; 2.0 mg calcium; 0.0 mg iron; 158.8 IU vitamin A; 1.0 mg vitamin C.

Fish Sticks 👫

These fish sticks would also be excellent in Fish Tacos (page 221). The tempura and panko mixes make these fish sticks light and crunchy on the outside and flaky on the inside. Panko mix is available in the ethnic food section of most supermarkets. If you cannot find them, use Dixie Fry Coating Mix, Italian bread crumbs, or make your own fresh bread crumbs. Serve with Sweet Potato Fries (page 101) and green beans and watermelon (rind and seeds removed) for dessert.

- 1 pound (455 g) fresh or frozen boneless skinless cod (be absolutely sure that every bone has been removed)
- 1/2 cup (60 g) Sun Luck Tempura Batter Mix
- 1 egg
- 1/4 cup (60 ml) milk
- 1/2 cup (30 g) Sun Luck Panko Japanese Style Breading, or more, if needed
- 1 tablespoon (14 ml) olive oil, or more if needed

Preheat the oven to 475°F (240°C, or gas mark 9). Cut the fish into 8 even stick-shaped pieces, about 3 1/2 x 1 1/2 inches.

Place the tempura batter mix on one plate. Whisk the egg and milk together in a small, shallow bowl. Place the panko on a second plate. Coat the fish sticks first in the tempura batter mix, then dip in the egg-milk mix, then coat with the panko.

Heat 1 tablespoon of the oil in a frying pan over medium high. Place the fish sticks in the frying pan and cook the fish 1 minute on each side. Transfer the fish to an ovenproof baking dish. Bake 5 minutes, until the fish is cooked through. Serve your toddler 1 or 2 sticks.

YIELD: *Makes 1 toddler serving AND 2 adult servings*

EACH WITH: 111.9 calories; 2.2 gm total fat; 0.4 gm saturated fat; 50.6 mg cholesterol; 107.5 mg sodium; 2.5 gm carbohydrate; 0.1 gm dietary fiber; 19.3 gm protein; 19.6 mg calcium; 0.5 mg iron; 48.1 IU vitamin A; 2.4 mg vitamin C.

Spaghetti with Tomato Sauce 👨‍👧

This is a quick dinner if you have homemade sauce or a good commercial sauce on hand. I sometimes add meatballs to the sauce. Serve with a good whole-wheat sourdough bread and a green salad. Pineapple or other sorbet for dessert completes the meal.

- 9 to 12 ounces (225 to 340 g) whole-wheat spaghetti
- 1 cup (240 g) Tomato Sauce (right), or more as needed
- 3 to 4 frozen meatballs per person (optional)
- 1/4 cup (25 g) grated Parmesan cheese

◎ Bring 3 quarts water to a boil in a large pot over high heat. Add the pasta and cook according to package direction until just tender, 9 to 14 minutes. Drain in a colander and return the spaghetti to the cooking pot. Stir in a little sauce (or olive oil) to prevent sticking.

Meanwhile, heat the sauce in a medium saucepan over medium heat. Add the frozen meatballs, if using, and follow the cooking directions on the package. With tongs, transfer the spaghetti to individual bowls and pass the sauce and grated cheese in separate bowls. Serve your toddler about 1/4 cup pasta (and 1 meatball cut into small pieces).

YIELD: *Makes 1 toddler serving AND 2 adult servings*

EACH WITH: 11.4 calories; 0.2 gm total fat; 0.1 gm saturated fat; 0.4 mg cholesterol; 7.9 mg sodium; 1.9 gm carbohydrate; 0.2 gm dietary fiber; 0.5 gm protein; 6.4 mg calcium; 0.1 mg iron; 18.4 IU vitamin A; 0.6 mg vitamin C.

Tomato Sauce 👨‍👧

This makes a large quantity, which can be divide into smaller portions for freezing. I prefer Muir Glen Organic Diced Tomatoes and/or Progresso Peeled Tomatoes with Basil. When using whole, canned tomatoes, process them in a blender for a couple of seconds.

- 3 tablespoons (45 ml) olive oil
- 1 medium onion, finely chopped
- 6 cloves garlic, peeled
- 4 cans (28 ounces each) whole tomatoes, crushed
- 1 can (6 ounces) tomato paste
- 1/4 cup chopped fresh oregano
- 1/4 cup chopped fresh basil
- 2 tablespoons (36 g) kosher salt, or to taste

◎ Heat the oil in a large, heavy-bottomed lidded pot over medium heat. Add the onion and garlic and sauté until soft, but not brown. Add the tomatoes, tomato paste, oregano, basil, and salt. Bring to a boil, stir, and reduce the heat. Simmer, covered, 1 hour, stirring every 15 minutes.

YIELD: *Makes 1 toddler serving AND 3 to 4 adult servings*

EACH WITH: 91.7 kcal calories; 5.0 gm total fat; 0.7 gm saturated fat; 0.0 mg cholesterol; 1678.9 mg sodium; 11.7 gm carbohydrate; 3.0 gm dietary fiber; 2.3 gm protein; 89.0 mg calcium; 2.7 mg iron; 677.0 IU vitamin A; 16.0 mg vitamin C.

Meatballs 👪

- 1 slice white bread

- 2 tablespoons (28 g) butter

- $1/4$ cup (33 g) minced onions

- $1/2$ pound (455 g) finely ground beef

- 1 egg

- $1/2$ teaspoon salt

- $1/8$ teaspoon pepper

- $1/4$ teaspoon freshly ground nutmeg

- $1/2$ teaspoon dried thyme or basil, or 1 tablespoon chopped parsley or chives

- $1/4$ cup (60 ml) olive oil

◎ Cut and discard the crusts from the white bread, then soak in water or milk. Melt the butter in a large skillet and sauté the onion for 3 minutes over medium-high heat. Press the water from the bread. Add to the onion mixture, the bread, meat, salt, pepper, nutmeg, spices, and 1 beaten egg. Mix the ingredients lightly with a fork. Shape them without pressure into 1-inch balls. Pour the oil into a large frying pan and heat over medium heat. Add the meatballs and brown, turning once. Drop them into boiling soup, stock, spaghetti sauce, or stew. Simmer them until done for about 10 minutes.

YIELD: *12 meatballs*

EACH WITH: 132.9 kcal calories; 12.6 gm total fat; 4.1 gm saturated fat; 37.5 mg cholesterol; 130.3 mg sodium; 1.5 gm carbohydrate; 0.1 gm dietary fiber; 3.5 gm protein; 11.9 mg calcium; 0.5 mg iron; 106.2 IU vitamin A; 0.6 mg vitamin C.

Garlic Bread 👨‍👩‍👧

- 4 (¹/₂-inch-thick) slices of whole-wheat sourdough bread
- Extra-virgin olive oil
- 2 large cloves garlic, peeled and halved
- ¹/₄ cup (25 g) grated Parmesan cheese

▥ Preheat the oven to 325°F (170°C, or gas mark 3). Brush the bread slices lightly with the oil and rub with the garlic. Sprinkle 1 tablespoon cheese on each slice. Place the slices on a baking sheet; bake 5 minutes, or until the bread turns golden and cheese is melted.

YIELD: *Makes 4 slices bread*

EACH WITH: 128.5 kcal calories; 6.2 gm total fat; 1.8 gm saturated fat; 5.5 mg cholesterol; 228.9 mg sodium; 13.5 gm carbohydrate; 1.2 gm dietary fiber; 5.0 gm protein; 103.7 mg calcium; 1.0 mg iron; 27.6 IU vitamin A; 1.4 mg vitamin C.

Acorn Squash Stuffed with Apple 👨‍👩‍👧

Serve this with plain rice. Splurge with white chocolate ice cream with fresh raspberries, for dessert.

- 1 acorn squash
- 1 apple, peeled, cored, and grated
- 1 tablespoon (14 g) butter, melted
- 1 teaspoon brown sugar

▥ Preheat the oven to 350°F (180°C, or gas mark 4). Wash the acorn squash, cut it in half, and remove seeds and strings. Place each half, cut side down, in a shallow 8 x 11-inch (20 x 27.5-cm) ovenproof baking dish with ¹/₄ inch of water (about 2 cups, or 470 ml). Bake 35 minutes, or until tender. Turn the squash over. In a bowl, mix together the apple, butter, and sugar. Spoon the apple mixture into the squash halves. Bake 5 minutes more, until the apple is soft.

YIELD: *Makes 2 adult AND 1 toddler servings*

EACH WITH: 72.7 kcal calories; 2.4 gm total fat; 1.5 gm saturated fat; 6.1 mg cholesterol; 3.5 mg sodium; 13.7 gm carbohydrate; 2.0 gm dietary fiber; 0.8 gm protein; 31.6 mg calcium; 0.7 mg iron; 402.2 IU vitamin A; 10.8 mg vitamin C.

FIFTEEN MONTHS

Oh, Pillykin, Willykin, Winky Wee!
How does the president take his tea?
He takes it with melons, he takes it with milk,
He takes it with syrup and sassafras silk;
He takes it without and he takes it within,
Oh, Pinky-doodle and Jollapin!

—OH, PILLYKIN, WILLYKIN, WINKY WEE!

TAKING TODDLERS SHOPPING AND TO RESTAURANTS

Taking small children shopping is usually done out of a necessity, not choice. Little ones get bored and restless very easily, and by the time parents decide to stop for a snack or lunch, baby is too tired to eat. One of the most common reasons for poor appetite is fatigue. It is wise not to wait too long before stopping for a break; both parents and child will benefit.

Sitting in a chair for any length of time is also very trying for a child. Look for alternatives to going to restaurants and coffee shops. If the weather is fine, find a park, small grassy area, or even a bench and have a mini-picnic. Either bring food from home or buy take-out restaurant food. Cheese and crackers, fruit, milk, or juice, packed in a little ice chest, will be plenty for a shopping lunch. If you feel like restaurant food, many restaurants now have take-out.

Taking the whole family to a restaurant requires a little more planning. If your baby is very young, take a small food mill so you can puree vegetables, meat, or starchy food. Do keep in mind that restaurant food will probably contain quite a lot of salt.

As your baby grows, you will be able to share restaurant meals.

A bigger concern will be how to keep your little one entertained while waiting for food. A story, simple puzzle, or a couple of favorite toys usually keep a toddler occupied, but your attention and participation will be needed. Expecting a small child to entertain herself for a long period of time is unreasonable.

Typical Daily Meals for a Fifteen-Month-Old

Continue to serve whole milk and whole-milk dairy products.

MEAL	FOODS
Breakfast	Winnie the Pooh's Favorite Breakfast (page 179), 1/4 toasted English muffin with Honey Butter, 1 small piece honeydew melon, and 1/2 cup (120 ml) Honey Milk (page 179)
Snack	3 cucumber slices with 3 rice cakes, and 1/2 cup (120 ml) milk
Lunch	1/4 cup Roasted Tomato Soup (page 182), 2 whole-wheat crackers, avocado-peach salad (1/4 avocado cubed and 1/4 cubed peach), and 1/4 cup (60 ml) milk
Snack	1/2 banana with 1 teaspoon smooth peanut butter, and 1/2 cup (120 ml) milk
Dinner	Toddler's Shepherd's Pie (cooked ground turkey, mashed potatoes and cheddar page 149), 1/4 cup cooked mashed peas, 1 slice peeled orange, and 1/4 cup (60 ml) milk

BREAKFAST

Low-Sugar Cereal with Fruit

- $1/4$ cup (12 g) whole-grain wheat cereal, such as plain Shredded Wheat (spoon size)
- $1/4$ cup ripe fruit, chopped into small pieces (mango, halved and seeded grapes, strawberries, or blueberries)
- $1/2$ cup (120 ml) milk

Serve the cereal and fruit as finger food with the milk to drink or soak the cereal in the milk if preferred.

YIELD: *Makes 1 toddler serving*

EACH WITH: 133.7 calories; 4.3 gm total fat; 2.3 gm saturated fat; 12.2 mg cholesterol; 50.8 mg sodium; 20.4 gm carbohydrate; 2.4 gm dietary fiber; 5.5 gm protein; 145.1 mg calcium; 3.3 mg iron; 144.0 IU vitamin A; 3.5 mg vitamin C

Winnie the Pooh's Favorite Breakfast

- 1 teaspoon Honey Butter (right)
- $1/4$ toasted whole-wheat English muffin
- 1 small piece honeydew melon, chopped into small pieces or lightly mashed
- $1/2$ cup (120 ml) Honey Milk (right)

Spread the Honey Butter on the muffin and serve with the melon and Honey Milk.

YIELD: *Makes 1 toddler serving*

EACH WITH: 204.4 calories; 8.3 gm total fat; 4.8 gm saturated fat; 22.4 mg cholesterol; 128.8 mg sodium; 28.7 gm carbohydrate; 1.8 gm dietary fiber; 6.0 gm protein; 173.0 mg calcium; 0.7 mg iron; 312.1 IU vitamin A; 24.9 mg vitamin C..

Honey Butter

- 4 tablespoons ($1/2$ stick/55 g) unsalted butter, room temperature
- 1 tablespoon (20 g) honey

With an electric mixer, whip the butter until light and creamy. Add the honey and whip until fluffy. Keep in the refrigerator for 3 to 4 days, or freeze for up to 1 month.

YIELD: *Makes about 4 tablespoons or $1/4$ cup*

EACH WITH: 117.8 calories; 11.5 gm total fat; 7.3 gm saturated fat; 30.5 mg cholesterol; 1.8 mg sodium; 4.3 gm carbohydrate; 0.0 gm dietary fiber; 0.1 gm protein; 3.7 mg calcium; 0.0 mg iron; 354.9 IU vitamin A; 0.0 mg vitamin C.

Honey Milk

This comforting warm drink makes a delicious treat for adults, too, especially with a pinch of saffron added.

- $1/2$ cup (120 ml) milk
- $1/2$ teaspoon honey

Place the milk in a microwave-safe container and microwave on high 30 to 45 seconds, until warmed. Add the honey and stir until the honey is dissolved. Test the milk to be sure it is not too hot.

YIELD: *Makes 1 toddler serving*

EACH WITH: 83.7 calories; 4.0 gm total fat; 2.3 gm saturated fat; 12.2 mg cholesterol; 48.9 mg sodium; 8.4 gm carbohydrate; 0.0 gm dietary fiber; 3.9 gm protein; 138.1 mg calcium; 0.1 mg iron; 124.4 IU vitamin A; 0.0 mg vitamin C.

Bacon and Egg 🧒

Bacon contains protein, B vitamins, iron, and zinc. Unfortunately, it may also contain large amounts of unhealthy fats and nitrates. So if you'd like to treat your family to bacon and eggs or a BLT, look for low-fat bacon without nitrates (Apple Gate Farms Sunday Bacon or Wellshire Farms are good choices) or buy bacon made from soy or turkey. Serve with 1/4 toasted English muffin, buttered, and 1/2 cup (120 ml) freshly squeezed orange juice.

* 1 strip bacon
* 1/2 teaspoon olive oil
* 1 egg

⬛ ◎ Place the bacon between two layers of plain paper towels (whitened without chlorine bleach). Microwave on high 1 minute, or until the bacon is crisp. Discard the towels and place the bacon on a plate.

Heat the oil in a small frying pan over medium heat. Crack the egg into the pan and cook until the egg white is completely cooked. (I will some-times cover the pan with a lid to be sure all the egg is firm.) Place the egg next to the bacon and cut up into small pieces.

YIELD: *Makes 1 toddler serving*

EACH WITH: 224.7 calories; 16.9 gm total fat; 5.0 gm saturated fat; 241.9 mg cholesterol; 609.0 mg sodium; 0.7 gm carbohydrate; 0.0 gm dietary fiber; 16.3 gm protein; 29.4 mg calcium; 1.3 mg iron; 253.1 IU vitamin A; 0.0 mg vitamin C.

SNACKS

Graham Crackers and Cheese Stick 🧒

Serve this with 1/4 cup (60 ml) milk.

* 2 graham crackers
* 1 mozzarella cheese stick
* 2 slices apple, peeled and cored

Serve the graham crackers with the cheese and apple.

VARIATIONS: Instead, offer 1 piece of string cheese and a whole-wheat bread stick served with 1/4 cup (60 ml) grape juice.

YIELD: *1 toddler serving*

EACH WITH: 266.2 calories; 16.1 gm total fat; 8.8 gm saturated fat; 51.0 mg cholesterol; 465.2 mg sodium; 14.8 gm carbohydrate; 0.4 gm dietary fiber; 15.5 gm protein; 359.1 mg calcium; 0.8 mg iron; 446.5 IU vitamin A; 0.0 mg vitamin C.

Vegetable Snack 🧒

Offer your toddler 1/2 cup (120 ml) milk.

* 3 peeled cucumber slices, cut into small pieces
* 1 rice cake

Serve the cucumber with the rice cake.

YIELD: *1 toddler serving*

EACH WITH: 3.7 calories; 0.0 gm total fat; 0.0 gm saturated fat; 0.0 mg cholesterol; 2.0 mg sodium; 0.7 gm carbohydrate; 0.3 gm dietary fiber; 0.2 gm protein; 1.4 mg calcium; 0.0 mg iron; 243.3 IU vitamin A; 0.2 mg vitamin C.

Whole-Wheat Toast with Apricot Puree

Serve with ¹/₂ cup (120 ml) milk

- ¹/₂ slice toasted whole-wheat bread, halved
- 2 teaspoons butter
- 2 teaspoons Apricot Puree (page 98)

Spread ¹/₄ slice of the bread with the butter and ¹/₄ slice of the bread with the apricot puree. Fold the two slices together.

YIELD: *Makes 1 toddler serving*

EACH WITH: 104.9 calories; 8.2 gm total fat; 4.9 gm saturated fat; 20.1 mg cholesterol; 75.1 mg sodium; 7.2 gm carbohydrate; 1.1 gm dietary fiber; 1.5 gm protein; 13.2 mg calcium; 0.5 mg iron; 359.0 IU vitamin A; 0.6 mg vitamin C.

Banana with Nut Butter

- ¹/₂ slightly frozen banana
- 1 teaspoon smooth peanut butter, almond butter, or cashew butter

Let your toddler dip the banana in the nut butter or cover the banana lightly with the nut butter and freeze lightly.

YIELD: *Makes 1 toddler serving*

EACH WITH: 85.9 kcal calories; 3.3 gm total fat; 0.4 gm saturated fat; 0.0 mg cholesterol; 1.2 mg sodium; 14.6 gm carbohydrate; 1.7 gm dietary fiber; 1.4 gm protein; 17.2 mg calcium; 0.3 mg iron; 37.8 IU vitamin A; 5.2 mg vitamin C.

LUNCH

Roasted Tomato Soup

This soup can be made ahead and frozen. For your toddler, add half a hard-cooked egg or a couple of tablespoons of cooked elbow macaroni to the soup. Serve with crackers or bread, and a piece of fresh fruit (peach, cantaloupe, or nectarine) for dessert.

- 2 tablespoons (28 ml) olive oil
- 1 medium onion, sliced
- 4 cloves garlic, peeled
- 1/4 cup (10 g) chopped fresh basil
- 1/4 cup (15 g) chopped fresh oregano
- 4 large tomatoes, each cut into 4 thick slices
- 1 tablespoon salt (optional)
- 1/4 cup (50 g) low-fat cottage cheese
- 2 cans (14 ounces each) nonfat chicken broth or 3 cups (705 ml) homemade chicken or vegetable broth

Preheat the oven to 425°F (220°C, or gas mark 7). Oil an 11 x 9-inch (27.5 x 22.5-cm) baking dish with 1 tablespoon of the olive oil. Place the onion and garlic on the bottom of the dish and sprinkle with the basil and oregano. Cover with the tomatoes and sprinkle with the remaining 1 tablespoon (14 ml) oil and 1 teaspoon salt, if using. Roast on the middle rack, uncovered, 45 minutes.

With a shallow ladle, transfer half of the roasted tomato/onion mixture to a blender. Add 2 tablespoons (15 g) of the cottage cheese and 1 can of the broth. Blend for 1 minute, until smooth. Add more liquid if needed. Pour the soup into a saucepan. Repeat with the remaining tomato/onion mixture, cottage cheese, and broth. Heat the soup over low heat until heated through. If the soup is too thick, add more broth until desired consistency. Serve your toddler 1/4 to 1/2 cup.

YIELD: *Makes 4 to 6 adult servings AND 1 toddler serving*

EACH WITH: 24.4 calories; 1.2 gm total fat; 0.2 gm saturated fat; 0.5 mg cholesterol; 128.9 mg sodium; 2.2 gm carbohydrate; 0.5 gm dietary fiber; 1.4 gm protein; 13.1 mg calcium; 0.4 mg iron; 205.5 IU vitamin A; 6.8 mg vitamin C.

Journey Cakes 👪

These cakes are delicious hot or cold and, as their name suggests, they travel well. Throw the cakes in a resealable plastic bag when you are running errands or on an outing with the kids and offer them when the little ones complain of hunger. You can quickly shred the vegetables in a food processor. You can cool any leftover cakes and wrap in foil or clear wrap and freeze for later use. Serve with 1/4 pear, peeled and cored.

- 2 tablespoons (28 ml) olive oil
- 1 large onion, shredded
- 1 large carrot, shredded
- 1 small zucchini, shredded
- 2 cloves garlic, crushed
- Dash low-sodium soy sauce
- 2²/₃ cups (260 g) whole-wheat flour, plus up to 1/2 cup (50 g) more if needed
- 5 teaspoons instant dry milk
- 1/2 cup (80 g) raisins
- 2 tablespoons (30 g) tahini (sesame seed paste)
- 2 teaspoons honey
- 1 egg, beaten
- Enough water to make a thick batter

◎ Heat 1 tablespoon (14 ml) of the oil in a large frying pan over medium heat. Add the onion, carrot, zucchini, and garlic and cook, stirring, until soft and golden. Sprinkle with the soy sauce.

In a medium bowl, combine the flour, dry milk, and raisins. Add the sautéed vegetables, tahini, honey, and egg. Blend well. Add just enough water to make a thick batter.

Wipe the frying pan clean. Add the remaining 1 tablespoon (14 ml) oil and heat over medium heat. Drop the batter into the pan to make cakes about 3 inches wide. Cook the cakes, turning with a wide spatula, until lightly browned and cooked through. (You may have to reduce the heat to avoid overbrowning.)

YIELD: *Makes 8 to 10 cakes*

APPROXIMATE SERVING SIZE: 1 cake. **EACH WITH:** 231.9 calories; 5.9 gm total fat; 1.1 gm saturated fat; 28.4 mg cholesterol; 57.7 mg sodium; 40.4 gm carbohydrate; 5.8 gm dietary fiber; 8.0 gm protein; 51.0 mg calcium; 2.1 mg iron; 1112.8 IU vitamin A; 1.8 mg vitamin C.

Silken Apple Smoothie 👶

- 1/4 sweet apple (Fuji, gala, or golden delicious), peeled, cored, and cut into very small pieces
- 1/3 cup (75 ml) cold apple juice
- 1 tablespoon (15 g) applesauce
- 2 tablespoons (30 g) soft silken tofu

Place the apple and juice in a blender and process until the apple is pureed.

Add the applesauce and tofu and process until smooth.

YIELD: *Makes 1 toddler serving*

EACH WITH: 73.8 calories; 0.7 gm total fat; 0.1 gm saturated fat; 0.0 mg cholesterol; 10.3 mg sodium; 16.0 gm carbohydrate; 0.7 gm dietary fiber; 1.6 gm protein; 14.6 mg calcium; 0.6 mg iron; 17.4 IU vitamin A; 2.2 mg vitamin C.

Chicken with Peanut Sauce 👨‍👧

Serve with slices of cantaloupe and kiwi.

- 1 tablespoon (14 ml) olive oil
- 1 pound (455 g) ground chicken
- 2 tablespoons (28 ml) lime juice
- 1/4 cup (5 g) chopped fresh cilantro
- 3 inner leaves romaine lettuce
- Peanut Sauce (recipe below)

◎ Heat the oil in a large skillet over medium heat. Add the chicken and cook, breaking it up with a wooden spoon and adding a little water to prevent sticking if needed. Cook 4 to 6 minutes, or until cooked through. Stir in the lime juice and sprinkle with the cilantro.

To assemble, place 1 to 2 tablespoons chicken on one lettuce leaf for your toddler and divide the remaining chicken between the two remaining leaves. Drizzle your toddler's chicken with about 1 tablespoon peanut sauce and the adult servings as desired.

YIELD: *Makes 1 toddler serving AND 2 adult servings*

EACH WITH: 86.5 calories; 1.7 gm total fat; 0.5 gm saturated fat; 43.6 mg cholesterol; 35.8 mg sodium; 0.3 gm carbohydrate; 0.0 gm dietary fiber; 16.4 gm protein; 8.0 mg calcium; 0.5 mg iron; 21.7 IU vitamin A; 1.2 mg vitamin C.

Peanut Sauce 👨‍👧

I like to use Adams natural peanut butter in this not-spicy peanut sauce. The sauce is also good with Chicken Fingers (page 200) and Fried Tofu with Steamed Vegetables (page 209) can refrigerate the sauce for up to 7 days.

- 1 tablespoon (14 ml) olive oil
- 1/2 cup (65 g) finely chopped onion
- 1 clove garlic, pressed through a garlic press or minced
- 1 nickel-size peeled fresh ginger, minced
- 1/2 cup (130 g) natural smooth peanut butter
- 2 teaspoons brown sugar
- 1/8 teaspoon cayenne pepper
- 3/4 to 1 cup (175 to 235 ml) water

◎ Heat the oil in a small saucepan over medium heat; add the onion, garlic, and ginger. Sauté 3 to 5 minutes, or until the onion is soft. Add the peanut butter, brown sugar, cayenne, and water and whisk until smooth. (It should be the consistency of pancake batter; if it's too thick, thin with a little bit more water.) Reduce the heat, cover, and simmer 10 minutes, or until you have the desired sauce consistency. Stir often to prevent burning. Serve at room temperature. (Oil will gather on top, so stir well before serving)

YIELD: *Makes about 16 tablespoons or 1 cup*

EACH WITH: 59.3 calories; 4.9 gm total fat; 0.9 gm saturated fat; 0.0 mg cholesterol; 1.8 mg sodium; 2.6 gm carbohydrate; 0.6 gm dietary fiber; 2.1 gm protein; 5.4 mg calcium; 0.2 mg iron; 6.0 IU vitamin A; 0.4 mg vitamin C.

DINNER

Macaroni–Broccoli Sauté 👪

If you want to make this for your toddler only, quarter the recipe. Serve a favorite sorbet for dessert.

* ¼ cup (60 ml) olive oil
* 1 clove garlic, minced
* 1 cup (180 g) finely diced tomatoes
* 2 cups (370 g) broccoli, steamed and chopped
* 1 cup (140 g) cooked whole-wheat elbow macaroni
* Salt (for adults)
* A pinch of cayenne (for adults)

◎ Heat the oil in a heavy-bottomed pan over medium heat. Add the garlic and sauté 30 seconds. Add the tomatoes and sauté 3 minutes. Add the broccoli and sauté 2 minutes more. Reduce the heat to low and add the macaroni. Stir to blend well and simmer until heated through. Serve your toddler ¼ cup. Season the adults' servings with salt and cayenne.

YIELD: *Makes 1 toddler serving AND 2 adult servings*

EACH WITH: 96.5 calories; 7.0 gm total fat; 1.0 gm saturated fat; 0.0 mg cholesterol; 10.5 mg sodium; 7.5 gm carbohydrate; 1.1 gm dietary fiber; 1.5 gm protein; 10.9 mg calcium; 0.4 mg iron; 523.7 IU vitamin A; 18.6 mg vitamin C.

Cheese Omelet 👪

If you make this for your toddler only, quarter the recipe. Serve with a piece of buttered toast, Carrot Puree with Parmesan (page 186), and a slice of peeled seedless orange.

* 1 tablespoon (14 ml) oil
* 4 eggs, beaten
* ½ cup (50 g) grated Jarlsberg or Swiss cheese
* ¾ cup (135 g) small pieces cooked asparagus
* ½ cup (90 g) chopped tomato

◎ Heat the oil in a frying pan over medium heat. Whisk the eggs and pour into the pan. Rotate the pan until the eggs cover the entire bottom of the pan. With a rubber spatula, move the cooked egg toward the middle and let the uncooked egg spread to the sides. Reduce the heat and add the cheese, asparagus, and tomatoes; allow eggs to set and the cheese to melt. Carefully fold the omelet in half and cook for another minute or two. Slide the omelet onto a warm plate. Serve about one-fourth of the omelet to your toddler. The rest of the omelet is for you.

YIELD: *Makes 1 toddler serving AND 1 to 2 adult servings*

EACH WITH: 152.7 calories; 11.7 gm total fat; 4.1 gm saturated fat; 181.7 mg cholesterol; 161.0 mg sodium; 3.0 gm carbohydrate; 0.5 gm dietary fiber; 8.8 gm protein; 124.1 mg calcium; 0.8 mg iron; 594.3 IU vitamin A; 5.8 mg vitamin C.

Carrot Puree with Parmesan

- 1 cup (125 g) baby carrots
- 1/2 cup (120 ml) water
- 1/4 cup (60 ml) warm whole milk
- 2 tablespoons (10 g) finely grated Parmesan cheese
- 1 tablespoon (14 g) butter

Heat the carrots and water, covered, in a medium saucepan over high heat. Bring to a boil, reduce the heat to low, and simmer 15 minutes, or until the carrots are soft.

Drain and mash well. Whisk in the milk, cheese, and butter.

YIELD: *Makes 1 toddler serving AND 1 adult serving*

EACH WITH: 41.8 calories; 3.3 gm total fat; 2.0 gm saturated fat; 9.1 mg cholesterol; 45.3 mg sodium; 1.9 gm carbohydrate; 0.5 gm dietary fiber; 1.3 gm protein; 41.8 mg calcium; 0.1 mg iron; 2775.8 IU vitamin A; 0.6 mg vitamin C.

Plum Yum

- 1/2 cup (120 ml) plum syrup (use leftover juice from Stewed Plums on page 94)
- 1 1/2 teaspoons cornstarch or arrowroot
- Water
- 2 tablespoons (28 ml) half-and-half

Heat the plum syrup in a small saucepan over medium heat until boiling. In a cup, mix the cornstarch with a little water to a smooth and runny consistency. Slowly add to the boiling syrup, stirring constantly until the syrup is clear and thickened. Remove from the heat to cool. Top with the half-and-half.

YIELD: *Makes about 8 tablespoons or 1/2 cup*

EACH WITH: 24.9 calories; 0.4 gm total fat; 0.3 gm saturated fat; 1.4 mg cholesterol; 4.7 mg sodium; 5.3 gm carbohydrate; 0.2 gm dietary fiber; 0.2 gm protein; 5.4 mg calcium; 0.1 mg iron; 55.0 IU vitamin A; 0.1 mg vitamin C.

Teriyaki Chicken 👪

If making this dish for your toddler only, quarter the recipe. This dish is very quick to make, and it's a toddler favorite. Serve with basmati rice and steamed asparagus, a green salad, and Plum Yum (page 186) for dessert.

- 1 pound (455 g) chicken tenders or 4 skinless, boneless chicken breast halves
- ½ cup (120 ml) low-salt teriyaki sauce

▦ Place the chicken between two sheets of plastic wrap; with a mallet, pound lightly to an even thickness. Cut the chicken into 1-inch wide strips. Place the chicken in a bowl and add the teriyaki sauce; toss to evenly coat the chicken. Marinate at least 10 minutes in the refrigerator.

Preheat the broiler. Spray a broiler pan with nonstick cooking spray. Arrange the chicken strips in a single layer on the broiler pan. Broil 2 to 3 minutes on each side, or until cooked through. Finely chop 1 or 2 strips for your toddler, and the rest is for the family.

YIELD: *Makes 1 toddler serving AND 3 adult servings*

EACH WITH: 48.7 calories; 0.9 gm total fat; 0.2 gm saturated fat; 21.8 mg cholesterol; 143.4 mg sodium; 1.1 gm carbohydrate; 0.0 gm dietary fiber; 8.6 gm protein; 5.4 mg calcium; 0.4 mg iron; 5.7 IU vitamin A; 0.0 mg vitamin C.

SIXTEEN MONTHS

Augustus was a chubby lad;

Fat ruddy cheeks Augustus had:

And everybody saw with joy

The plump and hearty, healthy boy.

He ate and drank as he was told,

And never let his soup get cold.

But one day, one cold winter's day,

He screamed out "Take the soup away!

O take the nasty soup away!

I won't have any soup today."

—THE STORY OF AUGUSTUS
WHO WOULD NOT HAVE ANY SOUP

ASSERTING INDEPENDENCE

Feeding problems may create trying times for parents, calling for tremendous patience and understanding. As difficult as this may be, it is important not to discourage your toddler's independence, including their self-feed.

Self-feeding is one of the first steps towards a child's autonomy and need to control his environment. Yes, the learning process can be frustrating at this age, because motor skills are not well developed. But part of your parental role now becomes that of a teacher. Show your child how to hold a spoon, gently bringing the hand to the mouth, until the necessary movements are fluid. Children tend to fluctuate between resistance and cooperation, so it can be a long, slow process. But your efforts will be rewarded when he demonstrates his new skill and exclaims "All by myself!"

Coercion doesn't work well with toddlers, but they are quick to follow good examples. Trying to force your child may only bring defiance and tantrums. At this age they have little understanding of rules or warnings. But praising and encouragement will bring smiles and better cooperation. Discipline gently.

Typical Daily Meals for a Sixteen-Month-Old

Continue to give whole milk and whole-milk dairy products.

MEAL	FOODS
Breakfast	1 small Banana Buttermilk Pancake (page 190) with butter and Maple Cream (page 190), and $1/4$ cup (60 ml) freshly squeezed orange juice
Snack	1 small microwaved broccoli crown with 1 tablespoon grated melted cheese, 2 rye crackers, and $1/2$ cup (120 ml) milk
Lunch	$1/2$ cup Peanut Butter-Date Milk Shake (page 220) and $1/4$ toasted bagel with butter
Snack	2 Corn Thin crackers with 1 tablespoon ricotta cheese (or mascarpone if you have it), topped with 1 grated carrot, and $1/2$ cup (120 ml) milk
Dinner	2 ounces cooked cod fillet served with Egg Butter (page 199), one small cooked potato, $1/4$ cup cooked spinach, 3 halved seedless grapes, and $1/2$ cup (120 ml) milk

FOOD GAMES

When your baby starts playing with the food, he is full. Remove the dish and let him get down if he wants to. It is not reasonable to expect an active toddler to sit quietly for long periods of time. It takes many years to grow up, and there will be plenty of opportunities to teach table manners.

SOUTHPAW?

Left- or right-handed dominance has not yet been established at sixteen months and should not be enforced. Allow your child to grab the spoon with either hand. In another three or four months, handedness will probably be evident and finer control of the wrist and fingers will be established, so self-feeding will be considerably more efficient and speedy.

BREAKFAST

Banana Buttermilk Pancakes 👨‍👩‍👧

These pancakes are delicious. Serve with Maple Cream (right) or your toddler's favorite jam and 1/4 cup (60 ml) grape juice.

- 1 cup (235 ml) buttermilk
- 1 egg
- 3 tablespoon (45 ml) olive oil, plus more for cooking the pancakes
- 1/2 cup (50 g) whole-wheat flour
- 1/4 cup (25 g) all-purpose flour
- 1/4 cup (35 g) cornmeal
- 1 teaspoon baking soda
- 1/2 teaspoon baking powder
- 1/2 banana, cut into small pieces or mashed

◎ Mix the buttermilk, egg, and 3 tablespoons oil in a large bowl. Combine the whole-wheat flour, all-purpose flour, cornmeal, baking soda, baking powder, and banana in a smaller bowl. Mix well with a fork. Add the dry ingredients to the wet ingredients and stir just enough to moisten all the ingredients. (Small lumps are okay.)

Heat a griddle or skillet to medium hot, or until a drop of water bounces off the surface. Coat lightly with oil. With a 1/4-cup measure, pour batter onto hot griddle, making a few pancakes at a time. (If the batter seems too thick, thin by stirring in water, a little at a time.) Spread the batter a bit with the bottom of a spoon. Cook until a few bubbles show on the surface of the pancakes, then turn with a wide spatula, and cook until both sides are golden brown. Transfer pancakes to warmed platter. Repeat with remaining batter, coating the griddle with oil each time.

YIELD: *Makes about six 4-inch pancakes*

EACH WITH: 178.1 calories; 9.0 gm total fat; 1.2 gm saturated fat; 37.4 mg cholesterol; 282.4 mg sodium; 20.3 gm carbohydrate; 2.1 gm dietary fiber; 5.0 gm protein; 77.6 mg calcium; 0.9 mg iron; 71.5 IU vitamin A; 1.3 mg vitamin C.

Maple Cream 👨‍👩‍👧

Use this in place of maple syrup, which is very sweet. Maple cream is a healthier sweet alternative. Refrigerate leftover Maple Cream and use on waffles or French toast.

- 1/2 cup (120 g) plain whole-milk yogurt
- 1/3 cup (75 ml) pure maple syrup

Whisk the yogurt and maple syrup together until very smooth.

YIELD: *Makes about 11 tablespoons or 2/3 cup*

EACH WITH: 29.5 calories; 0.1 gm total fat; 0.1 gm saturated fat; 0.5 mg cholesterol; 7.0 mg sodium; 6.8 gm carbohydrate; 0.0 gm dietary fiber; 0.5 gm protein; 21.6 mg calcium; 0.1 mg iron; 4.1 IU vitamin A; 0.1 mg vitamin C.

Tofu and Scrambled Eggs

Serve this with a small piece of toast lightly spread with a favorite jam and 1/2 cup (120 ml) freshly squeezed orange juice.

- 1 teaspoon butter or oil
- 2 tablespoons (1 ounce, or 28 g) silken tofu, mashed
- 1 egg
- 1 teaspoon milk
- 1 teaspoon grated Parmesan cheese

Heat the oil or butter in a small frying pan over medium heat. In a small bowl, whisk the tofu and egg together. Add the milk and cheese and whisk until well blended. Pour into the frying pan and scramble until well done.

YIELD: *Makes 1 toddler serving*

EACH WITH: 168.8 calories; 13.4 gm total fat; 3.1 gm saturated fat; 216.7 mg cholesterol; 208.4 mg sodium; 2.3 gm carbohydrate; 0.0 gm dietary fiber; 9.5 gm protein; 76.5 mg calcium; 1.0 mg iron; 333.3 IU vitamin A; 0.1 mg vitamin C.

Strawberry-Banana-Tofu Smoothie

- 1 small banana, lightly mashed
- 6 large fresh or frozen strawberries, hulled and quartered
- 1/3 cup (1/4 package, or 75 g) silken tofu
- 1 cup (235 ml) soy milk or whole milk

In a blender, combine the banana, strawberries, tofu, and milk. Process until smooth.

YIELD: *Makes 2 cups; 1 toddler serving AND 1 adult serving*

APPROXIMATE SERVING SIZE: 0.25 cup. **EACH WITH:** 38.1 calories; 1.0 gm total fat; 0.1 gm saturated fat; 0.0 mg cholesterol; 20.9 mg sodium; 5.7 gm carbohydrate; 1.0 gm dietary fiber; 2.3 gm protein; 17.8 mg calcium; 0.5 mg iron; 197.1 IU vitamin A; 9.0 mg vitamin C.

Bulgur with Sliced Peaches 👪

Bulgur wheat is whole-wheat that has been pre-cooked (steamed) then dried and cracked. I like the Hodgson Mill brand.

- 2 1/4 cups (525 ml) water
- 1 cup (140 g) dry bulgur wheat
- 1/2 cup (80 g) raisins (optional)
- 1/2 teaspoon salt (optional)
- 1/4 cup (60 ml) half-and-half (Per serving)
- 1 peach, pitted and sliced

◎ Combine the water, bulgur and raisins and salt if using in a medium saucepan over medium-high heat. Bring to a boil, stir, and reduce the heat. Cover and simmer 15 minutes. Ladle into bowls and add a little half-and-half to each serving. Top with the peaches.

YIELD: *Makes 1 toddler serving OR 2 adult servings*

EACH WITH: 39.9 calories; 0.2 gm total fat; 0.0 gm saturated fat; 0.0 mg cholesterol; 2.9 mg sodium; 8.9 gm carbohydrate; 2.1 gm dietary fiber; 1.4 gm protein; 5.0 mg calcium; 0.3 mg iron; 1.1 IU vitamin A; 0.0 mg vitamin C.

SNACKS

Broccoli with Melted Cheddar 🧒

Serve this with one wheat or rye cracker and 1/4 cup (60 ml) cran-apple juice.

- 1 small piece broccoli
- 1 tablespoon (7 g) grated cheddar cheese

▭ In a microwave-safe bowl, microwave the broccoli on high until tender, about 1 minute. Sprinkle the cheese on top and microwave on high 1 to 3 seconds, until the cheese has melted.

YIELD: *Makes 1 toddler serving*

EACH WITH: 77.5 kcal calories; 2.9 gm total fat; 1.6 gm saturated fat; 7.4 mg cholesterol; 101.3 mg sodium; 10.1 gm carbohydrate; 4.6 gm dietary fiber; 5.1 gm protein; 106.9 mg calcium; 1.0 mg iron; 2824.6 IU vitamin A; 90.9 mg vitamin C.

Cucumber Sandwich

Serve with 1/2 cup (120 ml) carrot juice.

* 2 slices whole-wheat bread, crust removed
* 1 tablespoon (15 g) mayonnaise
* 4 slices peeled cucumber

Cut the bread into a favorite shape with a cookie cutter. Spread the bread lightly with the mayonnaise. Place 2 slices of the cucumber on each piece of bread. Serve open-faced or combine slices to make a sandwich.

YIELD: *Makes 2 toddler servings*

EACH WITH: 76.2 kcal calories; 1.9 gm total fat; 0.3 gm saturated fat; 0.6 mg cholesterol; 150.2 mg sodium; 12.7 gm carbohydrate; 1.2 gm dietary fiber; 2.4 gm protein; 28.6 mg calcium; 0.9 mg iron; 15.5 IU vitamin A; 0.4 mg vitamin C.

Corn Thins with Ricotta Cheese and Grated Carrot

* 1 tablespoon (15 g) whole-milk ricotta cheese
* 1 Corn Thin (crisp cracker from Real Foods)
* 1 baby carrot, grated

Spread the ricotta cheese on the cracker and sprinkle with the carrot.

YIELD: *Makes 1 toddler serving*

EACH WITH: 65.1 calories; 2.2 gm total fat; 1.3 gm saturated fat; 7.8 mg cholesterol; 23.2 mg sodium; 8.8 gm carbohydrate; 0.2 gm dietary fiber; 2.5 gm protein; 36.7 mg calcium; 0.3 mg iron; 1469.2 IU vitamin A; 0.8 mg vitamin C.

Blueberry Muffins 👨‍👧

Although the recipe calls for fresh blueberries, you can use frozen. Add them to the batter frozen, but be careful not to stir too much or the batter may turn purple. Also, you have to bake the muffins 3 to 5 minutes longer.

- ³⁄₄ cup (150 g) sugar
- ¹⁄₂ cup (120 g) plain whole-milk yogurt or buttermilk
- ¹⁄₄ cup (60 ml) oil
- 2 eggs
- 1 teaspoon vanilla extract
- 1¹⁄₂ cups (240 g) fresh blueberries
- 2 cups (200 g) all-purpose flour
- 2 teaspoons baking soda
- ¹⁄₂ teaspoon salt

▥ Preheat the oven to 375°F (190°C, or gas mark 5). Lightly grease 24 mini-muffin cups. In a large bowl, mix the sugar, yogurt or buttermilk, oil, eggs, and vanilla. Fold in the blueberries. In a small bowl, combine the flour, baking soda, and salt. Add the wet ingredients to the dry ingredients and blend together gently. Spoon the batter into prepared mini-muffin cups. Bake 18 minutes, until lightly golden, or a cake tester inserted in center comes out clean. Remove from pan and cool on a rack.

YIELD: *Makes 24 mini muffins*

EACH WITH: 96.9 calories; 3.0 gm total fat; 0.6 gm saturated fat; 18.3 mg cholesterol; 161.9 mg sodium; 15.8 gm carbohydrate; 0.5 gm dietary fiber; 1.8 gm protein; 10.6 mg calcium; 0.6 mg iron; 30.2 IU vitamin A; 0.9 mg vitamin C.

VARIATIONS: Substitute 1¹⁄₂ cups chopped peeled pears, peaches, nectarines, diced rhubarb, or cranberries for the blueberries.

💡 *The muffins will keep for about 4 days. To freeze extras, put them in a plastic bag, removing as much air as possible to prevent freezer burn. To defrost, leave out overnight. Do not defrost in the refrigerator.*

LUNCH

Miso Soup 👫

Miso is a soybean paste used as a soup base in Asian cooking. The lighter miso is less strongly flavored than the darker pastes. Miso is available in health food stores, Asian markets, and in some supermarkets. Serve this soup with a rice cake and a piece of mango.

- 2 tablespoons (28 ml) olive oil
- 1 small onion, finely chopped
- 3 cloves garlic, peeled and minced
- 1/2 teaspoon fresh ginger, peeled and minced
- 3 tablespoons (50 g) miso (any kind: white, yellow, or red)
- 1 cup (30 g) spinach, washed and chopped
- 1/2 cup (70 g) cooked noodles or cooked rice
- 1/2 package (12.3 ounces, or 349 g) silken tofu, cubed
- Salt, pepper, or light soy sauce

◎ Heat 4 cups (940 ml) water in a large pan. Heat the oil in a separate pan and add the onion, garlic, and ginger and sauté until soft. Add the miso to the hot water and stir until dissolved. Add the spinach to the onion, garlic, and ginger. Cook until wilted, then add to the miso and water. Add the noodles or rice and tofu and heat through. (To maintain optimum nutrition, do not boil the miso soup.) Season to taste with salt, pepper, or soy sauce.

YIELD: *Makes 4 cups*

APPROXIMATE SERVING SIZE: 0.25 cup. **EACH WITH:** 47.9 calories; 2.6 gm total fat; 0.3 gm saturated fat; 1.7 mg cholesterol; 134.2 mg sodium; 3.9 gm carbohydrate; 0.6 gm dietary fiber; 2.5 gm protein; 22.3 mg calcium; 0.5 mg iron; 720.0 IU vitamin A; 0.9 mg vitamin C.

Chicken Salad 👪

Serve plain chicken salad to your toddler with crackers or in an ice cream cone. For the adults, spice up the chicken with horseradish and mustard and make a sandwich with a slice of tomato.

- ¼ cup (60 g) mayonnaise
- 2 tablespoons (30 g) plain whole-milk yogurt
- 1 can (12.5 ounces, or 355 g) chicken (premium chunk chicken breast packed in water), drained
- 1 tablespoon (10 g) chopped tomato (optional)
- Whole-wheat crackers
- 1 teaspoon whipped horseradish (for the adults)
- ½ teaspoon Grey Poupon mustard (for the adults)
- 5 to 10 drops Tabasco sauce (for the adults)
- 4 slices whole-wheat bread (for the adults)
- 2 slices tomato (for the adults)

Mix together the mayonnaise and the yogurt. For your toddler: Add 1 tablespoon of the mayonnaise mixture to ½ cup chicken. Mix well with a fork. Fold in 1 tablespoon chopped tomato, if desired. Spread 1 tablespoon chicken salad on each cracker or fill an ice cream cone with the chicken salad.

FOR THE ADULTS: Stir the horseradish, mustard, and Tabasco into the remaining mayonnaise mixture. Blend well and spread a bit onto the bread. Stir the remaining mayonnaise mixture into the remaining chicken. Place the tomato slices on two slices of bread and divide the chicken salad between the two; top with the remaining slices of bread.

YIELD: *Makes 1 toddler serving AND 2 adult servings*

EACH WITH: 102.9 calories; 5.7 gm total fat; 1.3 gm saturated fat; 21.9 mg cholesterol; 106.8 mg sodium; 2.2 gm carbohydrate; 0.0 gm dietary fiber; 10.1 gm protein; 11.1 mg calcium; 0.5 mg iron; 64.1 IU vitamin A; 0.0 mg vitamin C.

Date Milk Shake 👶

- 4 soft, pitted dates, cut into small pieces
- ½ cup (120 ml) milk

Combine the dates and milk in a blender and process until smooth.

VARIATION: You can substitute 4 soft pitted prunes or ¼ cup (60 g) prune puree for the dates.

YIELD: *Makes 1 toddler serving*

APPROXIMATE SERVING SIZE: 0.25 cup. **EACH WITH:** 169.6 calories; 2.1 gm total fat; 1.1 gm saturated fat; 6.1 mg cholesterol; 24.9 mg sodium; 38.7 gm carbohydrate; 3.2 gm dietary fiber; 2.8 gm protein; 99.6 mg calcium; 0.5 mg iron; 133.7 IU vitamin A; 0.0 mg vitamin C.

Asparagus and Cottage Cheese with Egg 👶

Serve with a small piece of toast and a few halved and pitted cherries. Save the asparagus stems for Asparagus Soup (page 198).

- 1 teaspoon olive oil
- ¼ cup (35 g) 1-inch asparagus tips
- 2 tablespoons (28 ml) water
- 1 egg
- ¼ cup (55) small-curd cottage cheese
- 1 tablespoon (5 g) grated Parmesan cheese (optional)

Heat the oil in a saucepan over low heat. Add the asparagus and sauté 3 minutes. Add the water, cover, and cook 5 minutes more, until the asparagus is tender. In a bowl, whisk the egg with cottage cheese and pour over the asparagus. Stir, cover, and cook over low heat until the egg mixture is cooked through. Sprinkle with the cheese if desired.

YIELD: *Makes 1 toddler serving*

EACH WITH: 25.5 calories; 1.8 gm total fat; 0.6 gm saturated fat; 27.9 mg cholesterol; 50.3 mg sodium; 0.5 gm carbohydrate; 0.1 gm dietary fiber; 1.8 gm protein; 10.4 mg calcium; 0.1 mg iron; 79.9 IU vitamin A; 0.2 mg vitamin C.

Asparagus Soup 👪

Serve with fresh French bread.

- 1¹/₂ pounds (680 g) fresh asparagus, washed and trimmed
- 3 cans (14 ounces, or 425 ml, each) nonfat chicken broth or 4 cups (940 ml) homemade
- ¹/₄ cup (60 ml) olive oil
- ¹/₂ cup (65 g) chopped onion (about ¹/₂ onion)
- 1 cup (90 g) chopped well-washed leeks, white part only (2 leeks)
- ¹/₂ cup (50 g) washed and chopped celery
- 1 baking potato (about ¹/₂ pound, or 225 g), peeled and cubed
- 1 tablespoon (14 ml) fresh lemon juice
- Salt
- 1 dollop for each plate creme fraiche or plain yogurt with a sprinkle of paprika (optional)

◎ Snap off asparagus tips and save. Place stalks in a saucepan with 3 cups chicken broth. Bring to a boil, cover, reduce heat to low, and simmer for 45 minutes. Drain and save the broth. Discard the stalks. Add oil to a large, heavy-bottomed pot. Add onion, leeks, celery, potato, and asparagus tips. Cover and cook on the lowest heat for 40 minutes or until vegetables are soft. Check and stir occasionally to prevent sticking. Add a little broth if necessary. When done, add lemon juice and divide into two batches.

Place the first batch in a blender, with 1¹/₂ cups (355 ml) of broth (or more if needed) and blend for 30 seconds. Repeat the same with the second batch. Return the soup to the saucepan, add salt to taste and reheat. Thin soup to desired consistency by adding additional broth. Add a dollop of crème fraîche or whipped yogurt and a sprinkle of paprika, if desired.

YIELD: *Makes 6 servings*

EACH WITH: 220.6 calories; 11.2 gm total fat; 1.8 gm saturated fat; 4.8 mg cholesterol; 271.0 mg sodium; 23.7 gm carbohydrate; 4.0 gm dietary fiber; 8.1 gm protein; 53.5 mg calcium; 3.6 mg iron; 1151.7 IU vitamin A; 22.8 mg vitamin C.

DINNER

Poached Cod

Serve with boiled, baked, or microwaved potato and cooked spinach. Other fish that may be prepared this way include haddock and sole.

- 2 ounces (55 g) cod fillet (fresh or frozen), skin and bones removed
- 1 small carrot, sliced
- 3-inch piece celery, sliced
- 1/4 cup (60 ml) water
- Egg Butter (recipe below)

◎ Place the fish, carrot, celery, and water in a small pan. Slowly bring to a simmer and cook 5 minutes. Lightly mash the fish with carrots and celery and top with the Egg Butter.

YIELD: *Makes 1 toddler serving*

EACH WITH: 198.0 calories; 1.5 gm total fat; 0.2 gm saturated fat; 79.9 mg cholesterol; 198.4 mg sodium; 4.5 gm carbohydrate; 1.7 gm dietary fiber; 39.5 gm protein; 37.0 mg calcium; 0.8 mg iron; 8075.9 IU vitamin A; 7.9 mg vitamin C.

Egg Butter

- 2 tablespoons (28 g) butter
- 1/2 hard-cooked egg, cut into small pieces

◎ Melt the butter in a small pan over low heat. Stir in the egg.

YIELD: *Makes 1 toddler serving*

EACH WITH: 242.4 calories; 25.7 gm total fat; 15.4 gm saturated fat; 167.1 mg cholesterol; 34.1 mg sodium; 0.3 gm carbohydrate; 0.0 gm dietary fiber; 3.4 gm protein; 19.3 mg calcium; 0.3 mg iron; 856.2 IU vitamin A; 0.0 mg vitamin C.

Tubettini with Peas

This is a quick dish to make when your tot is hungry and can't wait for dinner. Substitute any of your little one's favorite vegetables for the peas, if you wish. If you have some fresh or defrosted ground beef or turkey, fry up a couple of tablespoons and add to the pasta. Offer a 100 percent fruit Popsicle for dessert.

- 4 cups (940 ml) water
- 1/4 cup (25 g) whole-wheat tubettini
- 1/4 cup (40 g) frozen petite peas
- 2 teaspoons olive oil
- 1 to 2 tablespoons (5 to 10 g) grated Parmesan cheese

◎ Bring the water to a boil. Add the pasta and cook 5 minutes. Add the peas and cook 5 minutes more, until pasta is just tender and peas are heated through. Drain the pasta and peas and place in small bowl. Stir in the oil and cheese.

YIELD: *Makes 1 toddler serving*

EACH WITH: 325.2 calories; 28.7 gm total fat; 4.5 gm saturated fat; 4.4 mg cholesterol; 92.0 mg sodium; 13.0 gm carbohydrate; 1.6 gm dietary fiber; 4.6 gm protein; 63.0 mg calcium; 0.7 mg iron; 442.1 IU vitamin A; 2.0 mg vitamin C.

Chicken Fingers with Peanut Sauce 👩‍🍳

Serve this with lightly cooked julienned carrot sticks, rice, and thin slices of apple. The carrot and apple can also be dipped in the peanut sauce.

* 1 cup (235 ml) water
* 1 teaspoon salt
* 1 teaspoon whole peppercorns
* 1 bay leaf
* 2 chicken tenders
* 2 tablespoons (28 ml) Peanut Sauce (page 184), warmed

◎ Bring the water, salt, peppercorns, and bay leaf to a boil in a saucepan. Add the chicken and cover. Reduce the heat and simmer 20 minutes, until the chicken is cooked through. Cool the chicken and cut it into small, finger-size pieces. Let your toddler dip the chicken fingers into the sauce.

YIELD: *Makes 1 toddler serving*

EACH WITH: 13.2 calories; 0.3 gm total fat; 0.1 gm saturated fat; 6.7 mg cholesterol; 5.5 mg sodium; 0.0 gm carbohydrate; 0.0 gm dietary fiber; 2.5 gm protein; 1.1 mg calcium; 0.1 mg iron; 1.8 IU vitamin A; 0.0 mg vitamin C.

SEVENTEEN MONTHS

There was once a fish.

(What more could you wish?)

He lived in the sea.

(Where else would he be?)

He was caught on a line.

(Whose line if not mine?)

So I brought him to you.

(What else should I do?)

—THERE WAS ONCE A FISH

ACCEPTING CHANGES IN YOUR TODDLER'S EATING PATTERNS

Developing independence, which starts at about nine months of age, can be both exciting and distressing to parents. Behavior patterns—both good and bad—are forming, and your toddler will start displaying them. As problematic as this may be at times, it is important to be flexible and tolerant.

During the first years, infants and toddlers have tremendous adjustments to make and new experiences to absorb. These include adapting to a large variety of foods and methods of eating. Rebellion against unfamiliar foods can be lessened, and long-term refusals prevented, once parents learn to recognize their child's eating habits. For instance, acknowledging that a seventeen-month-old may have a sporadic appetite, which is no cause for undue alarm, may prevent mealtime battles. In the same way, perhaps your child takes awhile to wake up in the morning and may not be ready for breakfast until she's had some time to adjust to the new day. There's no reason you can't delay breakfast for a bit if that is the case.

During very hot weather, appetites often diminish, so you may want to keep meals light. Serve tuna, cheese, eggs, salads, and other dishes that are simple to prepare and eat. A variety of fresh fruits and vegetables will provide sufficient vitamins and minerals when supplemented with a little cereal, beans, rice, and nut butters.

Keep fresh fruit-juice pops in your freezer for healthy and refreshing treats, and don't hesitate to whip up smoothies made with berries, bananas, yogurt, tofu, and milk or ice cream.

Typical Daily Meals for a Seventeen-Month-Old

Continue serving whole milk and whole-milk dairy products.

MEAL	FOODS
Breakfast	Banana Split with Cereal (banana, yogurt, peach jam, and dry cereal page 203), and $1/4$ cup (60 ml) milk
Snack	Ham, Cream Cheese, and Asparagus Roll (page 204), 2 bread sticks, and $1/4$ cup (60 ml) milk
Lunch	$1/4$ cup Cup-of-Noodle Soup (page 206), $1/4$ slice whole-wheat buttered bread, 4 thin apple slices, and $1/2$ cup (120 ml) milk
Snack	1 Nut-Butter Kiss (page 205), $1/4$ pear (seeds removed), and $1/2$ cup (120 ml) milk
Dinner	Fried Tofu with Steamed Vegetables (carrot, broccoli and cauliflower) and Peanut Sauce (page 209), with $1/4$ cup rice, and water to drink

BREAKFAST

English Muffin 👶

Serve with 1/2 hard-cooked egg, 1/2 cup (120 ml) milk, and 1/2 small peeled and sliced kiwi.

- 1/4 English muffin, toasted
- 1 teaspoon butter
- 1/2 teaspoon apricot jam

Spread the muffin with the butter and jam.

YIELD: *Makes 1 toddler serving*

EACH WITH: 58.5 calories; 2.2 gm total fat; 0.4 gm saturated fat; 0.0 mg cholesterol; 89.6 mg sodium; 8.7 gm carbohydrate; 0.4 gm dietary fiber; 1.1 gm protein; 8.8 mg calcium; 0.4 mg iron; 90.8 IU vitamin A; 0.3 mg vitamin C.

Banana Split with Cereal 👶

- 1/4 small banana, split lengthwise
- 1 tablespoon (15 g) vanilla whole-milk yogurt
- 2 teaspoons Peachy Plum (page 95) or jam of choice
- 2 tablespoons (5 g) low-sugar dry cereal, such as Grape-Nuts

Place the banana on a small plate. Cover with the yogurt and Peachy Plum and sprinkle with the cereal.

YIELD: *Makes 1 toddler serving*

EACH WITH: 50.3 calories; 0.4 gm total fat; 0.2 gm saturated fat; 0.8 mg cholesterol; 37.8 mg sodium; 11.6 gm carbohydrate; 1.4 gm dietary fiber; 1.4 gm protein; 30.0 mg calcium; 1.1 mg iron; 139.8 IU vitamin A; 2.8 mg vitamin C.

Strawberry Omelet 👫

- 1 teaspoon butter
- 1/4 cup (40 g) washed and sliced strawberries
- 1 teaspoon sugar
- 1 egg
- 1 teaspoon water
- 2 tablespoons (15 g) plain yogurt
- 1/2 teaspoon sugar

◎ Heat the butter on low in a frying pan. Mix the strawberries with the sugar. Whisk the egg and the water and pour into the frying pan. Tilt the pan until the egg covers the whole bottom. Lift the sides of the egg with a plastic spatula and let the runny part of the egg run underneath.

When the egg has cooked firmly, add the strawberries. Fold the omelet in half and press down lightly. Mix the yogurt with the sugar. Cut off a piece of the omelet for your toddler and top it with 1 tablespoon of yogurt. What is left of the omelet is for you. Top it with the rest of the yogurt and enjoy.

YIELD: *Makes 1 toddler AND 1 adult serving*

EACH WITH: 86.6 calories; 6.2 gm total fat; 2.7 gm saturated fat; 114.4 mg cholesterol; 93.0 mg sodium; 3.8 gm carbohydrate; 0.4 gm dietary fiber; 4.1 gm protein; 43.8 mg calcium; 0.5 mg iron; 237.0 IU vitamin A; 11.3 mg vitamin C.

Couscous Breakfast Cereal with Raisin Puree 👶

- ¼ cup (60 ml) milk, plus more as desired
- ½ tablespoon butter
- 2 tablespoons (20 g) plain couscous (I like the Near East brands.)
- 2 tablespoons (30 g) Raisin Puree (page 133)

◎ Bring ¼ cup (60 ml) of the milk and the butter just to a boil in a small saucepan over medium heat. Stir in the couscous, cover, and remove from the heat. Let stand 5 minutes. Swirl in the raisin puree and add more milk as desired.

YIELD: *Makes 1 toddler serving*

EACH WITH: 152.9 calories; 6.9 gm total fat; 4.2 gm saturated fat; 18.3 mg cholesterol; 16.2 mg sodium; 22.3 gm carbohydrate; 1.0 gm dietary fiber; 2.4 gm protein; 48.1 mg calcium; 0.5 mg iron; 208.5 IU vitamin A; 0.5 mg vitamin C.

SNACKS

Ham, Cream Cheese, and Asparagus Roll 🧒

- 1 thin slice cooked ham
- 1 teaspoon cream cheese
- 1 stalk cooked asparagus

Spread the ham with the cream cheese. Place the asparagus on top of the cream cheese and roll it up. Cut into small pieces for finger food.

YIELD: *Makes 1 toddler serving*

EACH WITH: 75.7 calories; 4.2 gm total fat; 1.9 gm saturated fat; 21.3 mg cholesterol; 387.8 mg sodium; 3.7 gm carbohydrate; 1.6 gm dietary fiber; 6.5 gm protein; 24.4 mg calcium; 0.9 mg iron; 668.6 IU vitamin A; 5.7 mg vitamin C.

Hawaiian Chiffon 🧒

- 1 tablespoon (8 g) chopped macadamia nuts
- ¼ cup (60 ml) pineapple juice
- 2 tablespoons (30 g) vanilla whole-milk yogurt
- ¼ cup (40 g) pineapple chunks (fresh or canned), cut into small pieces

Process the macadamia nuts and juice in a blender until smooth. Add the yogurt and pineapple and continue to process until creamy.

YIELD: *Makes 1 toddler serving*

EACH WITH: 138.6 calories; 6.9 gm total fat; 1.3 gm saturated fat; 1.5 mg cholesterol; 21.6 mg sodium; 18.5 gm carbohydrate; 0.8 gm dietary fiber; 2.6 gm protein; 73.9 mg calcium; 0.5 mg iron; 36.4 IU vitamin A; 13.5 mg vitamin C.

Nut-Butter Kisses 🧑‍🍳

Serve one kiss with 1/4 pear.

- 1/3 cup (45 g) chopped cashews
- 1/4 cup (65 g) smooth peanut butter
- 1/4 cup (30 g) dry milk powder
- 1 tablespoon (20 g) honey
- 1 teaspoon pure vanilla extract

Pulse the cashews in a food processor until finely ground but not pureed. Add the peanut butter, milk powder, honey, and vanilla and pulse just until blended. With your hands, roll the peanut butter mixture into 8 "kisses." (The consistency of the mixture will be soft.) Refrigerate in an airtight container for 3 or 4 days.

YIELD: *Makes 8 "kisses"*

EACH WITH: 107.9 calories; 7.7 gm total fat; 2.0 gm saturated fat; 3.9 mg cholesterol; 17.1 mg sodium; 6.9 gm carbohydrate; 0.7 gm dietary fiber; 4.0 gm protein; 42.5 mg calcium; 0.5 mg iron; 36.6 IU vitamin A; 0.4 mg vitamin C.

The Red, White, and Blue 🧑‍🍳

If you have time and want to be creative, fill a pastry bag with the yogurt cheese and make the American flag, the Norwegian, or French flag, or any country's flag that is red, white, and blue.

- 1/4 cup (30 g) fresh raspberries
- 1/4 cup yogurt cheese (See "Yogurt Cheese" on page 114.)
- 1/4 cup (40 g) fresh blueberries

On a plate, make a row of the raspberries, a row of the yogurt cheese, and a row of blueberries. If your toddler cannot master a spoon yet, he can use a finger to lick up the yogurt cheese.

YIELD: *Makes 1 to 2 toddler servings*

EACH WITH: 74.0 calories; 2.3 gm total fat; 1.3 gm saturated fat; 8.0 mg cholesterol; 28.8 mg sodium; 11.8 gm carbohydrate; 2.9 gm dietary fiber; 2.8 gm protein; 84.0 mg calcium; 0.3 mg iron; 90.4 IU vitamin A; 11.9 mg vitamin C.

LUNCH

Cup-of-Noodle Soup
👶

This soup takes about 5 minutes to make, about the same time as preparing the commercial brand. Serve with a seed-free, peeled clementine.

* 1 can (14 ounces, or 425 ml) chicken broth (or 1½ cups homemade)
* 1 baby carrot, shredded
* 2 tablespoons (20 g) frozen corn or 1 tablespoon each frozen corn and peas
* 1 piece (3 inches) green onion, thinly sliced
* 1 ounce (about ¾ cup, or 15 g) egg noodles (Chow mein stir-fry noodles)
* ½ teaspoon tamari (natural soy sauce) or light soy sauce (optional)

◎ Bring the broth to a boil in a small pan over medium-high heat. Add the carrot, corn, and green onion and cook 2 minutes. Add the noodles and cook 3 more minutes. Season with the soy sauce if desired.

YIELD: *Makes 1½ cups*

APPROXIMATE SERVING SIZE: 0.25 cup. **EACH WITH:** 58.1 calories; 2.8 gm total fat; 0.5 gm saturated fat; 0.5 mg cholesterol; 354.2 mg sodium; 5.6 gm carbohydrate; 0.6 gm dietary fiber; 3.0 gm protein; 8.1 mg calcium; 0.6 mg iron; 1402.3 IU vitamin A; 1.2 mg vitamin C.

Grilled Cheese Sandwich 👪

Serve with a thin slice of pickle or lightly microwave a few carrot sticks. Add a piece of fruit for dessert.

* Butter
* 2 slices whole-wheat bread
* 2 slices cheddar cheese

◎ Heat a frying pan on medium. Butter both slices of the bread, place 1 cheese slice on each, and fold them together. Butter the outside of both bread slices and place buttered side down in the frying pan. Fry until first side is golden brown. Flip and fry the second side until golden brown and the cheese has melted. Cut a quarter piece of the sandwich for your toddler. Cool before serving.

YIELD: *Makes 1 toddler AND 1 adult serving*

EACH WITH: 78.3 calories; 4.9 gm total fat; 3.0 gm saturated fat; 13.9 mg cholesterol; 122.7 mg sodium; 4.9 gm carbohydrate; 0.4 gm dietary fiber; 3.7 gm protein; 91.5 mg calcium; 0.4 mg iron; 137.2 IU vitamin A; 0.0 mg vitamin C.

Tuna Fish Salad 👫

This salad can be served with crackers, in pita bread with tomato and/or alfalfa sprouts, or in a sandwich. A toddler may prefer the tuna fish mixed only with mayonnaise. Serve with pear slices and ¹/₂ cup (120 ml) milk.

- 2 cans (6 ounces, or 170 g each) chunk light tuna, drained
- ¹/₃ cup (30 g) finely chopped celery
- 2 hard-cooked eggs, chopped
- 3 to 4 tablespoons (45 to 60 g) mayonnaise
- 1 teaspoon mustard
- Salt
- Whole-wheat crackers
- ¹/₄ cup chopped onion (for the adults)
- 2 tablespoons (20 g) finely chopped pickles (for the adults)
- 4 slices whole-wheat bread (for the adults)

Combine the tuna, celery, eggs, mayonnaise, and mustard and salt to taste in a medium bowl. Mix well. For your toddler, spread 1 tablespoon tuna salad on each cracker or serve in an ice cream cone.

For the adults: Stir the onion and pickles into the tuna salad. Blend well and spread a bit onto the bread. Divide the remaining tuna salad between two slices of bread; top with the remaining slices of bread.

YIELD: *Makes 1 toddler serving AND 2 adult servings*

APPROXIMATE SERVING SIZE: 0.25 cup. **EACH WITH:** 89.7 calories; 3.5 gm total fat; 0.8 gm saturated fat; 66.8 mg cholesterol; 85.7 mg sodium; 1.6 gm carbohydrate; 0.1 gm dietary fiber; 12.2 gm protein; 13.7 mg calcium; 0.8 mg iron; 128.2 IU vitamin A; 0.1 mg vitamin C.

DINNER

Macaroni, Sausage, and Beans
👪

If you have some pantry staples and sausage, this is a quick dish to make. For the precooked sausage, I recommend Aidell's sun-dried tomato, artichoke and garlic, or chicken and apple varieties. Serve with steamed broccoli and strawberries for dessert.

* 4 cups (940 ml) water
* 1/2 cup (50 g) uncooked whole-wheat elbow macaroni
* 1 can (15 ounces, or 420 g) white beans, drained, or 1 1/2 cups cooked white beans
* 1 cup (245 g) Tomato Sauce (page 174) or store-bought tomato sauce
* 1 or 2 precooked sausage links, sliced
* 1/4 cup (15 g) chopped fresh parsley
* 1/4 cup (25 g) grated Parmesan or Romano cheese

◎ Bring the water to a boil in a large pot over high heat and add the macaroni. Cook according to package instructions until al dente. Drain, reserving 1/2 cup (120 ml) of the cooking liquid. Combine the macaroni, beans, tomato sauce, sausage, and 1/4 cup pasta water in a saucepan over low heat; simmer 5 minutes, stirring occasionally. Add more pasta water if it seems too dry. Garnish with the parsley and cheese. Serve 1/4 cup to your toddler, cutting the sausage into small pieces.

YIELD: *Makes 1 toddler serving AND 2 adult servings*

EACH WITH: 155.6 calories; 5.4 gm total fat; 2.1 gm saturated fat; 11.8 mg cholesterol; 417.0 mg sodium; 19.1 gm carbohydrate; 3.7 gm dietary fiber; 8.9 gm protein; 114.7 mg calcium; 2.5 mg iron; 376.4 IU vitamin A; 6.4 mg vitamin C.

Fried Tofu with Steamed Vegetables and Peanut Sauce

- 1 teaspoon olive oil
- 1 small slice extra-firm tofu
- 1 baby carrot
- 1 small broccoli floret
- 1 small cauliflower floret
- 1 tablespoon (14 ml) Peanut Sauce (page 184), warmed

◎ Heat the oil in a small frying pan over medium heat; add the tofu and cook until nicely browned. Turn the tofu and brown the other side. Cut the tofu into small pieces.

Place the carrot, broccoli, and cauliflower in a small steamer basket. Place the basket in a pot with 1 inch of boiling water. Cover and steam 3 to 5 minutes, until tender. Cut the carrot diagonally in half.

Assemble a plate with the broccoli, cauliflower, carrot, and tofu and drizzle with the peanut sauce. Or place the peanut sauce on the side and let your toddler use it as dipping sauce.

YIELD: *Makes 1 toddler serving*

EACH WITH: 188.9 calories; 8.1 gm total fat; 1.5 gm saturated fat; 0.0 mg cholesterol; 124.2 mg sodium; 20.7 gm carbohydrate; 8.1 gm dietary fiber; 12.6 gm protein; 110.7 mg calcium; 2.3 mg iron; 10679.2 IU vitamin A; 116.9 mg vitamin C.

Hearts, like doors,

will open with ease

To very, very little keys,

And don't forget

that two of these

Are "I thank you"

and "If you please."

—HEARTS, LIKE DOORS,
WILL OPEN WITH EASE

EIGHTEEN MONTHS

At eighteen months, your toddler's eating habits may be very erratic. He may eat a lot at one meal and nothing at another. He may want to eat the same food over and over again, and then, suddenly one day refuse to eat it at all. It can be a difficult time, but never force food or make a big issue out of it. If your toddler continues to grow and stays healthy, he is getting adequate nutrition.

Continue to give your toddler iron-fortified cereals, whole milk, and whole-milk dairy products. Your toddler still needs three small meals, plus one morning and one afternoon snack.

Typical Daily Meals for an Eighteen-Month-Old

Continue serving whole milk and whole-milk dairy products.

MEAL	FOODS
Breakfast	1/3 Avocado and cheddar Omelet (page 214), 1/3 slice buttered whole-grain toast, and 1/4 cup (60 ml) freshly squeezed orange juice
Snack	1/2 kiwi sliced, 3 strawberries sliced, 1/4 cup blueberries, 1 to 2 tablespoons Vanilla Yogurt-Cream Cheese Dip (page 217), and 1/2 cup (120 ml) milk
Lunch	1/3 cup Roasted Carrot Soup (page 219), 3 rye crackers, and 1/2 cup (120 ml) milk
Snack	1 Stuffed Campari Tomato (hard-cooked egg, page 217), 3 whole-wheat crackers, and 1/2 cup (120 ml) milk
Dinner	Fish Taco (1 fish stick, shredded cabbage, avocado, and tomato, page 221), small piece watermelon (rind and seeds removed), and 1/2 cup (120 ml) milk

BREAKFAST

Cream of Rice

Topping with 1 tablespoon Strawberry Sauce (recipe below) turns this porridge into a favorite.

- $^1/_4$ cup (60 ml) water
- 1 tablespoon (10 g) uncooked Cream of Rice
- 1 tablespoon (10 g) raisins
- Milk to thin, if needed

Bring the water to a boil in a small saucepan over medium heat. Stir in the Cream of Rice and raisins. Cook, stirring, 30 seconds. Remove from the heat, cover, and let stand 1 minute. Stir in enough milk to achieve a desired creamy consistency.

YIELD: *Makes 1 toddler serving*

EACH WITH: 68.6 calories; 0.1 gm total fat; 0.0 gm saturated fat; 0.0 mg cholesterol; 2.9 mg sodium; 16.6 gm carbohydrate; 0.5 gm dietary fiber; 1.0 gm protein; 8.8 mg calcium; 0.3 mg iron; 0.0 IU vitamin A; 0.2 mg vitamin C.

Strawberry Sauce

This sauce can be swirled on top of cooked Cream of Rice or yogurt, ice cream, pancakes, waffles, or banana splits.

- $^1/_2$ cup (130 g) frozen sweetened strawberries, partially thawed
- 1 tablespoon (28 ml) fruit juice or nectar (apple, pear, pineapple, peach, or apricot)

Place the strawberries and juice in a blender and puree.

YIELD: *Makes about 8 tablespoons or $^1/_2$ cup*

EACH WITH: 53.4 calories; 0.1 gm total fat; 0.0 gm saturated fat; 0.0 mg cholesterol; 0.9 mg sodium; 14.3 gm carbohydrate; 1.2 gm dietary fiber; 0.3 gm protein; 7.6 mg calcium; 0.3 mg iron; 17.3 IU vitamin A; 25.3 mg vitamin C.

RITUAL AND COPYING BEHAVIOR

As any parent who has had to read the same bedtime story exactly the same way every night can tell you, ritual is very important to toddlers. Behaviors performed the same way several times need to be repeated diligently by your child. The good news is that this offers you marvelous opportunities to establish positive habits—but it also means that, for better or worse, young children will mimic virtually everything adults do. Parents may be surprised at the mirror image they receive. Just keep in mind that we can learn from our children, as they can learn from us, making these challenging times a positive experience for everyone.

Whole-Wheat Waffles 👪

For tasty toppings, try Maple Cream (page 190), Strawberry Sauce (page 211), or any favorite topping. For a treat, add fresh berries or peach slices and top with a little whipped cream. Leftover waffles, once cooled, may be frozen. Place a sheet of waxed paper between each waffle, pop into a resealable plastic bag, and freeze. Just pop a frozen waffle into the toaster for a fast breakfast.

+ $3/4$ cup (90 g) whole-wheat flour

+ $3/4$ cup (90 g) all-purpose flour

+ 2 tablespoons (25 g) sugar

+ 2 teaspoons baking powder

+ $3/4$ teaspoon baking soda

+ $1/4$ teaspoon salt

+ 3 eggs (or 2 eggs plus 2 egg whites)

+ $1^1/2$ cups (355 ml) buttermilk

+ $1/2$ cup (1 stick, or 112 g) butter, melted, or $1/2$ cup (120 ml) olive oil

Preheat a waffle iron according to manufacturer's instructions. In a large bowl, combine the whole-wheat flour, all-purpose flour, sugar, baking powder, baking soda, and salt; mix with a whisk or a fork. In a medium bowl, beat the eggs until blended; add the buttermilk and butter. Stir the wet ingredients into the dry ingredients. If the mixture seems too thick (it should pour off a spoon, not plop), add a bit of water.

Lightly oil the waffle iron. Pour the batter into the waffle iron and bake according to the manufacturer's instruction until crisp and golden. Repeat to make 6 or 7 waffles.

YIELD: *Makes 6 or 7 waffles*

EACH WITH: 36.0 calories; 2.1 gm total fat; 1.2 gm saturated fat; 16.1 mg cholesterol; 43.8 mg sodium; 3.4 gm carbohydrate; 0.2 gm dietary fiber; 1.0 gm protein; 19.0 mg calcium; 0.1 mg iron; 69.5 IU vitamin A; 0.1 mg vitamin C.

Crackers, Berries, and Milk 👫

Sometimes toddlers prefer to have crackers, milk, and berries separately. But they may like it served as a "cold cereal" for a change.

* 1 graham cracker (or other favorite cracker)
* ¼ cup (40 g) favorite berries
* ¼ cup (60 ml) milk

In a small bowl, crumble the cracker into small pieces, top with the berries, and pour the milk over it.

YIELD: *Makes 1 toddler serving*

EACH WITH: 86.9 calories; 2.8 gm total fat; 1.3 gm saturated fat; 6.1 mg cholesterol; 67.1 mg sodium; 13.4 gm carbohydrate; 1.1 gm dietary fiber; 2.7 gm protein; 72.8 mg calcium; 0.4 mg iron; 81.9 IU vitamin A; 3.5 mg vitamin C.

Salsa 👫

This salsa is good with tacos, scrambled eggs, and tortilla chips.

* 3 cups (450 g) plum tomatoes, washed, seeded, and chopped
* ¼ cup (33 g) onion, finely chopped
* 2 tablespoons (8 g) (packed) fresh cilantro, chopped
* ¼ cup (60 ml) fresh lime juice
* 1 large garlic clove, minced
* 2 jalapeño chiles, washed, seeded, and minced
* ¼ teaspoon salt or to taste

Combine tomatoes, onion, cilantro, lime juice, garlic, chiles, and salt in a medium bowl, and toss to blend well. Add seasoning to taste. Let stand at least 30 minutes for flavors to develop.

YIELD: *Makes 3 cups*

APPROXIMATE SERVING SIZE: 0.5 cup. **EACH WITH:** 27.0 calories; 0.4 gm total fat; 0.0 gm saturated fat; 0.0 mg cholesterol; 106.7 mg sodium; 6.2 gm carbohydrate; 1.3 gm dietary fiber; 1.0 gm protein; 10.5 mg calcium; 0.5 mg iron; 771.9 IU vitamin A; 29.8 mg vitamin C.

Avocado and Cheddar Omelet
👨‍👧

Serve with ¹/₄ piece of whole-wheat toast and ¹/₄ cup (6o ml) freshly squeezed orange juice.

- 1 teaspoon butter or oil
- 2 eggs
- 2 teaspoons water
- 1/4 cup (60 g) mashed avocado
- 2 heaping tablespoons (15 g) shredded cheddar cheese
- 2 tablespoons (25 g) yogurt cheese (See "Yogurt Cheese" on page 114) or light sour cream
- Salsa (optional)

◎ Melt the butter in a frying pan over medium heat. Whisk the eggs and water vigorously with a fork and pour into the pan. Rotate the pan until the eggs cover the whole bottom of the pan. With a rubber spatula, move the cooked egg toward the middle of the pan and let the uncooked egg spread to the sides. Continue to cook, moving the cooked egg toward the center, until the egg is almost set. Spoon the avocado and cheese on top. Fold the omelet in half and continue to cook until the cheese has melted. Cut a small piece (about one-third of the omelet) for your toddler and top with 1 tablespoon of the yogurt cheese. The rest of the omelet and yogurt cheese is for you. Serve with salsa if desired.

YIELD: *Makes 1 toddler serving AND 1 adult serving*

EACH WITH: 81.6 calories; 6.7 gm total fat; 2.4 gm saturated fat; 91.7 mg cholesterol; 89.7 mg sodium; 1.9 gm carbohydrate; 0.8 gm dietary fiber; 3.9 gm protein; 46.9 mg calcium; 0.4 mg iron; 203.3 IU vitamin A; 1.1 mg vitamin C.

Mango Salsa 👪

- 1 ripe mango, peeled, cut away from the stone, and cut into small pieces
- 1/3 cup (43 g) corn, fresh or frozen, cooked, and cooled
- 1/4 cup (38 g) washed and sliced green onion
- 1 or 2 jalapeño peppers, washed, seeded, and finely chopped
- 2 to 3 tablespoons (28 to 40 ml) fresh lime juice
- 1 teaspoon olive oil
- 1 teaspoon salt or to taste
- 2 tablespoons (8 g) washed and chopped fresh cilantro

Combine mango, corn, green onion, jalapeño chile, lime juice, olive oil, and salt. Stir in cilantro. Cover and chill before serving.

YIELD: *Makes about 1 1/2 cups*

APPROXIMATE SERVING SIZE: 0.25 cup. **EACH WITH:** 39.3 calories; 1.0 gm total fat; 0.1 gm saturated fat; 0.0 mg cholesterol; 391.4 mg sodium; 8.1 gm carbohydrate; 1.1 gm dietary fiber; 0.6 gm protein; 8.9 mg calcium; 0.2 mg iron; 519.7 IU vitamin A; 13.1 mg vitamin C.

Guacamole 👪

- 5 medium ripe avocados, peeled and pitted
- 3 tablespoons (40 ml) freshly squeezed lime juice
- 1/3 cup (43 g) peeled and finely chopped red onion
- 2 to 3 jalapeño peppers, seeded and minced
- 1 teaspoon kosher salt, or to taste
- 1/3 cup (20 g) chopped fresh cilantro

Place the peeled avocados in a large bowl and mash with a potato masher or a fork. Add the lime juice, onion, jalapeños, and cilantro. Add salt to taste and garnish with the cilantro.

YIELD: *Makes 6 servings*

EACH WITH: 275.4 calories; 24.6 gm total fat; 3.6 gm saturated fat; 0.0 mg cholesterol; 38.1 mg sodium; 16.2 gm carbohydrate; 11.5 gm dietary fiber; 3.5 gm protein; 23.9 mg calcium; 1.0 mg iron; 310.0 IU vitamin A; 22.3 mg vitamin C.

SNACKS

Refried Bean Paté ⬤

When creating this recipe, I had a large crowd of friends and family at my house, ranging from very young to very old. Everyone tasted this paté, including my oldest son, who normally refuses to eat beans. Everybody liked it. Spread it on crackers, tortillas, or pita bread. Double this recipe to use the whole can of refried beans or use the leftovers in a Tostada (page 161).

* ¹/₂ cup (125 g) full-fat canned refried beans
* ¹/₄ cup (30 g) shredded Monterey Jack cheese
* ¹/₄ cup (30 g) shredded cheddar cheese
* 2 tablespoons (25 g) light sour cream (or 1 tablespoon, or 15 g, sour cream plus 1 tablespoon, or 15 g, plain whole-milk yogurt)
* 1¹/₂ teaspoons low-salt tamari (natural soy sauce) or light soy sauce
* 1 teaspoon crushed garlic

Place the beans, Monterey Jack cheese, cheddar cheese, sour cream, soy sauce, and garlic in a food processor. Pulse 1 to 2 minutes, stopping to scrape down the sides, if necessary.

With a spatula, remove the bean puree from the food processor into a small bowl.

YIELD: *Makes about 16 tablespoons or 1 cup*

EACH WITH: 24.2 calories; 1.4 gm total fat; 0.9 gm saturated fat; 4.8 mg cholesterol; 76.2 mg sodium; 1.4 gm carbohydrate; 0.4 gm dietary fiber; 1.4 gm protein; 31.0 mg calcium; 0.2 mg iron; 38.2 IU vitamin A; 0.5 mg vitamin C.

Vanilla Yogurt–Cream Cheese Dip 👪

This can also be used as a dessert or in a smoothie. To add balance to the nutritional intake, serve this with fresh fruit. Choose two or three different types and colors of fruit that combined should be ¹/₃ to ¹/₂ cup: honeydew melon, cantaloupe, watermelon, orange segments (with the seeds removed), fresh figs, mango, papaya, kiwi slices, strawberries, pears, peaches, plums, fresh pineapple, banana, blueberries, blackberries, cherries, or seedless grapes (cut in half). Wash, peel, pit, hull, seed, and core all fruit as needed. Cut into finger-food sizes.

* ¹/₄ cup (60 g) vanilla whole-milk yogurt
* ¹/₄ cup (60 g) cream cheese

Place the yogurt and cream cheese in blender and process 45 seconds. Refrigerate for up to 1 week.

YIELD: *Makes about 8 tablespoons or ¹/₂ cup*

EACH WITH: 31.8 calories; 2.6 gm total fat; 1.7 gm saturated fat; 8.4 mg cholesterol; 26.5 mg sodium; 1.2 gm carbohydrate; 0.0 gm dietary fiber; 0.9 gm protein; 18.9 mg calcium; 0.1 mg iron; 100.9 IU vitamin A; 0.1 mg vitamin C.

Stuffed Campari Tomatoes 👪

Camparis are vine-ripened tomatoes, about 2 inches (5 cm) in diameter, with a wonderful flavor. I usually have a bowl of them on the kitchen table, and everyone eats them like candy.

* 2 Campari tomatoes
* 1 hard-cooked egg
* 1 teaspoon mayonnaise
* 1 small sprig fresh parsley

With a sharp knife, thinly slice off the bottom of each tomato; with a small spoon, scrape out the seeds and liquid of the tomatoes and discard. Cut the egg into small pieces. In a small bowl with a fork, mash the egg with the mayonnaise. Mince the parsley and stir into the egg. (Or you can omit the parsley from the egg filling and serve the sprig separately on the plate, next to the tomato.) With a small spoon, fill the tomatoes with the egg mixture. If it is too difficult for your toddler to handle the whole tomato, cut it in half.

YIELD: *Makes 2 filled tomatoes; 2 toddler servings OR 1 adult serving*

EACH WITH: 75.9 calories; 3.9 gm total fat; 1.0 gm saturated fat; 106.6 mg cholesterol; 62.3 mg sodium; 6.9 gm carbohydrate; 1.5 gm dietary fiber; 4.4 gm protein; 25.9 mg calcium; 1.2 mg iron; 1339.4 IU vitamin A; 38.6 mg vitamin C.

LUNCH

Bacon, Lettuce, and Tomato Sandwich (BLT) 👪

I prefer to microwave my bacon between white, non-chlorine bleached paper towels. The towels absorb the grease. Throw the paper towels away, and you have an easy cleanup. Use Apple Gate Farms Sunday Bacon or Wellshire Farm's bacon or any bacon without nitrates. Serve with 1/4 pear (core removed).

- 4 slices bacon
- 4 slices whole-wheat bread
- 2 tablespoons (30 g) mayonnaise
- 2 lettuce leaves, washed
- 1 large tomato, sliced

⬛ Place the bacon between double layers of paper towels. Place on a microwave-safe plate and microwave on high 3 to 4 minutes, depending on the thickness of the bacon and how crisp you like it. Spread the bread slices thinly with mayonnaise. Cover one slice with a lettuce leaf, 2 slices bacon, and 2 slices tomato. Place the other slice on top. Repeat for the second sandwich. Serve your toddler one-fourth to one-half of one sandwich.

YIELD: *Makes 1 toddler serving AND 2 adult servings*

EACH WITH: 117.7 calories; 5.5 gm total fat; 1.3 gm saturated fat; 8.7 mg cholesterol; 307.2 mg sodium; 12.9 gm carbohydrate; 1.4 gm dietary fiber; 4.7 gm protein; 27.9 mg calcium; 1.0 mg iron; 952.9 IU vitamin A; 11.2 mg vitamin C.

Rice, Vegetables, and Fruit 👶

If you have leftover vegetables, this is a quick and simple dinner for a hungry and impatient toddler. If you need to cook the rice, use quick-cooking instant rice.

- 2 tablespoons (20 g) cooked rice
- 1 tablespoon (15 g) chopped carrots, green beans, corn, zucchini, asparagus, or peas
- 1 tablespoon (10 g) chopped tomato or avocado
- 1 tablespoon (10 g) chopped melon, peach, pear, or orange

⬛ ◎ Reheat the rice. Microwave or steam the vegetables of choice. Mix together the rice, vegetables, tomato or avocado, and fruit of choice.

YIELD: *Makes 1 toddler serving*

EACH WITH: 39.7 calories; 0.1 gm total fat; 0.0 gm saturated fat; 0.0 mg cholesterol; 4.6 mg sodium; 8.7 gm carbohydrate; 0.5 gm dietary fiber; 0.9 gm protein; 3.6 mg calcium; 0.5 mg iron; 651.5 IU vitamin A; 6.8 mg vitamin C.

Roasted Carrot Soup 👫

For adults or company, add 1 tablespoon (14 ml) sherry and 3 table-spoons (45 ml) half-and-half after removing your toddler's portion. Serve with toasted whole-wheat bread.

- 2 cups (250 g) baby carrots
- 1/2 cup (65 g) chopped onion
- 3 cloves garlic
- 1/4 cup (15 g) chopped fresh dill, plus more for garnish
- 2 teaspoons kosher salt or 1/4 teaspoon regular salt
- 1 tablespoon (14 ml) olive oil
- 2 to 3 cans (14 ounces, or 425 ml, each) vegetable or nonfat chicken broth or 3 to 4 cups (705 to 940 ml) homemade
- Plain yogurt (optional)

⊞ ◎ Preheat the oven to 400°F (200°C, or gas mark 6). Toss the carrots, onion, garlic, dill, and salt with the oil in a 9 x 11-inch (22.5 x 27.5-cm) ovenproof dish. Mix well. Bake 1 hour, stirring every 20 minutes, until the carrots are soft and lightly browned.

Transfer the carrot mixture to a blender, add 2 cups of the broth, and blend 45 seconds. Transfer the soup to a saucepan and place over low heat until heated through. Add additional broth for desired consistency. Serve your toddler 1/4 to 1/2 cup. Garnish individual servings with dollops of plain yogurt (if you like) and chopped dill.

VARIATION: For people who like curry, add 1 tablespoon (6 g) minced fresh ginger and 1 tablespoon (6 g) curry powder to the carrots before roasting.

YIELD: *Makes 1 toddler AND 5 adult servings*

EACH WITH: 42.2 calories; 1.0 gm total fat; 0.3 gm saturated fat; 2.3 mg cholesterol; 180.5 mg sodium; 6.1 gm carbohydrate; 0.6 gm dietary fiber; 2.3 gm protein; 16.1 mg calcium; 0.4 mg iron; 3152.1 IU vitamin A; 3.5 mg vitamin C.

Toddler Quesadilla 👶

Serve with a piece of a ripe, sweet pear.

- ¹/₂ teaspoon olive oil
- ¹/₂ of an 8-inch tortilla (flour, corn, or a mix of the two)
- ¹/₄ ripe avocado, mashed
- 1 tablespoon (7 g) shredded four-cheese Mexican blend, cheddar, or Monterey Jack cheese

◎ Heat the oil in a small frying pan over medium heat. Place the tortilla in the hot oil and cook 30 seconds. Turn and cook the other side 30 seconds. Drain on a paper towel. Spread the mashed avocado on the tortilla. Add the cheese and fold the tortilla over, lightly pressing the two pieces together. Cut the tortilla in half.

YIELD: *Makes 2 toddler servings*

EACH WITH: 96.2 calories; 6.5 gm total fat; 1.6 gm saturated fat; 3.7 mg cholesterol; 96.8 mg sodium; 7.8 gm carbohydrate; 1.8 gm dietary fiber; 2.3 gm protein; 43.1 mg calcium; 0.5 mg iron; 67.2 IU vitamin A; 1.9 mg vitamin C.

👨‍👧 **MAKE IT FOR GROWN-UPS:** Adults can make themselves quesadillas with the leftover avocado, adding canned chiles, salsa, corn, or whatever your heart desires (or what you have in the fridge).

Peanut Butter–Date Milk Shake 👶

- 4 soft pitted dates, cut into small pieces
- 1 tablespoon (15 g) smooth natural peanut butter
- ¹/₂ cup (120 ml) whole milk

Combine the dates, peanut butter, and 4 tablespoons (56 ml) of the milk in a blender and process 30 to 45 seconds, until completely smooth. Add the remaining milk and blend a few more seconds.

YIELD: *Makes 1 toddler serving*

EACH WITH: 527.3 calories; 20.2 gm total fat; 5.6 gm saturated fat; 12.2 mg cholesterol; 55.2 mg sodium; 83.7 gm carbohydrate; 8.4 gm dietary fiber; 13.7 gm protein; 213.1 mg calcium; 1.5 mg iron; 267.5 IU vitamin A; 0.0 mg vitamin C.

Fish Taco

Your toddler may prefer to eat just the fish, chopped tomato, shredded cabbage, and avocado out of a non-sugar ice cream cup. Serve fresh peaches for dessert.

- 2 corn tortillas
- 4 Fish Sticks (page 173) or 4 pieces thawed frozen cod, cooked
- 1/2 cup (45 g) finely shredded cabbage
- 1/2 lime
- 2 tablespoons (28 ml) Fish Taco Sauce (right)
- 2 slices avocado
- 1/2 tomato, chopped

Preheat the oven to 350°F (180°C, or gas mark 4). Wrap the tortillas in foil and heat in oven 5 to 10 minutes, until hot. Or heat a frying pan on medium and dry fry the tortillas, turning once. To assemble the taco, divide the fish and cabbage between the two tortillas. Squeeze on lime juice and cover each with 1 tablespoon (14 ml) taco sauce. Top with the avocado and tomato.

YIELD: *Makes 2 tacos*

EACH WITH: 342.6 calories; 10.8 gm total fat; 1.7 gm saturated fat; 99.7 mg cholesterol; 185.2 mg sodium; 17.3 gm carbohydrate; 5.0 gm dietary fiber; 44.1 gm protein; 77.5 mg calcium; 1.7 mg iron; 467.7 IU vitamin A; 24.8 mg vitamin C.

Fish Taco Sauce

- 2 tablespoons (30 g) mayonnaise
- 2 tablespoons (25 g) plain whole-milk yogurt or yogurt cheese (See "Yogurt Cheese" on page 114.)
- Pinch kosher salt

Mix together the mayonnaise, yogurt or yogurt cheese, and salt. Refrigerate, covered, for up to 3 days.

YIELD: *Makes about 1/4 cup; 4 servings*

EACH WITH: 55.4 calories; 6.0 gm total fat; 0.9 gm saturated fat; 0.8 mg cholesterol; 78.1 mg sodium; 0.3 gm carbohydrate; 0.0 gm dietary fiber; 0.2 gm protein; 8.1 mg calcium; 0.0 mg iron; 6.2 IU vitamin A; 0.0 mg vitamin C. .

NINETEEN MONTHS

Do you carrot all for me?

My heart beets for you

With your turnip nose

And your radish face.

You are a peach.

If we cantaloupe,

Lettuce marry;

We'd make a swell pear.

—HEART BEET

SHARING FAMILY MEALS

Eating together as a family builds closeness and solidarity. Unfortunately, this wonderful custom seems to happen less and less as we lead busier and busier lives and become a society of snackers, often eating hurriedly or alone in front of the television. Sharing meals in a warm and cheerful environment evokes positive reactions toward specific foods, going far beyond their nutritional values—often creating memories for life. The toddler years are the time to start a tradition of family meals. As your child grows, you'll find that she'll look forward to the special time each evening when the family sits down together and shares a meal.

Typical Daily Meals for a Nineteen-Month-Old

Continue to serve whole milk and whole-milk dairy products.

MEAL	FOODS
Breakfast	1/3 cup homemade Granola (page 225), 1/4 ripe peach cut into small pieces, and 1/2 cup (120 ml) milk
Snack	100 percent juice pop, and 1/3 muffin with butter
Lunch	1/3 cup Black Bean Soup (page 227), small piece buttered cornbread, and 1/2 cup (120 ml) milk
Snack	Ants on a Log (peanut butter and raisins, page 226), 2 graham crackers, and 1/2 cup (120 ml) milk
Dinner	2 homemade chicken nuggets (page 228), 4 to 6 Sweet Potato Fries (page 101), 2 slices tomato, and small slice watermelon (peeled and seeds removed)

BREAKFAST

Hot Peanut Cereal 👨‍🍳

- 1¼ cups (295 ml) water
- ½ cup (75 g) peanut meal
- ¼ cup (30 g) whole-wheat flour
- ¼ teaspoon salt
- ¼ cup (40 g) raisins
- 1 tablespoon (20 g) honey
- ½ cup (120 ml) milk

◎ Bring the water to a simmer in a saucepan over medium heat. Add the peanut meal, flour, and salt; whisk until smooth. Stir in the raisins and honey and continue to stir until the cereal comes to a boil. Add the milk and reduce the heat. Simmer, stirring occasionally, 10 minutes, until you have a desired consistency. The cereal will thicken as it cools.

💡 *To make peanut meal, grind ¹/₂ cup (75 g) unsalted peanuts in the food processor or blender to the consistency of meal (flour).*

YIELD: *Makes 1 cup*

EACH WITH: 49.3 calories; 2.6 gm total fat; 0.5 gm saturated fat; 0.8 mg cholesterol; 40.5 mg sodium; 5.8 gm carbohydrate; 0.7 gm dietary fiber; 1.7 gm protein; 13.5 mg calcium; 0.2 mg iron; 7.9 IU vitamin A; 0.1 mg vitamin C.

Pear Omelet 👨‍🍳

- 1 teaspoon butter
- 1 egg
- 1 teaspoon water
- ¼ cup (40 g) grated peeled pear
- 1 tablespoon (15 g) yogurt cheese (See "Yogurt Cheese" on page 114)

◎ Melt the butter in a small frying pan over low heat. Whisk the egg with the water and pour into the pan. Cook, turning once, until the egg is well set. Add the pear and fold the omelet in half. Top the omelet with the yogurt cheese.

YIELD: *Makes 1 toddler serving*

EACH WITH: 168.4 calories; 11.8 gm total fat; 5.0 gm saturated fat; 226.9 mg cholesterol; 178.8 mg sodium; 8.4 gm carbohydrate; 1.3 gm dietary fiber; 7.5 gm protein; 66.7 mg calcium; 0.8 mg iron; 463.7 IU vitamin A; 1.9 mg vitamin C.

Plain Granola 👪

This is a granola that works well for toddlers, because it is without nuts, raisins, or pieces of dried fruit, which can be a choking hazard. Serve this with whole-milk or plain yogurt topped with your favorite fresh fruit and berries (e.g., blueberries, kiwi, strawberries, raspberries, peaches, and bananas). Use old-fashioned rolled oats.

- 4 cups (320 g) rolled oats
- 1/3 cup (75 ml) maple syrup
- 1/3 cup (75 ml) olive oil
- 1/4 teaspoon salt

Preheat the oven to 325°F (170°C, or gas mark 3). Place the oats in a large bowl. Combine the syrup, oil, and salt in a small pan and heat over medium a few minutes, until warmed through. Do not let it boil. Add the syrup mixture to the oats and stir until completely blended.

Spread the granola on an 11 x 17-inch (27.5 x 42.5-cm) baking sheet. Bake on the middle rack, stirring and re-spreading every 5 minutes, 15 to 20 minutes, until the oats have turned golden. Cool completely before you store the granola in an air-tight container. It will keep at room temperature for up to 4 weeks.

YIELD: *Makes about 3 1/2 cups; 7 servings*

EACH WITH: 476.4 calories; 16.4 gm total fat; 2.5 gm saturated fat; 0.0 mg cholesterol; 86.5 mg sodium; 69.3 gm carbohydrate; 9.4 gm dietary fiber; 15.1 gm protein; 58.5 mg calcium; 4.5 mg iron; 0.0 IU vitamin A; 0.0 mg vitamin C.

SNACKS
Goat Cheese Toast 🧒

Serve with 1/2 cup (120 ml) carrot juice.

- 1/4 slice rye or oat bread, toasted
- 1 teaspoon soft, mild goat cheese
- 1 slice pear

Spread the bread with the cheese and top with the pear.

YIELD: *1 toddler serving*

EACH WITH: 39.4 calories; 1.2 gm total fat; 0.7 gm saturated fat; 2.2 mg cholesterol; 61.1 mg sodium; 5.8 gm carbohydrate; 0.9 gm dietary fiber; 1.5 gm protein; 12.9 mg calcium; 0.3 mg iron; 53.3 IU vitamin A; 0.7 mg vitamin C.

Yogurt Cheese with Topping 🧒

- 1 ice-cream cone
- 1/4 cup yogurt cheese (See "Yogurt Cheese" on page 114.)
- 1 tablespoon Prune Puree (page 93), Peach Puree (page 94), or mashed, fresh strawberries.

Fill the ice-cream cone with the cheese and top with the Prune Puree, Peach Puree, or strawberries.

YIELD: *1 toddler serving*

EACH WITH: 94.1 calories; 2.4 gm total fat; 1.3 gm saturated fat; 8.0 mg cholesterol; 60.3 mg sodium; 15.6 gm carbohydrate; 0.7 gm dietary fiber; 3.1 gm protein; 81.5 mg calcium; 0.5 mg iron; 113.6 IU vitamin A; 0.8 mg vitamin C.

Ants on a Log 🧒

This is a favorite snack for older kids. Toddlers can enjoy it as well, as long as the raisins are chopped so they are not a choking hazard.

- 5 raisins
- $1/4$ cup (60 ml) water
- $1/3$ stalk celery
- 1 tablespoon (15 g) cream cheese or peanut butter

▦ Place the raisins and water in a microwave-safe container; microwave on high 1 minute. Let the raisins cool in the water until they are soft and plump. Chop them into small pieces. Fill the celery with the cream cheese and dot with the raisins (they'll look like ants).

YIELD: *Makes 1 toddler serving*

EACH WITH: 441.2 calories; 5.7 gm total fat; 3.3 gm saturated fat; 16.0 mg cholesterol; 67.9 mg sodium; 103.7 gm carbohydrate; 5.0 gm dietary fiber; 5.2 gm protein; 81.9 mg calcium; 2.6 mg iron; 255.0 IU vitamin A; 3.4 mg vitamin C.

LUNCH

Apple Witch (Apple-Cheddar Sandwich) 🧒

Serve with cold or hot milk with Ovaltine—$1/2$ cup (120 ml) milk mixed with 3 teaspoons Ovaltine.

- 1 teaspoon butter
- $1/2$ slice whole-grain bread
- 1 slice cheddar cheese
- 2 thin slices apple

Spread the butter on the bread. Add the cheese and top with the apple. Cut in half and sandwich the two pieces together.

YIELD: *Makes 1 toddler serving*

EACH WITH: 186.8 calories; 13.6 gm total fat; 6.7 gm saturated fat; 29.4 mg cholesterol; 281.5 mg sodium; 8.5 gm carbohydrate; 1.0 gm dietary fiber; 8.4 gm protein; 215.9 mg calcium; 0.7 mg iron; 454.5 IU vitamin A; 0.7 mg vitamin C.

Black Bean Soup 👪

*Use canned beans if you must, but this soup is best
when made from scratch. I like to use the small,
black turtle beans. Serve with Super Moist Cornbread
(page 281).*

* 1½ cups (290 g) dried black beans, soaked in 8
  cups (1880 ml) water overnight, drained
* 8 to 10 cups (1880 to 2350 ml) water
* 2 bay leaves
* 3 tablespoons (45 ml) olive oil
* 1 large onion, chopped
* 1 red, green, or yellow bell pepper, seeded and
  chopped
* 3 cloves garlic, chopped
* 1 tablespoon (6 g) ground cumin
* 1 tablespoon (18 g) salt
* 1 teaspoon coriander
* ¼ teaspoon hot red pepper flakes, or to taste
  (optional)
* 1 large tomato, chopped
* 1 can (7 ounces, or 200 g) diced green chiles
* ¼ cup (4 g) chopped fresh cilantro, plus more for
  garnishing
* 1 tablespoon (14 ml) fresh lemon or lime juice
* 1 tablespoon (12 g) sour cream mixed with
  1 tablespoon (15 g) nonfat plain whole-milk yogurt

◉ Rinse the beans and place in a 4-quart
saucepan with the water and bay leaves. Bring to
a boil over medium heat, skim off the foam, cover,
reduce the heat, and simmer 2 hours, until the
beans are tender. Discard the bay leaves.

Heat the oil in a frying pan over medium heat.
Add the onion, bell pepper, and garlic and cook,
stirring occasionally, 10 minutes. Add the cumin,
salt, coriander, and red pepper flakes if using, and
cook 3 minutes longer. Add the tomato and stir.
Transfer the sautéed vegetables to a blender and
add the green chiles and cilantro; blend until
smooth.

When the beans are tender, add the pureed vegetables to the beans and simmer, stirring occasionally, 20 minutes. Add the lemon juice. For
smoother and thicker soup, puree or mash a cup of
beans with some liquid. Serve your toddler ¼ to
½ cup. Garnish individual servings with the sour
cream mixture and cilantro.

YIELD: *Makes 1 toddler serving and 7 adult servings*

EACH WITH: 105.8 calories; 3.3 gm total fat; 0.5 gm saturated fat; 0.4
mg cholesterol; 499.4 mg sodium; 15.3 gm carbohydrate; 3.5 gm
dietary fiber; 4.8 gm protein; 40.9 mg calcium; 1.4 mg iron; 353.9 IU
vitamin A; 21.3 mg vitamin C.

> **BEAN YIELDS**
>
> 1 cup dried beans uncooked =
> 2 cans (15 ounces, or 420 g, each) drained beans =
> 3 cups cooked
>
> 1 pound dried beans =
> 2 cups dried beans =
> 4 cans (15 ounces, or 420 g, each) drained beans =
> cups cooked beans

A Very Berry Smoothie 🧒

- ¹/₂ cup (80 g) frozen unsweetened mixed berries
- ¹/₂ banana
- 2 tablespoons (30 g) plain whole-milk yogurt
- 1 tablespoon (14 ml) frozen orange juice concentrate
- 1 cup (235 ml) whole milk

Place the berries, banana, yogurt, orange juice concentrate, and milk in a blender and blend 60 seconds.

YIELD: *Makes 2 cups*

EACH WITH: 42.5 calories; 4.8 gm total fat; 2.6 gm saturated fat; 14.2 mg cholesterol; 56.6 mg sodium; 21.1 gm carbohydrate; 1.9 gm dietary fiber; 5.1 gm protein; 163.4 mg calcium; 0.2 mg iron; 209.6 IU vitamin A; 15.8 mg vitamin C.

DINNER
Chicken Nuggets 👪

These are tasty and quick to make—and much healthier than fast food chicken nuggets. For the coating, grind bread crumbs seasoned with a little salt, pepper, and oregano in the food processor, or use tempura, panko crumbs, or Dixie Fry Coating mix. Serve with Sweet Potato Fries (page 101) or Potato Salad (page 273). Serve a peeled and de-seeded honeydew melon slice for dessert.

- 1 tablespoon (14 ml) olive oil, or more as needed
- 1 egg
- 2 tablespoons (28 ml) whole milk
- ¹/₂ cup (50 g) seasoned bread crumbs
- 1 pound (455 g) chicken tenders or 3 boneless and skinless chicken breasts, cut into nugget-size pieces

◎ ▨ Preheat the oven to 400°F (200°C, or gas mark 6). Heat the oil in a frying pan over medium-high heat. Whisk the egg and milk in a bowl. Place the bread crumbs on a plate. Dip each chicken tender first in the egg/milk mixture, then dredge in the bread crumbs, covering both sides. Cook in the hot oil 1 minute; turn and cook 1 minute more. Place the chicken in a baking dish and bake 15 minutes, or until meat is cooked through and any juices run clear. (Meat thermometer should register 160 to 180°F, or 70 to 82°C.)

YIELD: *Makes 1 toddler servings AND 3 adult servings*

EACH WITH: 172.0 calories; 7.5 gm total fat; 1.5 gm saturated fat; 82.0 mg cholesterol; 332.0 mg sodium; 10.9 gm carbohydrate; 0.7 gm dietary fiber; 14.4 gm protein; 51.2 mg calcium; 1.2 mg iron; 123.9 IU vitamin A; 0.4 mg vitamin C.

Chicken Omelet

Serve with a slice of tomato and a slice of avocado. A slice of halved orange (with peel and seeds removed) is a nice dessert.

* ¹/₂ teaspoon olive oil
* 1 egg
* ¹/₄ cup (35 g) shredded cooked chicken
* ¹/₄ teaspoon tamari (natural soy sauce)
* ¹/₂ teaspoon fresh snipped chives

Heat the oil in a small frying pan over medium heat. Lightly beat the egg in a cup or small bowl. Add the chicken and mix well. Stir the tamari and chives into the egg. Pour the egg mixture into the frying pan. Cook until the egg begins to set and the underside is golden brown. Then flip the omelet over and cook until the egg is completely set. Transfer to a small plate and cut into 1-inch-wide strips.

YIELD: *Makes 1 to 2 toddler servings*

EACH WITH: 82.5 calories; 4.8 gm total fat; 1.3 gm saturated fat; 120.8 mg cholesterol; 138.3 mg sodium; 0.7 gm carbohydrate; 0.0 gm dietary fiber; 8.5 gm protein; 24.2 mg calcium; 0.5 mg iron; 169.4 IU vitamin A; 0.1 mg vitamin C.

Avocado, Cucumber, and Tomato Salad

Your toddler may prefer the salad without onion and dressing.

* ¹/₂ cucumber, peeled and sliced
* 1 avocado peeled, pitted, and cubed
* 1 large, ripe tomato, washed and cubed
* ¹/₄ cup (40 g) small, sweet, white or red, thinly sliced onion rings, cut into 2-inch (5-cm) lengths (optional)
* Mild Vinaigrette (page 261) or dressing of choice

Halve the cucumber slices. Combine the avocado, cucumber, tomato, and onion if using, into a bowl and toss lightly with the dressing.

YIELD: *Makes 4 servings*

EACH WITH: 86.8 calories; 6.8 gm total fat; 0.9 gm saturated fat; 0.0 mg cholesterol; 8.1 mg sodium; 6.9 gm carbohydrate; 3.7 gm dietary fiber; 1.4 gm protein; 11.8 mg calcium; 0.5 mg iron; 359.2 IU vitamin A; 16.6 mg vitamin C.

THE AMAZING ARTICHOKE

Artichokes are available year-round, but their peak season is during spring, and it's then they are at their lowest price. Artichokes should be bright green and have leaves that are tightly packed and blemish free. Store artichokes unwashed in plastic bag in the refrigerator.

Before cooking the artichokes, wash them. Pull off outer lower leaves. Cut off stem. With a pair of scissors, snip tips off the remaining petals and cut off the top quarter of the artichoke.

◎ Steam 40 to 45 minutes until a leaf comes out easily. Or, stand up in a pan with about 3 inches of water. Cover and boil gently 25 to 45 minutes, according to size. Stand upside down to drain.

▭ Invert 1 large (about 12 ounces, or 340 g) prepared artichoke in a deep 1-quart microwave-safe cup or bowl. Add $^1/_3$ cup (75 ml) water. Cover and microwave on high about 7 minutes. Let stand 5 minutes. When done, petals will pull out easily.

TO EAT: Your toddler may enjoy the ritual of eating an artichoke. To eat, pull off petals one at a time. Dip base of petal into sauce or melted butter; pull the very bottom of the leaf through teeth to scrape off the soft, pulpy portion of the petal. When all the petals have been removed, spoon out and discard the fuzzy stuff (the choke) at the base. The bottom, or heart, is completely edible, and so-o-o delicious.

YIELD: *1 serving*

APPROXIMATE SERVING SIZE: 1/10 artichoke. **EACH WITH:** 6.0 calories; 0.0 gm total fat; 0.0 gm saturated fat; 0.0 mg cholesterol; 11.4 mg sodium; 1.3 gm carbohydrate; 0.6 gm dietary fiber; 0.4 gm protein; 5.4 mg calcium; 0.2 mg iron; 21.2 IU vitamin A; 1.2 mg vitamin C.

ARTICHOKE DIPS

◆ $^1/_4$ cup (60 g) mayonnaise and $^1/_2$ teaspoon lemon juice

◆ $^1/_4$ cup (60 g) mayonnaise and 1 teaspoon pesto

◆ 2 tablespoons (30 g) mayonnaise, 2 tablespoons (25 g) sour cream or plain yogurt, and $^1/_2$ teaspoon lemon juice (If you should happen to have some cooked crab, shred a tablespoon or two and blend it in with the mayo/sour cream mix.)

◆ 1 tablespoon (15 g) mayonnaise, 1 tablespoon (12 g) sour cream, $^1/_4$ teaspoon mustard, $^1/_2$ teaspoon ketchup, and 1 tablespoon (14 ml) fresh orange juice

◆ Plain melted butter

◆ Mild Vinaigrette (page 261)

Serve with a slice of peeled and seeds removed Asian pear.

TWENTY MONTHS

This little pig went to market;
*   This little pig stayed at home;*
This little pig had roast beef;
*   This little pig had none;*
*   This little pig said, "Wee, wee!*

I CAN'T FIND MY WAY HOME"
—THIS LITTLE PIGGY

By now, you and your toddler are settled into a good routine. He has lost many of his babyish qualities and is becoming more independent. At this age, children are learning to talk, and it's important that you encourage your baby's language development with a variety of stimulating activities. Tell your baby what you're giving her to eat, and when she mimics your words, reinforce her attempts with smiles and praise. Reading books that feature pictures of objects from your baby's world (such as toys, foods, and clothing) is also an important way to help build her vocabulary.

At twenty months, your toddler is still open to trying new foods. Continue to give him fresh fruits and vegetables when they're in season. A fun activity for the whole family is berry or apple-picking, and most toddlers love to snack on fruit they picked themselves. Combining fresh fruit with a protein such as cheese, milk, or peanut butter creates a well-balanced snack. Remember, your toddler still needs whole milk dairy products, so don't switch to lowfat milk yet.

Typical Daily Meals for a Twenty-Month-Old

Continue serving whole milk and whole-milk dairy products.

MEAL	FOODS
Breakfast	Scrambled Egg with Refried Beans (page 234), and $^1/_4$ cup (60 ml) apple juice
Snack	$^1/_2$ cup Banana Milk Shake (page 234) and 1 crostini (small Italian-style toast)
Lunch	1 Mini Pizza (page 235), $^1/_2$ pitted nectarine, and $^1/_2$ cup (120 ml) milk
Snack	2 whole-wheat crackers topped with 2 avocado slices, and $^1/_2$ cup (120 ml) milk
Dinner	Haddock and Tomatoes (page 239), $^1/_4$ cup (50 g) mashed potatoes, 4 cooked green beans, 2 kiwi slices, and $^1/_2$ cup (120 ml) milk

BREAKFAST

Aussie Smoothie

Since the macadamia nut originated in Australia, this is a tribute to the Australians.

- 1 tablespoon (8 g) chopped macadamia nuts
- ¼ cup (60 ml) orange juice
- 2 tablespoons (30 g) vanilla whole-milk yogurt
- 1 kiwi fruit, peeled and cut into small pieces

Combine the nuts and juice in a blender and puree. Add the yogurt and kiwi and process until smooth.

YIELD: *Makes 1 toddler serving*

EACH WITH: 153.1 calories; 7.9 gm total fat; 1.7 gm saturated fat; 4.0 mg cholesterol; 17.3 mg sodium; 20.1 gm carbohydrate; 3.1 gm dietary fiber; 3.0 gm protein; 75.6 mg calcium; 0.6 mg iron; 220.4 IU vitamin A; 101.7 mg vitamin C.

Milk Toast Cereal

Serve with ¼ cup (40 g) fresh blueberries on the side.

- ½ teaspoon butter
- ½ slice whole-wheat raisin bread, toasted
- ¼ cup (60 ml) whole milk
- ½ teaspoon honey or maple syrup

Spread the butter on the toast and cut into small pieces. Mix the milk and honey or syrup and warm in the microwave, on high for 30 seconds. Pour the milk mixture over the toast.

YIELD: *Makes 1 toddler serving*

EACH WITH: 99.9 calories; 4.5 gm total fat; 2.5 gm saturated fat; 11.2 mg cholesterol; 75.5 mg sodium; 12.4 gm carbohydrate; 0.6 gm dietary fiber; 3.0 gm protein; 78.3 mg calcium; 0.3 mg iron; 121.5 IU vitamin A; 0.0 mg vitamin C.

Little Stars and Raisins

This can be served plain or with milk and fruit (2 to 3 tablespoons of one of the following fruits or a combination): sliced banana, strawberries, or kiwi, blueberries, or chopped pineapple. The Little Stars are also good topped with 1 tablespoon (15 g) applesauce, Apricot Puree (page 98), or Prune Puree (page 93).

- 1 cup (235 ml) water
- 2 to 3 tablespoons (6 to 12 g) uncooked stellini (little stars) pasta
- 1 tablespoon (10 g) raisins
- ¼ cup (60 ml) milk
- Fruit of choice

Bring the water to a boil in a saucepan over medium-high heat. Add the pasta and raisins. Simmer, uncovered and stirring occasionally, 10 minutes, until the pasta is just tender. Drain. Add the milk and fruit of choice.

YIELD: *Makes 1 toddler serving*

EACH WITH: 16.9 calories; 0.3 gm total fat; 0.1 gm saturated fat; 1.6 mg cholesterol; 3.0 mg sodium; 3.5 gm carbohydrate; 0.1 gm dietary fiber; 0.4 gm protein; 8.8 mg calcium; 0.1 mg iron; 6.9 IU vitamin A; 0.1 mg vitamin C.

Scrambled Egg with Refried Beans 🧒

The remaining refried beans from the can may be used tomake Tostados (page 161) or Refried Bean Paté (page 216).

- 1 teaspoon olive oil
- 1 egg
- 2 tablespoons (30 g) full-fat canned refried beans
- 2 tablespoons (15 g) grated Monterey Jack cheese
- Mild salsa (optional)

◎ Lightly coat a frying pan with the oil and heat over medium heat. Whisk the egg. Pour the egg into the pan and cook, scrambling, until done. Push the egg to one side and add the refried beans; stir until heated through. Sprinkle with the cheese. Serve with a teaspoon of salsa, if desired.

YIELD: *Makes 1 toddler serving*

EACH WITH: 184.0 calories; 12.1 gm total fat; 5.1 gm saturated fat; 229.9 mg cholesterol; 342.2 mg sodium; 6.4 gm carbohydrate; 1.7 gm dietary fiber; 12.0 gm protein; 159.9 mg calcium; 1.4 mg iron; 429.5 IU vitamin A; 2.0 mg vitamin C.

SNACKS

Banana Milk Shake 🧒

- ½ cup (120 ml) milk
- 1 small, slightly frozen banana, cut into small pieces

Combine the milk and banana in a blender and process until well blended.

YIELD: *Makes 1 toddler serving*

APPROXIMATE SERVING SIZE: 0.25 cup. **EACH WITH:** 42.9 calories; 1.1 gm total fat; 0.6 gm saturated fat; 3.2 mg cholesterol; 13.1 mg sodium; 7.5 gm carbohydrate; 0.7 gm dietary fiber; 1.3 gm protein; 37.6 mg calcium; 0.1 mg iron; 49.8 IU vitamin A; 2.3 mg vitamin C.

Crackers, Avocado, and Cheese 🧒

Use saltine crackers without salt, Matzo crackers without salt, or whole-wheat crackers.

- 2 slices avocado
- 2 crackers
- 1 slice Monterey Jack cheese, halved

Place an avocado slice on each cracker and top with cheese.

YIELD: *Makes 1 toddler serving*

EACH WITH: 178.7 calories; 13.6 gm total fat; 6.1 gm saturated fat; 24.9 mg cholesterol; 198.4 mg sodium; 7.0 gm carbohydrate; 2.1 gm dietary fiber; 8.0 gm protein; 219.8 mg calcium; 0.7 mg iron; 257.8 IU vitamin A; 2.5 mg vitamin C.

Deviled Egg 👪

Although deviled eggs may be considered old-fash-ioned, I have noticed that when people bring them to a party, they're the first hors d'oeuvres to disappear. Here's an updated version, using flavored cream cheese dip. Although some dips can be a little spicy, once it is mixed with the egg, its flavor becomes mellow. You can also use regular cream cheese or cream cheese with different flavors.

- 1 hard-cooked egg, cut in half lengthwise
- 1 teaspoon flavored cream cheese dip
- 1 teaspoon mayonnaise

Scoop out the egg yolk and place on a plate. Add the dip and mayonnaise and mash well with a fork. Fill each egg white half with the yolk mixture.

YIELD: *Makes 2 toddler servings OR 1 adult serving*

EACH WITH: 56.7 calories; 4.3 gm total fat; 1.5 gm saturated fat; 109.3 mg cholesterol; 55.5 mg sodium; 0.9 gm carbohydrate; 0.0 gm dietary fiber; 3.3 gm protein; 14.8 mg calcium; 0.3 mg iron; 184.4 IU vitamin A; 0.0 mg vitamin C.

LUNCH
Mini Pizza 🍴

Serve with halved, pitted cherries, if in season, or other fresh fruit.

- ½ English muffin, lightly toasted
- 1½ tablespoons (20 g) Tomato Sauce (page 174) or store-bought tomato sauce
- 2 tablespoons (15 g) grated mozzarella cheese

Preheat the oven to 350°F (180°C, or gas mark 4). Spread the muffin with the tomato sauce and sprinkle with the cheese. Place the muffin on a cookie sheet or tinfoil. Bake about 1 minute, until the cheese has melted. Cut into bite-size pieces. Make sure the cheese is not too hot before serving.

YIELD: *Makes 1 toddler serving*

EACH WITH: 189.3 calories; 8.1 gm total fat; 2.6 gm saturated fat; 11.9 mg cholesterol; 1642.9 mg sodium; 23.3 gm carbohydrate; 3.3 gm dietary fiber; 7.5 gm protein; 165.6 mg calcium; 3.0 mg iron; 672.6 IU vitamin A; 13.5 mg vitamin C.

Vegetarian Borscht

Serve with good rye bread.

- 2 tablespoons (14 ml) olive oil
- 1/2 medium onion, chopped
- 2 large cloves garlic, peeled and finely chopped
- 4 medium beets, washed, peeled, and chopped
- 2 small carrots, washed and sliced
- 1/2 small celery (celeriac) root, peeled and chopped, or 1 cup (50 g) sliced celery
- 2 small potatoes, washed, peeled, and chopped
- 1 leek, white parts, cleaned and sliced
- 1/2 small head red cabbage, chopped
- 2 tablespoons (28 ml) balsamic vinegar
- 1/8 teaspoon cayenne, or to taste
- 4 large sprigs dill, fronds only, coarsely chopped
- 6 to 8 cups (1410 to 1880 ml) water, or more if needed
- 2 tablespoons (30 g) tomato paste
- Salt
- Fresh-ground black pepper
- Sour cream
- Chopped dill

Place the oil in a large, heavy-bottomed pot. Add the onion, garlic, beets, carrots, celeriac root or celery, potatoes, leek, cabbage, vinegar, cayenne, and dill to the pot. Cover and cook on the lowest heat 5 minutes. Check and stir occasionally to prevent sticking. Add the water and bring to a boil. Lower the heat to a simmer. Take 1/3 cup of the warm broth and mix it in a cup with the tomato paste. Pour it back into the soup. Stir. Replace the lid and simmer the soup until all the vegetables are soft. Add more water if needed. In batches, puree the soup and return it to the saucepan. Add salt and pepper to taste. Thin soup with additional water to desired consistency and reheat. Serve in bowls with a dollop of sour cream and a sprinkle of dill.

YIELD: *Makes 8 servings*

EACH WITH: 115.1 calories; 3.7 gm total fat; 0.5 gm saturated fat; 0.0 mg cholesterol; 655.5 mg sodium; 19.6 gm carbohydrate; 3.9 gm dietary fiber; 2.8 gm protein; 56.2 mg calcium; 1.5 mg iron; 2256.2 IU vitamin A; 35.5 mg vitamin C.

DINNER

Vegetarian "Meat" Balls 👫

Serve these nutty vegetarian morsels plain with pasta and cheese or simmer them for a few minutes in Tomato Sauce (page 174) and serve with spaghetti.

- 2 eggs
- 1/2 cup (50 g) pecan nuts
- 1/3 cup (40 g) grated sweet onion
- 1/2 teaspoon salt (optional)
- 3/4 cup (75 g) Italian-style seasoned bread crumbs
- 1 cup (115 g) grated 4-cheese Mexican blend or a mix of grated cheddar and Monterey Jack cheese
- 1 teaspoon chopped fresh parsley
- 1/4 cup (60 ml) olive oil

◉ In a food processor, combine the eggs, nuts, onion, and salt if using and process until the nuts are completely ground. Transfer to a large bowl. Stir in the bread crumbs, mixing well. Mix in the cheese and parsley. Form 12 small balls.

Heat the oil in a frying pan over medium heat. Add the vegetarian balls and fry, turning often so they will not burn, until nicely browned, about 10 minutes.

YIELD: *Makes 12 balls*

EACH WITH: 157.6 calories; 12.7 gm total fat; 3.6 gm saturated fat; 46.9 mg cholesterol; 212.4 mg sodium; 6.2 gm carbohydrate; 0.8 gm dietary fiber; 5.3 gm protein; 101.4 mg calcium; 0.8 mg iron; 176.7 IU vitamin A; 0.6 mg vitamin C.

Roasted Chicken with Lemon and Oregano

I made this dish for my family most Sundays for many years. Served with basmati rice and Roasted Vegetables (page 239), it was always a hit. The vegetables can be roasted in the oven, in their own pan, with the chicken, after the chicken has been cooking for 45 minutes.

- ½ onion, sliced
- 3 cloves garlic, peeled
- 4 small baby carrots
- 1 stalk celery, cut into thirds
- Salt
- Pepper
- 1 (3- to 4-pound, or 1.5 to 2 kg) chicken (giblets removed), washed and dried inside and out and trimmed of excess fat
- 1 small bunch parsley
- 2 tablespoons (6 g) chopped fresh oregano
- 1 cup (235 ml) nonfat chicken broth
- Juice of 1 lemon

Preheat the oven to 350°F (180°C, or gas mark 4). Place the onion, garlic, carrots, and celery in the bottom of a 13 x 9-inch (32.5 x 22.5-cm) baking dish. Rub salt and pepper over the chicken and sprinkle salt inside the cavity. Place the parsley in the cavity. Place the chicken on top of the vegetables and sprinkle the oregano over chicken. Pour the broth and lemon juice into the bottom of the dish.

Roast on the center rack about 1½ hours, basting every 20 minutes, adding more liquid to the pan if needed. The chicken is done when an instant-read thermometer registers 170 to 180°F (76 to 82°C) when inserted in the thickest part of the thigh. Serve your toddler 2 to 4 tablespoons of finely chopped chicken.

VARIATIONS: For Roasted Chicken in Tomato Sauce, omit the lemon and oregano and add 2 cups (490 g) Tomato Sauce (page 174 or store-bought) during the last 30 minutes of cooking. Baste the chicken with the sauce once or twice.

For Roasted Chicken with Tarragon and Wine, substitute 1 cup (235 ml) dry white wine for the lemon juice and chopped fresh tarragon for the oregano.

YIELD: *Makes 1 toddler and 3 to 5 adult servings*

EACH WITH: 74.3 calories; 1.6 gm total fat; 0.4 gm saturated fat; 37.1 mg cholesterol; 94.3 mg sodium; 2.5 gm carbohydrate; 0.5 gm dietary fiber; 12.0 gm protein; 24.4 mg calcium; 1.0 mg iron; 658.6 IU vitamin A; 5.0 mg vitamin C.

Roasted Vegetables 👪

- 1 cup (250 g) baby carrots or regular carrots, cut into 2-inch (5-cm) pieces
- 1 large sweet potato, peeled and cut into 2 x 2-inch (5 x 5-cm) cubes
- 4 small red or white potatoes, scrubbed and halved
- 1 onion, quartered
- 4 large cloves garlic, peeled
- 1 tablespoon (18 g) kosher salt or 1 teaspoon regular salt
- 2 tablespoons (28 ml) olive oil

Preheat the oven to 375°F (190°C, or gas mark 5). Place the carrots, sweet potato, potatoes, onion, and garlic in a 9 x 13-inch (22.5 x 32.5-cm) baking dish. Sprinkle the salt evenly over the vegetables and drizzle with the oil. With clean hands, mix the vegetables well, so each piece is coated with oil. Roast on the center rack 45 to 60 minutes, or until the vegetables are soft. Stir every 15 minutes to prevent sticking. Serve your toddler 2 to 3 tablespoons of vegetables, lightly mashed.

YIELD: *Makes 1 toddler AND 3 adult servings*

EACH WITH: 141.8 calories; 4.1 gm total fat; 0.6 gm saturated fat; 0.0 mg cholesterol; 362.3 mg sodium; 24.2 gm carbohydrate; 3.0 gm dietary fiber; 2.8 gm protein; 34.3 mg calcium; 1.0 mg iron; 4842.7 IU vitamin A; 23.3 mg vitamin C.

Haddock and Tomatoes 👪

This quick, easy, and delicious dish goes well with mashed potatoes and green beans; offer Kiwi Kwiki (page 240) for dessert.

- 2 tablespoons (28 g) butter
- 1 pound (455 g) frozen haddock, without skin and bone, partially defrosted
- Juice of 1/2 lemon
- Salt (optional)
- 1 large tomato, quartered
- 2 tablespoons (8 g) chopped fresh parsley

Melt the butter in a heavy-bottomed pan over medium-low heat. Cut the fish into two or three pieces. Add the fish to the pan and sprinkle with the lemon juice and a little salt, if using. Arrange the tomato around the fish. Cover the pan and simmer 5 to 10 minutes, until the fish flakes easily when prodded with a fork. Do not overcook the fish or it will be dry. Sprinkle with the parsley. Serve your toddler about 2 to 3 tablespoons of the fish and tomatoes.

YIELD: *Makes 1 toddler serving AND 2 adult servings*

EACH WITH: 286.7 calories; 6.7 gm total fat; 3.3 gm saturated fat; 167.3 mg cholesterol; 189.8 mg sodium; 2.2 gm carbohydrate; 0.5 gm dietary fiber; 51.9 gm protein; 95.4 mg calcium; 3.1 mg iron; 652.7 IU vitamin A; 13.6 mg vitamin C.

Basic Mashed Potatoes
👨‍👧

- 2 pounds (1 kg) potatoes, peeled and quartered (Russet or Yukon gold are best, but white or red potatoes are also fine.)
- $1/2$ to $3/4$ cup (120 to 175 ml) whole milk, heated
- 3 tablespoons (45 g) butter
- Salt

◎ Place the potatoes in a heavy-bottomed saucepan and add enough water to cover by 1 inch. Bring to a boil over high heat. Reduce to a simmer and cook 20 to 30 minutes, or until tender. Drain. Add $1/2$ cup (120 ml) of the milk and the butter and mash well. Season with salt and whisk the potatoes, adding more milk if needed. Serve in a warmed bowl as soon as possible. Serve your toddler about 2 tablespoons potatoes.

YIELD: *Makes 1 toddler AND 3 adult servings*

EACH WITH: 101.0 calories; 5.6 gm total fat; 3.5 gm saturated fat; 14.8 mg cholesterol; 94.3 mg sodium; 11.4 gm carbohydrate; 1.3 gm dietary fiber; 1.8 gm protein; 28.5 mg calcium; 0.5 mg iron; 171.1 IU vitamin A; 12.0 mg vitamin C. .

Kiwi Kwiki 👶

- 1 kiwi fruit, peeled, cut in half lengthways, and sliced
- $1/4$ banana, sliced
- 1 tablespoon (10 g) vanilla ice cream

Layer the kiwi and banana in a small bowl and top with the ice cream.

YIELD: *Makes 1 toddler serving*

EACH WITH: 92.7 calories; 1.6 gm total fat; 0.7 gm saturated fat; 4.4 mg cholesterol; 10.6 mg sodium; 20.2 gm carbohydrate; 3.1 gm dietary fiber; 1.5 gm protein; 40.1 mg calcium; 0.3 mg iron; 127.2 IU vitamin A; 73.1 mg vitamin C.

TWENTY-ONE MONTHS

How many miles to Babylon?

Three score miles and ten.

Can I get there by candlelight?

Yes, and back again.

If your heels are nimble and light,

You can get there by candlelight.

—HOW MANY MILES TO BABYLON?

TRAVELING WITH CHILDREN

Taking children on a trip can be an enjoyable and memorable experience. Without careful planning, however, it may be less pleasant, and a hungry, cranky child doesn't make it any more pleasant! Here are some of the basics you may want to take along when you're traveling with a little one.

- Individual bags of simple foods that will not spoil, are easy to eat, and are enjoyed by your child. Fruits and cooked vegetables, hard cheeses, and crackers or toast are good choices.

- Consider taking along a small insulated bag to keep cheeses and fruits chilled. Instead of ice packs, freeze juice boxes or small bottles of water and use them to keep your foods cold. The bonus is that you'll have more beverages to offer your toddler when the drinks defrost!

- Juice and milk should be kept in a Thermos. Pre-frozen cartons of juice are welcome when the weather is very warm.

- When flying, changes in air pressure can wreak havoc on little ears. Swallowing during cabin pressure changes minimizes the possibility of earaches or other discomforts. Be sure to keep several bottles of formula, juice, and water handy for takeoffs and landings.

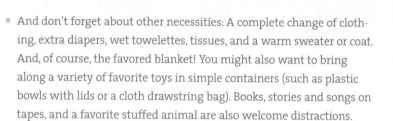
■ And don't forget about other necessities: A complete change of cloth-ing, extra diapers, wet towelettes, tissues, and a warm sweater or coat. And, of course, the favored blanket! You might also want to bring along a variety of favorite toys in simple containers (such as plastic bowls with lids or a cloth drawstring bag). Books, stories and songs on tapes, and a favorite stuffed animal are also welcome distractions.

Most of all, the success of a trip depends on your attitude and state of mind. If you can relax, be flexible, understand a toddler's rest-lessness or tiredness, and give a lot of attention (singing songs, telling stories, and encouraging him to observe the changing scenery when possible), the trip can be enjoyable for everyone.

Typical Daily Meals for a Twenty-One-Month-Old

Continue to serve whole milk and whole-milk dairy.

MEAL	FOODS
Breakfast	1/3 to 1/2 cup Malt-O-Meal Hot Wheat Cereal (page 243) with a dot of butter and 1/4 cup (60 ml) milk poured on top, 1/2 hard-cooked egg, 1/4 cup fresh raspberries
Snack	1/2 cup Emerald Nectar (apricot, avocado, and yogurt, page 246) and 2 Nut Butter Kisses (page 205)
Lunch	1/3 cup Butternut and Acorn Squash Soup (page 247), 1/3 slice buttered whole-grain bread, 1/2 cup (120 ml) milk
Snack	2 tablespoons Carrot–Peanut Butter, Cottage Cheese Spread (page 246) on 2 whole-wheat crackers, 1/2 cup (120 ml) milk
Dinner	Starry Night Broccoli Forest (pasta, broccoli, parmesan, page 251) and Apple Mist (page 249) 1/2 cup (120 ml) milk

BREAKFAST

Malt-O-Meal Hot Wheat Cereal 👶

Serve with a dot of butter and a little milk poured on top and 1/2 cup (120 ml) freshly squeezed orange juice to drink.

- 1/2 cup (120 ml) milk
- 1 1/2 tablespoons (15 g) Malt-O-Meal Hot Wheat Cereal

⊡ Stir the milk and Malt-O-Meal in a large microwave-safe bowl. Microwave on high 1 minute. Stir. Microwave 1 or 2 minutes more, until the cereal thickens, stirring every 30 seconds. Watch carefully to prevent boiling over. Stir and let stand until it is the desired consistency and the cereal is cool enough to eat.

◎ In a small saucepan, heat the milk to boiling, stirring and watching that the milk doesn't boil over. (It never seems to boil when you're watching, but inevitably will as soon as you turn your back.) Gradually stir in the Malt-O-Meal and bring to a boil. Reduce the heat and cook 2 1/2 minutes, or until it has thickened, stirring continuously.

YIELD: *Makes 1 toddler serving*

EACH WITH: 130.1 calories; 4.1 gm total fat; 2.3 gm saturated fat; 12.2 mg cholesterol; 49.9 mg sodium; 17.5 gm carbohydrate; 0.0 gm dietary fiber; 5.6 gm protein; 140.0 mg calcium; 4.5 mg iron; 124.4 IU vitamin A; 0.0 mg vitamin C.

Warm Grapefruit Crunch 👶

Serve with 1/2 cup (120 ml) warm Ovaltine.

- 1/4 sweet grapefruit, segmented
- Sprinkle brown sugar or honey
- 1 tablespoon (15 g) cottage cheese
- 1 tablespoon (7 g) Grape-Nuts

⊡ Place the grapefruit in a microwave-safe bowl and sprinkle with the brown sugar or honey. Microwave on high about 10 seconds, or until the sugar is melted. Cool, top with the cottage cheese, and sprinkle with Grape-Nuts.

To segment a grapefruit: Cut the fruit in half. Using a grapefruit knife, cut around the inside of the skin of the grapefruit, and then cut out each segment, removing all white pith.

YIELD: *Makes 1 toddler serving*

EACH WITH: 55.9 calories; 0.5 gm total fat; 0.2 gm saturated fat; 1.2 mg cholesterol; 104.0 mg sodium; 10.6 gm carbohydrate; 1.1 gm dietary fiber; 3.1 gm protein; 20.5 mg calcium; 2.0 mg iron; 455.8 IU vitamin A; 9.6 mg vitamin C.

Nut Butter Delight

- ¹/₂ banana
- ¹/₂ cup (120 ml) milk
- 2 tablespoons (30 g) smooth peanut, almond, or cashew butter

Combine the banana, milk, and nut butter in a blender; process until smooth. Add more milk, if needed.

YIELD: *Makes 1 toddler serving*

EACH WITH: 502.0 calories; 36.4 gm total fat; 8.9 gm saturated fat; 12.2 mg cholesterol; 60.3 mg sodium; 31.5 gm carbohydrate; 5.4 gm dietary fiber; 20.6 gm protein; 168.3 mg calcium; 1.4 mg iron; 162.2 IU vitamin A; 5.1 mg vitamin C. .

"Eggs Florentine"

Serve with ¹/₂ cup (120 ml) freshly squeezed orange juice.

- 2 eggs
- 1 tablespoon (15 g) cottage cheese
- 1 tablespoon (8 g) grated Swiss cheese
- 1 tablespoon (15 g) goat cheese
- ¹/₂ teaspoon butter
- ¹/₄ cup (40 g) chopped frozen spinach, thawed and drained
- Pinch grated nutmeg

Preheat the oven to 350°F (180°C, or gas mark 4). Grease a 6-ounce ramekin. Lightly beat the eggs in a small bowl; add the cottage cheese, Swiss cheese, goat cheese, and butter. Stir in the spinach and nutmeg. Pour the egg mixture into the prepared ramekin. Bake about 30 minutes, or until a knife inserted in the center comes out clean. Remove and cool.

YIELD: *Makes 2 toddler servings*

EACH WITH: 130.2 calories; 8.9 gm total fat; 4.1 gm saturated fat; 221.8 mg cholesterol; 150.3 mg sodium; 1.8 gm carbohydrate; 0.6 gm dietary fiber; 10.6 gm protein; 104.3 mg calcium; 1.5 mg iron; 2676.8 IU vitamin A; 4.7 mg vitamin C.

SNACKS

Smoked Salmon Logs 👪

Smoked salmon (lox) is a good source of omega-3 fatty acid. There are many ways to serve smoked salmon: on Rye Crisp crackers, on a small piece of bagel with cream cheese, with scrambled eggs, wrapped around a slice of avocado sprinkled with lime juice, or on a piece of bread topped with slices of hard-cooked eggs. Also see Smoked Salmon Spread (page 288).

- ¹/₂ cup (100 g) uncooked Calrose sticky rice
- ¹/₂ cup (120 ml) water
- Sprinkle seasoned rice vinegar
- 6 to 8 (2 x 1-inch, or 5 x 2.5-cm) slices smoked salmon

◎ Rinse the rice in a fine-mesh colander until the water runs clear; drain well. Combine the rice and water in a small pan and let stand 30 minutes. Bring the rice to a boil over medium-high heat; stir, cover tightly, reduce the heat to very low, and steam 20 minutes. Spread the rice on a flat dish to cool and sprinkle with the vinegar.

Lay the salmon slices on a large cutting board. When the rice is cool enough to handle, wet your hands (the rice will be very sticky) and roll rice into 1 x ¹/₂-inch (2.5 x 1.25-cm) logs. Roll the sliced salmon around the rice logs. Serve your toddler 1 or 2 logs as a snack.

VARIATIONS: You can also roll these logs in an egg "pancake"—beaten egg that has been cooked in a thin sheet in a frying pan. You could also arrange thin sticks of peeled cucumber, avocado, steamed carrot sticks, or roasted red pepper on top of the rice before rolling up the logs.

YIELD: *Makes 6 to 8 salmon logs*

EACH WITH: 67.8 calories; 0.8 gm total fat; 0.1 gm saturated fat; 10.3 mg cholesterol; 13.7 mg sodium; 9.9 gm carbohydrate; 0.4 gm dietary fiber; 4.8 gm protein; 3.3 mg calcium; 0.7 mg iron; 23.3 IU vitamin A; 0.0 mg vitamin C.

Avocado and Hard-Cooked Egg 🧒

- 1 hard-cooked egg
- 2 tablespoons (30 g) mashed avocado

Cut the egg in half and remove the yolk. Mash the avocado and yolk together. Spoon the mixture back into the hard-cooked egg halves.

YIELD: *Makes 1 to 2 toddler servings*

EACH WITH: 62.8 calories; 4.9 gm total fat; 1.1 gm saturated fat; 106.0 mg cholesterol; 32.0 mg sodium; 1.6 gm carbohydrate; 1.0 gm dietary fiber; 3.4 gm protein; 14.3 mg calcium; 0.4 mg iron; 168.4 IU vitamin A; 1.5 mg vitamin C.

Emerald Nectar 👪

- 1 cup (235 ml) apricot nectar
- 1/4 cup (60 g) vanilla whole-milk yogurt
- 1/2 ripe avocado, peeled and pitted

Combine the apricot nectar, yogurt, and avocado in a blender and process until smooth.

YIELD: *Makes about 2 cups; 4 toddler servings*

EACH WITH: 88.1 calories; 3.9 gm total fat; 0.7 gm saturated fat; 0.8 mg cholesterol; 13.5 mg sodium; 13.2 gm carbohydrate; 2.1 gm dietary fiber; 1.5 gm protein; 33.1 mg calcium; 0.4 mg iron; 868.9 IU vitamin A; 36.8 mg vitamin C.

Carrot–Peanut Butter Spread 👪

This healthy spread is good on crackers or pumpernickel or used as a dip for pita bread wedges or crudités. For adults, add a pinch of ground ginger, pepper, and salt.

- 1/2 cup (60 g) sliced carrots (about 3 small carrots)
- 2 tablespoons (28 ml) water
- 3 tablespoons (45 g) cottage cheese
- 1 tablespoon (14 ml) frozen orange juice concentrate
- 2 teaspoons smooth natural peanut butter

▭ Combine the carrots and water in a small microwave-safe bowl. Cover and microwave on high 3 minutes. Transfer to a food processor. Add the cottage cheese, orange juice concentrate, and peanut butter and process 1 minute, or until the spread is smooth. If needed, use a spatula and scrape down the spread from the sides. Serve your toddler about 2 tablespoons.

YIELD: *Makes about 1/3 cup or 5 tablespoons; About 2 toddler servings*

EACH WITH: 98.0 calories; 5.8 gm total fat; 1.4 gm saturated fat; 1.8 mg cholesterol; 114.3 mg sodium; 6.6 gm carbohydrate; 1.5 gm dietary fiber; 6.1 gm protein; 30.8 mg calcium; 0.3 mg iron; 3696.0 IU vitamin A; 4.5 mg vitamin C.

LUNCH

Butternut and Acorn Squash Soup 👪

This is a naturally sweet soup that appeals to toddlers. When I make it for adults only, I add cayenne; it makes a nice contrast to the sweetness. Serve with crostini with goat cheese or Roquefort Spread (page 290). Offer cold watermelon, with the seeds and rind removed, for dessert.

- 2 butternut squash, halved, seeds and membranes removed
- 1 acorn squash, halved, seeds and membranes removed
- 2 tablespoons (28 ml) olive oil
- 1 large onion, chopped
- 1 large Granny Smith apple, peeled, cored, and chopped
- 1 tablespoon (6 g) grated peeled fresh ginger
- 1 clove garlic, minced
- 1 tablespoon (18 g) salt
- 1/4 teaspoon ground cinnamon
- 1/4 teaspoon ground nutmeg
- 1/8 teaspoon cayenne (optional)
- 3 to 5 cans (14 ounces, or 425 ml, each) nonfat chicken broth or 5 to 7 cups homemade
- 2 tablespoons (30 g) nonfat plain yogurt
- 2 tablespoons (25 g) sour cream

🔲 ◎ Preheat the oven to 400°F (200°C, or gas mark 6). Oil a 15 x 11-inch (37.5 x 27.5-cm) baking dish.

Place the squash halves, cut sides down, in the baking dish and bake 30 to 45 minutes, or until soft. Cool, scrape out the flesh and place in a bowl.

Heat the oil in large saucepan over low heat. Add the onion, apple, ginger, and garlic and sauté 10 minutes. Add the salt, cinnamon, nutmeg, and cayenne if using and sauté 2 minutes more. Add 1 cup (235 ml) of the broth, cover, and simmer 5 minutes.

In batches, puree the squash flesh, the onion/apple spice mixture, and some of the remaining broth in a blender until smooth. Pour the puree back into the saucepan, stir in the remaining broth, and heat slowly. Adjust seasoning. Serve your toddler 1/4 to 1/2 cup soup.

In a bowl, mix the yogurt and sour cream. Garnish individual servings with the yogurt mixture.

YIELD: *Makes 1 toddler serving AND 5 to 7 adult servings*

EACH WITH: 87.0 calories; 3.7 gm total fat; 0.8 gm saturated fat; 4.0 mg cholesterol; 699.9 mg sodium; 10.6 gm carbohydrate; 1.0 gm dietary fiber; 3.4 gm protein; 28.8 mg calcium; 0.5 mg iron; 2344.4 IU vitamin A; 7.3 mg vitamin C. .

COOKING SQUASH

Other options for cooking the squash:

Butternut squash: Cut the squash in half and remove seeds and membranes. Place in a microwave-safe dish, cut sides down. Add 1/2 cup (120 ml) water and microwave on high 12 to 15 minutes, until tender. Cool and remove the flesh.

Acorn squash: Microwave the whole squash on high 1 minute. Cut in half and remove seeds and membranes. Place in a microwave-safe dish, cut sides down. Add 1/4 cup (60 ml) water and microwave on high 8 to 10 minutes, or until tender. Cool and remove the flesh.

Tuna Melt 👨‍👩‍👧

This is a quick, tasty, open-faced sandwich. Serve with tomato slices and dill pickles.

- 2 tablespoons (30 g) mayonnaise
- 2 tablespoons (30 g) plain whole-milk yogurt
- 2 cans (6 ounces, or 170 g, each) chunk light tuna, packed in water, drained
- 4 slices whole-wheat bread
- 4 slices mozzarella cheese

⬛ Preheat the broiler. Cover a baking sheet with tinfoil. In a medium bowl, combine the mayonnaise and yogurt; blend in the tuna. Spread the tuna evenly on each slice of bread and top with a cheese slice. Place the open-faced sandwiches on the prepared baking sheet. Broil until the cheese has melted. Let cool and cut one-third to one-half of the open-faced sandwiches into bite-size pieces for your toddler.

YIELD: *Makes 2 toddler and 3 adult servings*

EACH WITH: 372.4 calories; 23.9 gm total fat; 12.1 gm saturated fat; 85.7 mg cholesterol; 788.7 mg sodium; 8.5 gm carbohydrate; 1.0 gm dietary fiber; 30.5 gm protein; 449.9 mg calcium; 1.3 mg iron; 587.1 IU vitamin A; 0.0 mg vitamin C. .

Macaroni and Cheese 👨‍👩‍👧

Serve with Carrot and Avocado with Lime Dressing (page 158) and halved, pitted grapes for dessert.

- 1 cup (150 g) uncooked elbow macaroni
- 2 tablespoons (28 g) butter
- 1 tablespoon (8 g) flour
- 1 cup (235 ml) milk
- 1 cup shredded (115 g) cheddar cheese or $1/2$ cup cheddar plus $1/2$ cup Monterey Jack or Jarlsberg cheese

◎ Bring 2 quarts water to a boil in a large saucepan over high heat. Add the macaroni and cook 10 minutes, until just tender. Drain. In a small pan, melt the butter over medium heat; whisk in the flour. Add a little of the milk, whisking vigorously. Continue adding the milk, a little at a time, continuously whisking, until the mixture is smooth. Reduce the heat and simmer, stirring constantly, 5 minutes. Add the cheese and stir until melted. Stir in the drained macaroni. Serve your toddler $1/3$ cup.

YIELD: *Makes 2 cups; 1 toddler AND 1 or 2 adult servings*

EACH WITH: 297.1 calories; 18.7 gm total fat; 11.6 gm saturated fat; 54.9 mg cholesterol; 246.4 mg sodium; 19.5 gm carbohydrate; 1.9 gm dietary fiber; 14.3 gm protein; 340.1 mg calcium; 1.1 mg iron; 543.3 IU vitamin A; 0.0 mg vitamin C.

Spinach Salad 👪

Serve this with soup, a sandwich, or melon for dessert. Note that your toddler may prefer to eat the salad as finger food without the dressing.

- 1 small bunch spinach (about 3 cups, or 90 g), washed, dried, stems removed
- 3 slices cooked bacon
- 2 hard-cooked eggs, chopped
- $1/2$ cup (35 g) sliced white mushrooms
- 1 avocado, seeded, peeled, and cubed
- Warm Sherry Vinaigrette (below)

Tear the spinach into pieces and place in a salad bowl. Tear the bacon into pieces and add to the spinach. Add the eggs, mushrooms, and avocado. Add the dressing and toss gently to mix. Serve your toddler about $1/4$ cup salad.

YIELD: *Makes 1 toddler serving AND 2 adult servings*

EACH WITH: 268.5 calories; 26.0 gm total fat; 4.2 gm saturated fat; 90.1 mg cholesterol; 257.9 mg sodium; 5.1 gm carbohydrate; 3.2 gm dietary fiber; 5.8 gm protein; 34.0 mg calcium; 1.2 mg iron; 1866.1 IU vitamin A; 9.3 mg vitamin C.

Warm Sherry Vinaigrette 👪

- 6 tablespoons (85 ml) olive oil
- 3 tablespoons (45 ml) sherry vinegar
- $1/2$ teaspoon Dijon mustard
- $1/4$ teaspoon salt
- Pinch freshly ground pepper

▢ In a small, lidded microwave-safe container, combine the oil, vinegar, mustard, salt, and pepper; shake until you have a creamy consistency. Remove the lid and warm in the microwave on high 30 seconds.

YIELD: *Makes about 8 tablespoons or $1/2$ cup*

EACH WITH: 60.3 calories; 6.8 gm total fat; 0.9 gm saturated fat; 0.0 mg cholesterol; 51.0 mg sodium; 0.2 gm carbohydrate; 0.0 gm dietary fiber; 0.0 gm protein; 0.3 mg calcium; 0.0 mg iron; 0.3 IU vitamin A; 0.0 mg vitamin C.

Apple Mist 🍼

- $1/4$ sweet apple, peeled, cored, and sliced
- 2 tablespoons (28 ml) apple juice
- 1 tablespoon (14 ml) cream

◎ Combine the apple and juice in a small saucepan over medium heat and bring to a simmer. Reduce the heat and simmer until the apple is soft. Remove from the heat and mash. Whisk in the cream. Serve warm.

YIELD: *Makes 1 toddler serving*

EACH WITH: 59.2 calories; 3.0 gm total fat; 1.8 gm saturated fat; 9.9 mg cholesterol; 6.9 mg sodium; 8.3 gm carbohydrate; 0.4 gm dietary fiber; 0.5 gm protein; 18.2 mg calcium; 0.1 mg iron; 110.9 IU vitamin A; 1.7 mg vitamin C. .

VARIATIONS:

Lemon Risotto: Near the end of cooking, stir in the juice of 1½ lemons (about ¼ cup, or 60 ml juice); increase the Parmesan to 1 cup (50 g).

Tomato Risotto: Near the end of cooking, add 1 cup (245 g) tomato sauce.

Pesto Risotto: Near the end of cooking, add ½ cup (130 g) Pesto (page 251).

Basic Instruction for Risotto
👪

Serve with a green salad and fresh berries for dessert.

- 6 cups (1410 ml) nonfat chicken broth
- 2 tablespoons (28 g) unsalted butter
- 1 tablespoon (14 ml) extra virgin olive oil
- ½ small onion, finely chopped, or 2 shallots, minced
- 1½ cups (285 g) uncooked arborio rice
- ¼ cup (25 g) freshly grated Parmesan cheese

◎ Bring the broth to a simmer in a large saucepan; reduce the heat to low and keep warm.

In a large heavy-bottomed pot, melt 1 tablespoon of the butter in the oil. Add the onion and sauté until translucent and soft, about 3 minutes. Do not let the onion brown or burn. Add the rice and stir well, until all the grains are coated, about 1 minute. Add ½ cup (120 ml) of the hot broth and cook, stirring constantly, until the liquid is absorbed. Continue cooking slowly, stirring and adding stock when the rice is covered with just a veil of stock, until the stock is used up and the rice is just tender but firm with a creamy consistency. Do not let the rice cook dry. This should take 20 to 30 minutes. Toward the end, taste the rice frequently to be sure the rice does not overcook.

When the risotto is done, remove the pan from the heat, stir in the remaining 1 tablespoon butter and the cheese, and serve immediately. Serve your toddler ⅓ cup of risotto.

YIELD: *Makes 1 toddler AND 5 adult servings*

EACH WITH: 185.3 calories; 5.7 gm total fat; 2.3 gm saturated fat; 11.5 mg cholesterol; 222.6 mg sodium; 26.6 gm carbohydrate; 0.8 gm dietary fiber; 6.0 gm protein; 31.3 mg calcium; 1.5 mg iron; 78.6 IU vitamin A; 0.5 mg vitamin C.

Pesto 👪

This is a small-portion recipe for pesto. You may want to double or triple it. It freezes well and is a favorite on spaghetti.

- ¹/₂ cup (30 g) firmly packed fresh basil
- 1 teaspoon minced, fresh garlic
- 1 tablespoon pine nuts (or walnuts)
- 3 tablespoons (40 ml) extra virgin olive oil
- 1 tablespoon firmly packed, grated Parmesan or Romano
- Salt and pepper, optional

Wash and dry basil, and place in a food processor with garlic and pine nuts. Pulse into a coarse paste. Slowly add olive oil, and process until all the ingredients are well blended. Transfer mixture to a bowl, using a spatula. Stir in the cheese, and season with salt and pepper, if desired.

YIELD: *Makes about 8 tablespoons or ¹/₂ cup*

EACH WITH: 79.7 calories; 8.5 gm total fat; 1.3 gm saturated fat; 0.7 mg cholesterol; 14.9 mg sodium; 0.8 gm carbohydrate; 0.4 gm dietary fiber; 0.7 gm protein; 15.5 mg calcium; 0.2 mg iron; 180.2 IU vitamin A; 0.8 mg vitamin C.

Starry Night Broccoli Forest 👶

The cooked pastas are shaped like stars and moons, which makes this an appealing dish for little ones.

- 2 tablespoons (20 g) uncooked stelline pasta (stars)
- 1 tablespoon (10 g) uncooked acini di pepe (small peppercorn) pasta (moons)
- 3 or 4 small broccoli pieces (trees)
- Grated Parmesan or Romano (snow)

◎ Bring 1 cup (235 ml) water to a boil in a medium saucepan. Add the stelline and acini de pepe and reduce heat; simmer 5 minutes. Add the broccoli and cook 5 minutes more, stirring occasionally, until the pasta is soft and the broccoli is cooked. Add a little more water if the pasta becomes too dry. At the end of cooking, the water should be mostly absorbed by the pasta. Transfer the pasta and broccoli to a plate or bowl. Sprinkle with the cheese and let cool slightly before serving to your toddler.

YIELD: *Makes 1 toddler serving*

EACH WITH: 96.3 calories; 1.0 gm total fat; 0.3 gm saturated fat; 1.5 mg cholesterol; 41.1 mg sodium; 17.9 gm carbohydrate; 1.6 gm dietary fiber; 4.4 gm protein; 42.6 mg calcium; 1.1 mg iron; 297.7 IU vitamin A; 39.2 mg vitamin C. .

Summer Delight

If you make this for your toddler only, quarter the recipe.

- 1/2 cup (75 g) cubed ripe melon
- 1/2 cup (75 g) cubed fresh or canned pineapple
- 1/2 cup (80 g) diced ripe or canned pears
- 1 small banana, sliced
- 1/4 cup (60 ml) orange juice, frozen

Combine the melon, pineapple, pears, banana, and frozen orange juice in a bowl and toss. Chill at least 1 hour before serving. Lightly mash the fruit for your toddler.

YIELD: *Makes 1 toddler serving AND 2 adult servings*

EACH WITH: 46.0 calories; 0.1 gm total fat; 0.0 gm saturated fat; 0.0 mg cholesterol; 3.2 mg sodium; 11.8 gm carbohydrate; 1.4 gm dietary fiber; 0.6 gm protein; 7.1 mg calcium; 0.2 mg iron; 579.8 IU vitamin A; 18.8 mg vitamin C. .

Chicken Tacos

Serve with peeled and pitted watermelon.

- 2 hard taco shells or 2 soft tortillas
- 1/4 to 1/2 cup (15 to 30 g) shredded lettuce
- 1/2 cup (70 g) shredded cooked chicken
- 1 small tomato, chopped, or 1/3 cup salsa
- 1/2 avocado, peeled, pitted, and sliced
- 2 tablespoons (15 g) shredded cheddar cheese
- Light sour cream (optional)

Divide the lettuce, chicken, tomato, and avocado between the taco shells. Top with the cheese and sour cream, if desired. If you're feeding a younger toddler, you may want to fill one taco with smaller portions than the other. In addition, your toddler may prefer the taco un-assembled in a bowl or in a non-sugar ice cream cup.

YIELD: *Makes 1 toddler and 1 adult servings*

EACH WITH: 192.5 calories; 13.6 gm total fat; 3.4 gm saturated fat; 25.8 mg cholesterol; 90.6 mg sodium; 10.0 gm carbohydrate; 3.3 gm dietary fiber; 8.9 gm protein; 62.8 mg calcium; 1.0 mg iron; 809.5 IU vitamin A; 12.3 mg vitamin C.

TWENTY-TWO MONTHS

Dance to your daddy,

   Dance to your daddy, my bonnie lamb;

You shall get a fishy,

   On a little dishy;

You shall get a fishy,

   when the boat comes home.

—DANCE TO YOUR DADDY

Typical Daily Meals for a Twenty-Two-Month-Old

Continue to serve whole milk and whole-milk dairy products.

MEAL	FOODS
Breakfast	1 Whole-Wheat Waffle (page 212), cut into small pieces, with $^1/_4$ cup lightly crushed blueberries and 2 tablespoons whipped cream, $^1/_2$ cup (120 ml) milk
Snack	2 Rice Cakes with Almond Butter (page 255), $^1/_2$ cup (120 ml) milk
Lunch	$^1/_3$ cup Lentil Soup (page 257) $^1/_3$ of a slice of buttered rye bread, 2 pitted nectarines, $^1/_2$ cup (120 ml) milk
Snack	1 Campari tomato stuffed with 1 tablespoon Tuna Salad (page 255), 2 unsalted saltine crackers, $^1/_2$ cup (120 ml) grape juice
Dinner	Warm Vegetable Salad (page 261), 1 slice orange (rind and pits removed), $^1/_2$ cup (120 ml) milk

BREAKFAST

Fried Sweet Potatoes 👪

- 1 sweet potato, scrubbed
- Olive oil
- Salt (optional)

◎ Prick the sweet potato skin with a fork in several places and microwave on high 5 minutes. (Or bake; see page 91.) Cool and peel the potato. When cool enough to handle, halve the potato lengthwise and cut each half into about 1/2-inch (1.25-cm) slices.

Lightly coat a frying pan with oil and heat over medium heat. Add the potato slices, season lightly with salt if desired, and cook until nicely browned on the bottom. Turn the slices and cook until golden and crisp, about 1 minute more.

YIELD: *Makes 1 toddler and 1 adult serving*

EACH WITH: 116.8 calories; 9.0 gm total fat; 1.2 gm saturated fat; 0.0 mg cholesterol; 24.1 mg sodium; 8.7 gm carbohydrate; 1.3 gm dietary fiber; 0.7 gm protein; 13.1 mg calcium; 0.3 mg iron; 6147.7 IU vitamin A; 1.0 mg vitamin C.

Strawberry Milk 👶

- 1/2 cup (70 g) fresh sweet strawberries, hulled, or frozen strawberries lightly sweetened
- 1/2 cup (120 ml) milk

Place the strawberries and milk in a blender and process until smooth, 1 minute.

VARIATIONS: Substitute 1/2 cup fresh or frozen raspberries, blueberries, or pitted cherries for the strawberries.

YIELD: *Makes 1 toddler serving*

EACH WITH: 97.5 calories; 4.2 gm total fat; 2.3 gm saturated fat; 12.2 mg cholesterol; 49.6 mg sodium; 11.4 gm carbohydrate; 1.5 gm dietary fiber; 4.4 gm protein; 150.0 mg calcium; 0.4 mg iron; 133.6 IU vitamin A; 44.7 mg vitamin C.

Petite Omelet 🍼

Serve with Fried Sweet Potatoes (page 254), a small piece of toast, and a couple of kiwi slices.

- 1 teaspoon butter
- 1 egg, beaten with 1 teaspoon water
- 1 tomato slice, cut into small pieces
- 1 slice Jarlsberg or Swiss cheese, cut into small pieces

◎ Put butter in a small frying pan and heat over medium heat. Pour in the egg and rotate the pan so the egg covers the entire bottom. As the liquid sets, pull it gently to the edge of the pan and cook until all the egg has set. Add the tomato and cheese, and continue to cook until the cheese begins to melt. Carefully fold the omelet in half, turn, and continue cooking until the egg is fully cooked.

YIELD: *Makes 1 toddler serving*

EACH WITH: 389.2 calories; 35.9 gm total fat; 21.1 gm saturated fat; 298.3 mg cholesterol; 129.3 mg sodium; 3.2 gm carbohydrate; 0.3 gm dietary fiber; 14.3 gm protein; 256.1 mg calcium; 1.1 mg iron; 1353.8 IU vitamin A; 7.0 mg vitamin C.

SNACKS

Stuffed Tomato with Tuna Salad 🍼

Serve with 1/2 cup (120 ml) apple juice.

- 1 (2-inch, or 5-cm) tomato, halved
- 1 tablespoon (15 g) Tuna Fish Salad (page 207)

Scoop the seeds out of the tomato halves and stuff with the tuna salad.

YIELD: *Makes 1 toddler serving*

EACH WITH: 49.8 calories; 1.6 gm total fat; 0.3 gm saturated fat; 1.7 mg cholesterol; 62.6 mg sodium; 6.9 gm carbohydrate; 1.4 gm dietary fiber; 3.1 gm protein; 8.3 mg calcium; 0.7 mg iron; 778.7 IU vitamin A; 32.3 mg vitamin C.

Rice Cakes with Almond Butter 🍼

Serve with 1/2 cup (120 ml) milk and 1/4 cup (40 g) fresh blueberries.

- 2 mini rice cakes
- 2 teaspoons almond butter

Spread each rice cake with 1 teaspoon almond butter.

YIELD: *Makes 1 toddler serving*

EACH WITH: 101.0 calories; 6.6 gm total fat; 0.6 gm saturated fat; 0.0 mg cholesterol; 58.0 mg sodium; 9.4 gm carbohydrate; 0.7 gm dietary fiber; 2.4 gm protein; 29.5 mg calcium; 0.5 mg iron; 0.1 IU vitamin A; 0.1 mg vitamin C. .

Apricot Whip 👤

- 3 tablespoons (45 g) vanilla whole-milk yogurt
- 1 tablespoon (15 g) Apricot Puree (page 98)

Whip the yogurt vigorously with a fork. Whip in the apricot puree.

YIELD: *Makes 1 toddler serving*

EACH WITH: 27.4 calories; 1.5 gm total fat; 0.9 gm saturated fat; 5.9 mg cholesterol; 20.7 mg sodium; 2.1 gm carbohydrate; 0.0 gm dietary fiber; 1.6 gm protein; 54.4 mg calcium; 0.0 mg iron; 44.5 IU vitamin A; 0.2 mg vitamin C.

Banana-Raspberry Dream 👤

- 1 small ripe banana
- 1/2 cup (60 g) fresh or frozen raspberries, sweetened
- 1/2 cup (120 ml) Rice Dream or vanilla soy milk

Place the banana, raspberries, and Rice Dream in a blender and process until smooth.

YIELD: *Makes 2 toddler servings*

EACH WITH: 139.3 calories; 0.8 gm total fat; 0.1 gm saturated fat; 0.0 mg cholesterol; 22.6 mg sodium; 34.1 gm carbohydrate; 4.1 gm dietary fiber; 1.1 gm protein; 16.8 mg calcium; 0.6 mg iron; 71.0 IU vitamin A; 15.0 mg vitamin C.

Avocado with Strawberry Cream Cheese 👪

If your toddler is getting tired of the blandness of the avocado, try adding the fresh taste of strawberry cream cheese; it combines nicely with creamy avocado. The leftover filling is also good stuffed in fresh apricot halves or peaches or on top of pear or apple slices. The strawberry cream cheese will keep, tightly covered, in the refrigerator for 2 to 3 days.

- 1 cup (230 g) cream cheese
- 1/2 cup (130 g) frozen or dried pitted cherries
- 1 cup (165 g) sliced strawberries
- 1 avocado peeled, pitted, and cut into quarters or eighths

Combine 1/2 cup (115 g) of the cream cheese and the cherries in a food processor and process until smooth. Add the remaining 1/2 cup (115 g) cream cheese and the strawberries and continue processing until smooth. Fill each avocado quarter or eighth with 1/2 to 1 tablespoon strawberry cream cheese.

YIELD: *Makes about 1 1/2 cups*

APPROXIMATE SERVING SIZE: 0.25 cup. **EACH WITH:** 175.1 calories; 15.9 gm total fat; 7.9 gm saturated fat; 36.5 mg cholesterol; 100.3 mg sodium; 6.7 gm carbohydrate; 2.6 gm dietary fiber; 3.3 gm protein; 34.8 mg calcium; 0.7 mg iron; 497.3 IU vitamin A; 16.4 mg vitamin C.

LUNCH

Lentil Soup 👫

Serve with whole-wheat bread and a piece of honey-dew melon.

- 1 cup (190 g) lentils
- 6 cups (1410 ml) water for soaking
- 6 cups (1410 ml) water for cooking
- 2 bay leaves
- 2 tablespoon (28 ml) olive oil
- 1 small onion, peeled and finely chopped
- 1 teaspoon finely chopped garlic
- 1 cup (125 g) washed, scraped, and sliced carrots
- 1 cup washed and thinly sliced celery
- 4 small potatoes washed, peeled, and cubed (optional)
- 1 tablespoon (18 g) salt, or to taste
- ½ cup (30 g) fresh parsley, finely chopped

◉ Soak the lentils in 6 cups (1410 ml) water overnight. Next day, drain the lentils, rinse well, and transfer to a large, heavy-bottomed pot. Add 6 cups (1410 ml) water and the bay leaves. Bring to a boil, reduce heat, cover pot, and simmer 45 minutes, or until the lentils are soft. While the lentils are cooking, heat the oil in a frying pan. Add the onion and sauté for 5 minutes; add the garlic, carrots, celery, and potatoes if using and sauté for an additional 10 minutes, stirring often. Add the vegetables to the lentils and cook until soft. Salt to taste, and garnish with the parsley.

NOTE: The vegetables may be cooked with the lentils without sautéing them first. However, the sautéed vegetables add a richer flavor to the soup.

VARIATION: Add ½ pound (225 g) fresh spinach, washed and stems trimmed (or a 10-ounce, or 280 g, package frozen spinach), ½ cup (100 g) washed rice, and season the soup with 1 teaspoon cumin and the juice of ½ lemon.

YIELD: *Makes 1 toddler serving AND 5 to 7 adult servings*

EACH WITH: 255.9 calories; 5.4 gm total fat; 0.8 gm saturated fat; 0.0 mg cholesterol; 1203.3 mg sodium; 42.9 gm carbohydrate; 7.2 gm dietary fiber; 10.9 gm protein; 51.6 mg calcium; 3.8 mg iron; 3085.5 IU vitamin A; 32.2 mg vitamin C.

Tomato and Cucumber Sandwich ▮

Your toddler may prefer plain mayonnaise instead of the olive spread. Serve with half a pitted nectarine and 1/2 cup (120 ml) milk.

- 2 slices whole-wheat bread
- Olive Spread (right)
- 4 slices peeled cucumber
- 1 small tomato, sliced
- Crumbled feta cheese

Lightly toast the bread; cover with a thin layer of olive spread. Layer the cucumber and tomato on one slice of toast and sprinkle with the cheese. Cover with the second piece of toast. Serve one-fourth of the sandwich to your toddler.

YIELD: *Makes 1 adult serving AND 1 toddler serving*

EACH WITH: 234.9 calories; 20.1 gm total fat; 4.3 gm saturated fat; 11.1 mg cholesterol; 424.8 mg sodium; 11.4 gm carbohydrate; 2.0 gm dietary fiber; 4.0 gm protein; 88.1 mg calcium; 1.2 mg iron; 289.3 IU vitamin A; 8.3 mg vitamin C.

Olive Spread ▮

Refrigerate leftovers in an airtight container for up to 1 week.

- 1/4 cup (30 g) black California olives, pitted
- 1/4 cup (60 g) mayonnaise

Puree the olives in a blender until smooth. Add the mayonnaise and pulse until well blended.

YIELD: *Makes 1/2 cup*

EACH WITH: 33.0 calories; 2.9 gm total fat; 0.4 gm saturated fat; 1.9 mg cholesterol; 84.9 mg sodium; 2.0 gm carbohydrate; 0.1 gm dietary fiber; 0.1 gm protein; 4.3 mg calcium; 0.1 mg iron; 31.3 IU vitamin A; 0.0 mg vitamin C..

Pear Surprise ▮

- 2 ripe sweet pears, peeled, halved lengthwise, cored, and hollowed out with a melon scoop
- 4 tablespoons (60 g) chopped canned mandarin orange segments, juice from the can reserved
- 1/4 cup (60 g) vanilla whole-milk yogurt

Trim a very small slice from each pear half, so it will sit level on a plate. Whisk 1 tablespoon (14 ml) mandarin orange juice with the yogurt. Fill the cavities in the pear halves with about 1 tablespoon (15 g) mandarin orange each. Cover each with 1 tablespoon yogurt/juice mix.

YIELD: *Makes 1 toddler serving AND 3 adult servings*

EACH WITH: 36.0 calories; 0.3 gm total fat; 0.2 gm saturated fat; 1.1 mg cholesterol; 4.9 mg sodium; 8.6 gm carbohydrate; 1.5 gm dietary fiber; 0.5 gm protein; 15.8 mg calcium; 0.1 mg iron; 92.6 IU vitamin A; 5.0 mg vitamin C.

DINNER

Eggplant in Yogurt Sauce 👨‍👩‍👧

Serve the eggplant with cooked basmati rice.

- About 1 tablespoon (14 ml) olive oil
- 1 small eggplant (about 1 pound, or 455 g), cut into ½-inch (1.25-cm) slices
- Sprinkle salt
- ½ cup (120 ml) plain whole-milk yogurt

◎ Lightly coat a frying pan with some of the olive oil and heat over medium heat. Sprinkle each eggplant slice lightly with salt and brush both sides with olive oil. Place the eggplant in the frying pan. Cook 10 minutes, until the eggplant is browned; turn and cook the other side until browned. Warm the yogurt over low heat and pour over the eggplant. Remove the skin for your toddler's portion. Give your toddler 1 or 2 slices.

YIELD: *Makes 8 small slices; 1 toddler serving and 2 adult servings*

EACH WITH: 38.0 calories; 2.3 gm total fat; 0.6 gm saturated fat; 2.0 mg cholesterol; 8.2 mg sodium; 4.0 gm carbohydrate; 1.9 gm dietary fiber; 1.1 gm protein; 23.7 mg calcium; 0.2 mg iron; 30.6 IU vitamin A; 1.3 mg vitamin C.

Breaded Fillet of Sole 👨‍👩‍👧

Serve with Creamy Potato-Parsnip and Carrot Mash (page 125).

It is worth investing in the tempura batter mix and the panko breading (available in supermarkets), which makes the fish deliciously light and crisp. However, plain flour seasoned with salt and pepper also works well.

- ½ cup (60 g) (or more) tempura batter mix
- 1 egg, beaten, seasoned with a pinch of salt and pepper
- 1 cup (50 g) panko (Japanese bread crumbs)
- Olive oil
- 1 pound (455 g) skinless sole fillets
- 1 lemon, quartered, for garnish

◎ Place the tempura batter mix on a plate, the egg in a shallow bowl, and the panko crumbs on another plate. Heat enough oil to generously cover the bottom a frying pan over medium heat. Dip the fish first in the tempura mix, then the egg; then dredge in the panko crumbs. Fry the fillets, turning once, 4 to 6 minutes, until golden on both sides and opaque and flaky. Serve your toddler about 2 ounces of the fish.

YIELD: *Makes 1 toddler serving and 2 adult servings*

EACH WITH: 208.8 calories; 11.1 gm total fat; 2.5 gm saturated fat; 30.6 mg cholesterol; 478.8 mg sodium; 15.3 gm carbohydrate; 0.5 gm dietary fiber; 13.2 gm protein; 16.2 mg calcium; 1.9 mg iron; 34.2 IU vitamin A; 0.0 mg vitamin C.

Lime Dill Sauce 👨‍👩‍👧

This is a sauce for special meals; the luxury of butter makes it delicious. If you prefer, use olive oil instead of butter and emulsify the sauce with a food processor.

* Juice of 1 lime
* 1/4 cup (1/2 stick, or 55 g) butter or olive oil
* 1 tablespoon chopped fresh dill

◎ Heat the lime juice in a frying pan over very low heat. Add the butter and stir until the butter has melted and become opaque and thick. Stir in the dill.

YIELD: *Makes about 4 tablespoons or 1/4 cup*

EACH WITH: 106.1 calories; 11.5 gm total fat; 7.3 gm saturated fat; 30.5 mg cholesterol; 3.4 mg sodium; 1.2 gm carbohydrate; 0.1 gm dietary fiber; 0.3 gm protein; 18.6 mg calcium; 0.4 mg iron; 404.6 IU vitamin A; 3.2 mg vitamin C.

Lime Dill Chicken 👨‍👩‍👧

This is my grandchildren's favorite dinner; they usually request it for their birthdays, and I happily oblige. Serve with mashed potatoes, corn, and broccoli.

* 4 skinless boneless chicken breasts
* 1 egg, beaten and seasoned with a little salt and pepper
* 1 cup (100 g) seasoned bread crumbs (store-bought or homemade)
* 2 tablespoons (28 ml) olive oil, or more if needed
* Lime Dill Sauce (left)

◎ Place the chicken between 2 sheets of plastic food wrap, in a large plastic freezer bag rinsed with cold water, or between 2 pieces of waxed paper. Pound the chicken with a wooden mallet until very thin.

Pour the egg into a shallow bowl. Place the bread crumbs in another plate. Dip the chicken in the beaten egg, then dredge in the bread crumbs to coat completely. Heat the oil in a frying pan over medium heat. In batches if necessary, add the chicken and cook, turning once, 4 to 6 minutes, until cooked through. Transfer to a heatproof dish and keep warm in a low oven until all the chicken has been cooked. Spoon a little sauce over the chicken and serve the rest on the side. Serve your toddler 2 to 4 tablespoons of chicken chopped into small pieces with a little bit of sauce.

YIELD: *Makes 1 toddler AND 4 adult servings*

EACH WITH: 190.6 calories; 10.1 gm total fat; 4.2 gm saturated fat; 67.6 mg cholesterol; 278.0 mg sodium; 9.7 gm carbohydrate; 0.7 gm dietary fiber; 14.8 gm protein; 41.3 mg calcium; 1.3 mg iron; 243.1 IU vitamin A; 2.4 mg vitamin C.

Warm Vegetable Salad

Serve with a small plate of fresh fruit: a slice of orange, rind removed; a few halved grapes without seeds; and a few fresh raspberries.

- ½ cup (120 ml) water
- 1 baby potato, quartered
- 1 baby carrot, sliced
- 1 ear baby sweet corn
- 2 sugar peas, strings removed
- 1 teaspoon butter
- Mild Vinaigrette (right)

Bring the water to a boil in a small pan over medium-high heat. Add the potato and simmer 5 minutes. Add the carrot and simmer 5 minutes more. Add the sweet corn and sugar peas and simmer until they are heated through, about 30 seconds. Check to ensure that the potato and carrot are done and drain the vegetables. Add the butter and stir, add the vinaigrette, and toss with the vegetables.

YIELD: *Makes 1 toddler serving*

EACH WITH: 381.0 calories; 18.5 gm total fat; 4.4 gm saturated fat; 10.1 mg cholesterol; 33.8 mg sodium; 50.2 gm carbohydrate; 7.9 gm dietary fiber; 7.9 gm protein; 63.3 mg calcium; 3.8 mg iron; 2543.0 IU vitamin A; 80.6 mg vitamin C.

Mild Vinaigrette

- 1 tablespoon (14 ml) olive oil
- 1 teaspoon raspberry vinegar
- 1/2 teaspoon chopped fresh mint

Mix the oil, vinegar, and mint well in a small cup.

YIELD: *1 toddler serving*

EACH WITH: 121.7 calories; 13.5 gm total fat; 1.8 gm saturated fat; 0.0 mg cholesterol; 1.6 mg sodium; 0.6 gm carbohydrate; 0.3 gm dietary fiber; 0.1 gm protein; 7.9 mg calcium; 0.6 mg iron; 152.5 IU vitamin A; 0.5 mg vitamin C.

TWENTY-THREE MONTHS

Family Evenings and Reading

Not everyone has a fireplace, but family evenings in a cozy atmosphere can be created in any home. Shared pastimes, such as reading, games, singing, crafts, and discussions, foster a child's love for such activities in later years, and create a lifetime of memories. It is especially worthwhile to encourage a child to love books and reading.

My boys are now in their 40's, and my daughter and grandson are in their 20's. When we reunite during holidays, everyone's favorite diversion is still to take turns reading in front of the fire.

Typical Daily Meals for a 23-Month-Old

MEAL	FOODS
Breakfast	1/2 cup Sunrise Surprise (dates, oj, banana, yogurt and carrot puree) (page 264), 1/2 hard-cooked egg, and 2 or 3 oat crackers
Snack	1/2 unsalted pretzel dipped in peanut butter and 1/2 cup (120 ml) milk
Lunch	Cucumber, Shrimp, and Spinach Salad (page 265) and 1/2 cup (120 ml) milk
Snack	1/2 scone with 1 teaspoon Honey Butter (page 179) and 1/2 cup (120 ml) milk
Dinner	1/3 cup Farfalle Pasta with Tuna Fish (page 267), Kiwi Kwiki (page 240), and 1/2 cup (120 ml) milk

BREAKFAST

French Toast 👨‍🍳

If you are concerned that the egg may not be cooked well enough after cooking in the frying pan, place the toast on the wire rack and bake in a 400°F (200°C, or gas mark 6) oven for a minute or two. Serve with maple syrup or Maple Cream (page 190) and fresh strawberries on the side.

* 1 egg
* 1 tablespoon (14 ml) milk
* 1 slice whole-grain bread
* 2 teaspoons butter
* 1 teaspoon maple syrup or Maple Cream (page 190)

◎ Beat the egg and milk together in a shallow bowl. Add the bread, turning to coat thoroughly. Melt the butter in a small frying pan over medium heat. Add the egg-soaked bread and cook, turning once, until golden brown and cooked all the way through, 6 to 8 minutes. Drizzle the toast with syrup or Maple Cream. Serve half of the toast, cut up into bite-size pieces, to your toddler. Mom or Dad can have the other half.

YIELD: *Makes 2 toddler servings*

EACH WITH: 109.3 calories; 7.1 gm total fat; 3.5 gm saturated fat; 116.6 mg cholesterol; 112.3 mg sodium; 7.0 gm carbohydrate; 1.0 gm dietary fiber; 4.8 gm protein; 32.9 mg calcium; 0.9 mg iron; 246.9 IU vitamin A; 0.0 mg vitamin C. .

Granola with Yogurt and Berries 👶

* ¼ cup (30 g) Plain Granola (page 225)
* ¼ cup (60 g) plain whole-milk yogurt
* ¼ cup (40 g) mixed fresh blueberries and sliced strawberries

Pour the granola into a bowl and top with the yogurt and berries.

YIELD: *Makes 1 toddler serving*

EACH WITH: 57.3 calories; 2.1 gm total fat; 1.1 gm saturated fat; 6.1 mg cholesterol; 24.8 mg sodium; 8.0 gm carbohydrate; 0.9 gm dietary fiber; 2.2 gm protein; 71.1 mg calcium; 0.1 mg iron; 81.8 IU vitamin A; 3.5 mg vitamin C.

Pastina Breakfast 👨‍🍳

Serve with 3 fresh strawberries on the side.

* 1 cup (235 ml) water
* 3 tablespoons (12 g) uncooked pastina
* 1 teaspoon butter
* ¼ cup (60 ml) milk

⬛ Combine the water and pastina in a 4-cup microwave-safe bowl. Microwave on high 5 minutes. Let stand 1 minute. Dot with the butter and pour on the milk.

YIELD: *Makes 1 toddler serving*

EACH WITH: 167.6 calories; 6.2 gm total fat; 3.6 gm saturated fat; 16.2 mg cholesterol; 26.8 mg sodium; 22.4 gm carbohydrate; 0.6 gm dietary fiber; 5.4 gm protein; 74.8 mg calcium; 1.0 mg iron; 179.3 IU vitamin A; 0.0 mg vitamin C. .

Sunrise Surprise

- 3 dates, pitted and finely chopped
- 1/2 cup (120 ml) orange juice
- 1 tablespoon (15 g) mashed banana
- 1 tablespoon (15 g) plain whole-milk yogurt
- 1 tablespoon (15 g) Carrot Puree (page 98), or cooked and pureed leftover carrots

Combine the dates and 1/4 cup (60 ml) of the juice in a blender and process on high speed 45 seconds, until dates are well blended with the juice. Add the banana, yogurt, carrot puree, and remaining 1/4 cup (60 ml) juice, and blend well.

YIELD: *Makes 1 toddler serving*

EACH WITH: 181.7 calories; 1.2 gm total fat; 0.7 gm saturated fat; 4.1 mg cholesterol; 17.9 mg sodium; 43.5 gm carbohydrate; 2.8 gm dietary fiber; 2.3 gm protein; 52.2 mg calcium; 0.5 mg iron; 107.5 IU vitamin A; 21.5 mg vitamin C.

LUNCH

Broccoli-Cheddar Soup

Serve with whole-wheat bread and slices of a ripe pear washed and cored.

- 2 tablespoons (28 ml) olive oil
- 1 small onion, peeled and chopped
- 1 teaspoon chopped garlic
- 1 leek, white part only, cleaned well and sliced
- 2 small potatoes, washed, peeled, and cubed
- 1 pound (455 g) broccoli, washed and chopped
- 2 cans (14 ounces, or 425 ml) each) vegetable or nonfat chicken broth or 3 cups (705 ml) homemade
- 1 1/2 cups (355 ml) 2% milk
- 1/2 to 1 cup (60 to 115 g) packed, grated cheddar cheese
- Salt

 Heat the oil in a large saucepan over low heat. Add the onion and sauté 5 minutes. Add garlic and leek and continue to sauté 5 more minutes, stirring occasionally. Add the potatoes, broccoli, and broth. Cover and simmer 30 minutes, or until the vegetables are soft. Pulse or puree the mixture (depending on how smooth you like your soup) in two batches in the food processor. Add some of the milk if you need to thin the soup. Return the soup to the pan, add the milk and gently reheat. Stir in the cheese until melted. Salt to taste.

YIELD: *Makes 6 servings*

EACH WITH: 246.2 calories; 11.2 gm total fat; 4.1 gm saturated fat; 20.1 mg cholesterol; 307.9 mg sodium; 26.2 gm carbohydrate; 3.7 gm dietary fiber; 11.8 gm protein; 225.5 mg calcium; 1.7 mg iron; 860.6 IU vitamin A; 81.8 mg vitamin C. .

Avocado, Tomato, and Mozzarella Melt 👪

Serve with ¹/₂ cup (120 ml) grape juice.

* 1 slice whole-wheat or rye bread
* Mayonnaise
* 2 thin slices avocado
* 1 large slice tomato
* 1 thin slice mozzarella

🍳 Preheat the broiler. Lightly spread the bread with mayonnaise. Layer the bread with the avocado and tomato and top with the mozzarella. Place on a cookie sheet covered with tinfoil and broil until the cheese has melted. (It melts quickly; don't let it brown.)

Serve your toddler ¹/₄ to ¹/₃ of the open-faced sandwich.

YIELD: *Makes 1 toddler serving AND 1 adult serving*

EACH WITH: 248.7 calories; 18.8 gm total fat; 8.3 gm saturated fat; 44.8 mg cholesterol; 430.4 mg sodium; 7.0 gm carbohydrate; 1.6 gm dietary fiber; 13.8 gm protein; 295.1 mg calcium; 0.7 mg iron; 457.2 IU vitamin A; 3.6 mg vitamin C.

Cucumber, Shrimp, and Spinach Salad 🧒

* 1 cup (30 g) packed fresh spinach leaves, washed
* 4 slices peeled cucumber
* 2 or 3 large cooked shrimp, peeled, tails removed
* Creamy Lemon Dressing (below) (optional)

◎ With water droplets still clinging to the leaves, cook the spinach in a small skillet over medium heat, tossing, until soft, about 2 minutes. Drain the spinach, let cool, and squeeze into a square shape. Place the cucumbers on a plate in a nice pattern. Cut the shrimp into small pieces and arrange on top of the cucumbers. Place the spinach next to the cucumbers. Serve plain or with dressing.

YIELD: *Makes 1 toddler serving*

EACH WITH: 49.1 calories; 1.5 gm total fat; 0.7 gm saturated fat; 31.5 mg cholesterol; 65.6 mg sodium; 3.5 gm carbohydrate; 0.9 gm dietary fiber; 5.8 gm protein; 81.5 mg calcium; 1.3 mg iron; 2897.2 IU vitamin A; 9.8 mg vitamin C.

Creamy Lemon Dressing 🧒

* 2 tablespoons (30 g) plain whole-milk yogurt
* ¹/₂ teaspoon white wine vinegar
* ¹/₄ teaspoon lemon juice

Combine the yogurt, vinegar, and lemon juice and whisk together vigorously with a fork.

YIELD: *Makes 1 toddler serving*

EACH WITH: 19.7 calories; 1.0 gm total fat; 0.7 gm saturated fat; 4.1 mg cholesterol; 14.7 mg sodium; 1.6 gm carbohydrate; 0.0 gm dietary fiber; 1.1 gm protein; 38.5 mg calcium; 0.0 mg iron; 31.5 IU vitamin A; 0.2 mg vitamin C. .

LUNCH

Shepherd's Pie 👪

This is a simple dish to make with leftover mashed potatoes. It can be finished under the broiler or in the microwave oven. Serve with steamed broccoli and Kiwi Kwiki (page 240) or sliced kiwifruit for dessert.

- 1 tablespoon (14 ml) olive oil
- 1 medium onion, finely chopped
- 1 teaspoon minced garlic
- 1 pound (455 g) ground turkey or lean ground beef
- Salt
- Pepper
- 2 cups (200 g) Mashed Potatoes (page 240) or reheated leftover potatoes
- 1/2 cup (60 g) shredded cheese (Swiss, cheddar, and Parmesan are a nice combination.)

◎ 🍳 Preheat the broiler. Heat the oil in a frying pan over medium heat. Add the onion and garlic and sauté until translucent. Add the turkey or beef, breaking it into small pieces, and season with salt and pepper. Stir well and cook until the red or pink color has disappeared and the meat is browned and thoroughly cooked. Stir in a little broth or water to add moisture if necessary. Transfer to an ovenproof casserole dish. Cover the meat with hot mashed potatoes and sprinkle with the cheese. Broil the casserole about 4 inches (10 cm) from the heat until the potatoes are lightly browned and the cheese is bubbly. (Or cover the casserole and cook it in the microwave until the cheese has melted and the casserole is heated through.) Serve your toddler 1/3 cup.

YIELD: *Makes 1 toddler and 3 adult servings*

EACH WITH: 211.6 calories; 10.8 gm total fat; 3.9 gm saturated fat; 62.3 mg cholesterol; 301.5 mg sodium; 13.1 gm carbohydrate; 1.2 gm dietary fiber; 15.0 gm protein; 95.4 mg calcium; 1.1 mg iron; 109.0 IU vitamin A; 5.3 mg vitamin C. .

Farfalle Pasta with Tuna Fish 👫

- 1 cup (105 g) uncooked whole-wheat farfalle pasta
- 1 can (6 ounces, or 170 g) chunk light tuna packed in spring water, drained
- 2 tablespoons (28 ml) olive oil
- Salt
- Freshly ground pepper
- 1 tablespoon (14 ml) salad dressing (Ranch works well.)

◎ Bring 2 quarts (2 liters) water to a boil in a large saucepan. Add the pasta and boil 14 to 16 minutes, until cooked al dente. Drain. Combine the pasta and tuna in a bowl, sprinkle with the oil, and toss well. Season to taste with salt and pepper and dressing (ranch dressing works well). Serve your toddler 1/4 to 1/2 cup.

YIELD: *Makes 1 toddler serving AND 1 adult serving*

EACH WITH: 295.7 calories; 13.4 gm total fat; 2.1 gm saturated fat; 25.5 mg cholesterol; 254.6 mg sodium; 26.6 gm carbohydrate; 2.9 gm dietary fiber; 18.7 gm protein; 23.5 mg calcium; 1.9 mg iron; 13.1 IU vitamin A; 0.1 mg vitamin C.

Fava Spread (Yellow Split Peas) 👫

Spread on crackers or pita bread while still warm or use as a side dish for dinner. Serve with pitted and cut sweet orange segments.

- 1 cup (200 g) yellow split peas
- 1/2 cup (65 g) minced onion
- 2 cloves garlic, minced
- 1/2 cup (90 g) canned, crushed tomatoes
- 2 teaspoons kosher salt
- 2 tablespoons chopped parsley
- 2 teaspoons olive oil

◎ Rinse the peas thoroughly, place in a medium pan with 4 cups (940 ml) water, and bring to a boil. Skim off the foam and add the onion, garlic, tomatoes, and salt.

Reduce the heat to low, cover, and simmer 1 hour, or until the peas are mushy. Stir occasionally during cooking. When done, sprinkle with the parsley and oil and whisk to the desired texture with a fork.

YIELD: *Makes 4 servings*

EACH WITH: 211.6 calories; 2.9 gm total fat; 0.4 gm saturated fat; 0.0 mg cholesterol; 1205.6 mg sodium; 35.2 gm carbohydrate; 13.5 gm dietary fiber; 13.0 gm protein; 51.5 mg calcium; 2.8 mg iron; 408.6 IU vitamin A; 8.4 mg vitamin C. .

TWO YEARS . . . AND BEYOND

Two whole years have passed. In spite of anxieties, colic, teething, tantrums, and sleepless nights, you have survived! In this short time, you have become a family, an expert in juggling time, and survived with little sleep—and along the way you have already created priceless memories.

Now that your bundle of joy is an active, running, jumping two-year-old, remember that two- to three-year-olds need a wide variety of foods and the same numbers of servings as older children and adults, but they still need smaller portions. And keep in mind that young children's appetites can vary a lot from day to day. So long as your toddler is growing well and eating a variety of foods, she is probably getting the nutrients she needs.

BREAKFAST

Buttermilk Biscuits 👨‍👧

These are a wonderful treat for breakfast. For a dessert, they can be cut in half and filled with sliced fresh strawberries and a little whipped cream.

- 1 cup (120 g) all-purpose flour
- 1/2 tablespoon baking powder
- 1/2 teaspoon salt
- 1/4 teaspoon baking soda
- 2 1/2 tablespoons (30 g) chilled butter
- 1/2 cup (120 ml) buttermilk

▦ Preheat the oven to 425°F (220°C, or gas mark 7). In a large bowl, sift together the flour, baking powder, salt, and baking soda. With a pastry blender, cut the shortening into the flour mixture until coarse crumbs form. Add the buttermilk. Mix with a fork until dough forms.

Turn the dough onto a lightly floured surface and knead lightly until smooth. Don't overwork the dough. Flatten the dough with hands to a 3/4-inch (2-cm) thickness. Dip a biscuit cutter or glass in flour and cut out rounds. Place the rounds on an ungreased baking sheet. Bake 12 to 15 minutes, until golden.

YIELD: *Makes 6 biscuits*

EACH WITH: 157.8 calories; 5.6 gm total fat; 3.4 gm saturated fat; 19.6 mg cholesterol; 461.5 mg sodium; 21.2 gm carbohydrate; 0.6 gm dietary fiber; 5.6 gm protein; 213.2 mg calcium; 1.2 mg iron; 165.4 IU vitamin A; 0.6 mg vitamin C. .

SNACKS

Snacks play an important role in fulfilling nutritional needs for two-year-olds. Toddlers have small tummies, tend to have small appetites, and may not be able to consume a full serving at one time. Here are some snack suggestions that require little if any cooking or preparation.

GRAINS

- A variety of multigrain, wheat, and whole-wheat crackers.
- A variety of rye, rice, oat, or corn crackers and cakes.
- Non-sugar ready-to-eat cereals.
- Bread: multi-grain, rye, wheat, rice, oat, or corn.
- Pita bread, tortillas.
- Polenta, bagel, unsalted pretzels, Matzoh.
- Crumpets, English muffins, crostini.

VEGETABLES

- Steamed, microwaved, roasted, or sautéed broccoli, green beans, carrot sticks, cauliflower, asparagus tips.
- Roasted potato fingers, sweet potato fingers, peeled and seeded and sliced green/red/yellow/orange peppers, eggplant, mushrooms, summer and winter squash.
- Cherry tomatoes cut in small pieces, peeled sliced cucumbers, diced avocado.

- Vegetable spreads for bread or crackers: roasted garlic puree, cream cheese spreads (sun-dried tomatoes, spinach, lemon, avocado, mushroom, carrot, sweet potato, and herb spreads), bean spreads, pate.

FRUITS

- Apples, pears, Asian pears, oranges, tangerines, and pineapple peeled and cut into rings or wedges.
- Apricots, peaches, nectarines, banana, cherries (pitted and cut in small pieces) plums (stoned), varied melons and kiwis (peeled and seeded), strawberries, fresh figs, mangoes, papaya (peeled and seeded), black berries, blueberries, raspberries, fruit smoothies.
- Mix fresh fruit with cream cheese or mascarpone.

DAIRY

- Milk shakes, made with milk, soy, ice cream, or yogurt, fruit juices and fruit.
- Yogurt with fresh fruit.
- Cottage cheese or ricotta cheese with or without fresh fruit.

- Cheese: mozzarella, cheddar, Jarlsberg, fontina, Gouda or regular Swiss cheese, Jack, provolone.
- To spread on bread or crackers: Cream cheese, goat cheese, feta, blue cheese, (can all be mixed with yogurt-cheese ½ and ½).

PROTEIN

- Hard-cooked eggs (wedges or slices).
- Creamy peanut butter or other nut butters spread thin on crackers.
- Black or white bean dip spread thin on crackers.
- Crab, shrimp, or smoked salmon cut in small pieces or mixed with cream cheese to spread on crackers.
- Fish sticks, salmon cakes, crab cakes, chicken fingers, spring rolls.
- Canned chicken, turkey, salmon, sardines, or tuna salad.
- Small meat cakes or meatballs.
- Gardenburgers, quesadilla, pot stickers.

LUNCH

Corn, Crab, and Curry Soup 👪

This is a mild curried soup. An older child may enjoy the flavor, if he already has been exposed to spicy food. The soup is quick to make. You can use fresh crabmeat, canned, or imitation crabmeat with no MSG added. Serve with good whole-wheat bread.

* 1 tablespoon (14 ml) olive oil
* 1/3 cup (50 g) minced onion
* 1 tablespoon (9 g) curry powder
* 2 cans (14 ounces, or 425 ml) nonfat chicken broth (or 3 cups homemade)
* 1 cup (130 g) fresh or frozen corn
* 1 cup (235 ml) half-and-half
* 1 cup (125 g) lump crabmeat
* 1 teaspoon kosher salt or to taste, optional

◎ Heat the oil in a saucepan on medium, add the onion, and sauté for 3 minutes. Add the curry powder and sauté for 2 more minutes. Add broth and corn, bring to a boil, turn down the heat, and simmer for 5 minutes. Add the half-and-half and heat without boiling. Remove from heat and stir in the crabmeat.

YIELD: *Makes 4 servings*

EACH WITH: 365.0 calories; 15.0 gm total fat; 5.8 gm saturated fat; 160.4 mg cholesterol; 1368.8 mg sodium; 18.6 gm carbohydrate; 1.7 gm dietary fiber; 38.6 gm protein; 231.8 mg calcium; 2.4 mg iron; 323.9 IU vitamin A; 9.6 mg vitamin C.

Green Peas Soup 👪

Serve with whole-wheat bread and a pitted nectarine.

* 1/3 cup (80 ml) olive oil
* 1/2 onion, peeled and finely chopped
* 1 garlic clove, finely chopped
* 1 medium potato, washed, peeled, and cubed
* 1 leek, trimmed and carefully washed, white and light green parts sliced
* 1 stick celery, washed and sliced
* 2 cups (260 g) fresh or frozen peas
* 2 cans (14 ounces, or 425 ml) chicken broth
* 1 teaspoon lemon juice
* Salt and pepper to taste

◎ Heat oil in a heavy-bottomed 3-quart saucepan over the lowest heat. Add onion, garlic, potato, leek, and celery. Cover and simmer for 1 hour, until the vegetables are soft. Stir occasionally to make sure the vegetables do not stick or burn. Add a little broth, if necessary. Add peas and simmer for 10 more minutes. When the vegetables are cooked, process in two batches. Place half of the content in the blender with 1 can of broth, and blend for 45 seconds. Repeat with the second batch. Return the soup to the saucepan, add lemon juice, and season to taste.

YIELD: *Makes 4 servings*

EACH WITH: 355.2 calories; 20.4 gm total fat; 3.1 gm saturated fat; 5.4 mg cholesterol; 278.8 mg sodium; 34.0 gm carbohydrate; 6.0 gm dietary fiber; 10.4 gm protein; 57.5 mg calcium; 2.6 mg iron; 977.9 IU vitamin A; 45.9 mg vitamin C. .

Chicken Sandwich ⬤

*Serve with soup and a piece of fruit for lunch or a
light dinner.*

- 4 slices sourdough bread
- Olive Spread (page 258), salsa, or mayonnaise
- 2 lettuce leaves
- 4 tomato slices
- 2 large slices chicken breast

Toast the bread lightly. Spread the olive spread
lightly to cover 2 pieces of bread. Top each with a
lettuce leaf, 2 tomato slices, and a slice chicken
breast. Spread olive spread lightly on the remaining bread; place on top of chicken to make sandwiches. Cut in half diagonally.

If a piece of the sandwich is too difficult for your
toddler to eat, finely chop the ingredients and
serve separately, with a small piece of toast.

YIELD: *Makes 2 servings*

EACH WITH: 258.5 calories; 8.1 gm total fat; 1.3 gm saturated fat; 7.6
mg cholesterol; 666.1 mg sodium; 36.9 gm carbohydrate; 2.8 gm
dietary fiber; 9.9 gm protein; 61.1 mg calcium; 2.2 mg iron; 2113.6 IU
vitamin A; 18.4 mg vitamin C. .

Potato Latkes ⬤

*Serve plain, as finger food, or with applesauce or
apple butter.*

- 2 small red potatoes peeled and coarsely grated
  (about ¹/₂ cup, or 80 g)
- 1 egg
- 1 teaspoon finely grated onion
- ¹/₂ teaspoon kosher salt
- 2 tablespoons (15 g) all-purpose flour
- Oil for frying

◎ Soak the potatoes in a large bowl of water for
about 1 hour. Drain thoroughly and pat dry with a
paper towel.

In a small bowl, beat the egg, onion, and salt.
Place the potatoes in a large bowl and sprinkle
with the flour. Add the egg mixture and blend
well. Coat a frying pan with a thin layer of oil and
heat over medium heat. Drop the potato mixture
to the pan in 1-tablespoon amounts and flatten
with a spatula (take care the mixture does not
splatter). Cook the latkes 2 to 3 minutes, until
golden brown on the bottom. Turn over and cook
2 to 3 minutes more, until golden on the other
side. Drain on a paper towel and keep warm until
ready to serve.

YIELD: *Makes 6 to 8 latkes*

EACH WITH: 32.9 calories; 1.5 gm total fat; 0.3 gm saturated fat; 26.4
mg cholesterol; 154.6 mg sodium; 3.6 gm carbohydrate; 0.5 gm
dietary fiber; 1.4 gm protein; 5.2 mg calcium; 0.3 mg iron; 31.1 IU vitamin A; 0.9 mg vitamin C. .

Coleslaw 👪

This dish is great for a picnic.

* 2 cups (140 g) finely shredded cabbage
* 1 cup (120 g) finely shredded carrots
* ½ cup (113 g) mayonnaise
* ½ cup (123 g) nonfat plain yogurt
* 1 tablespoon (14 ml) white wine vinegar
* 1 teaspoon creamy horseradish
* 1 teaspoon salt
* 1 teaspoon sugar (optional)

Mix cabbage and carrots together in a large bowl. In a 1-cup measuring cup, blend mayonnaise, yogurt, white wine vinegar, horseradish, salt, and sugar if using. Add half of the dressing to the cabbage and carrots. Stir well, and add more dressing or seasoning to taste. Transfer to a lidded container and refrigerate.

YIELD: *3 cups*

EACH WITH: 162.3 calories; 15.6 gm total fat; 2.2 gm saturated fat; 0.4 mg cholesterol; 519.6 mg sodium; 4.9 gm carbohydrate; 1.1 gm dietary fiber; 1.7 gm protein; 59.7 mg calcium; 0.3 mg iron; 2247.9 IU vitamin A; 9.0 mg vitamin C.

Potato Salad 👪

This potato salad is a nice accompaniment with cold roasted chicken. Serve watermelon (peeled and seeded) for dessert.

* 8 small red potatoes, well scrubbed
* 4 hard boiled eggs
* ¾ cup (90 g) finely chopped, celery, leaves included
* ⅓ cup (43 g) finely chopped onion, optional
* ¼ cup (36 g) finely chopped pickles (preferably Claussen kosher dill)
* ¾ cup (170 g) mayonnaise
* 2 teaspoons Dijon mustard
* Dash of salt, or to taste
* Sprinkle of paprika

◎ Boil scrubbed potatoes for 30 to 45 minutes, or until soft. Drain. Cool, peel and cube. (If new potatoes, leave the skin on.) Peel eggs and chop into small pieces. Combine potatoes, onion if desired, celery, pickles, chopped eggs, mayonnaise, and mustard in a large bowl. Sprinkle with a little salt and mix well with a spatula. Sprinkle paprika on top.

YIELD: *Makes 6 servings*

EACH WITH: 424.3 calories; 26.9 gm total fat; 4.3 gm saturated fat; 141.0 mg cholesterol; 292.2 mg sodium; 37.9 gm carbohydrate; 4.3 gm dietary fiber; 8.7 gm protein; 49.9 mg calcium; 2.4 mg iron; 246.0 IU vitamin A; 45.7 mg vitamin C. .

Pasta Salad ⬤

Serve fresh blackberries or a blackberry sorbet for dessert.

- ¹/₂ pound (225 g) feta cheese
- 5 teaspoons olive oil
- 1 basket cherry tomatoes, washed and halved
- ¹/₃ cup (45 g) toasted pine nuts, optional (do not use for a toddler unless ground)
- ¹/₂ cup (30 g) chopped basil, washed
- ¹/₂ cup (50 g) pitted and halved Greek black or green olives, or black California olives
- ¹/₂ of a 1-pound (455 g) package of whole-wheat penne pasta

▣ ◎ Preheat the oven to 450°F (230°C, or gas mark 8). Place the cheese in tinfoil and sprinkle with 2 teaspoons olive oil. Wrap the foil around the cheese and place it on a baking sheet. Place tomatoes in a heatproof dish and sprinkle with 2 teaspoons olive oil. Place cheese and tomatoes in the oven and bake for about 15 minutes. Bring water to boil in a large pot, add pasta and cook until al dente. (Follow instructions on the package.) If using pine nuts: heat a frying pan on high and toast the pine nuts for a few seconds while stirring. Watch carefully to prevent burning. When pasta is cooked, drain and place in a large bowl. Stir in 1 table-spoon (14 ml) olive oil. Add cheese, tomatoes with their roasting juices, pine nuts if using, basil, and olives. Mix well and serve.

YIELD: *Makes 4 to 6 servings*

EACH WITH: 422.8 calories; 14.3 gm total fat; 6.5 gm saturated fat; 33.7 mg cholesterol; 531.2 mg sodium; 61.9 gm carbohydrate; 7.5 gm dietary fiber; 17.2 gm protein; 240.3 mg calcium; 3.8 mg iron; 887.1 IU vitamin A; 14.3 mg vitamin C.

Potato Kugel 👪

If you have a food processor with a grater disc, this is quick to make. Cut vegetables to fit feeder tube of the food processor, and use grater disc. Otherwise, grate by hand.

- 2 tablespoons whole-wheat bread crumbs (put 1 slice of whole-wheat bread in the food processor, and pulse until crumbled)
- 1 small red or white skinned potato, with peel, well scrubbed, and grated
- 1 tablespoon (10 g) grated onion
- 1 small carrot, scrubbed, and grated
- 1 small garlic clove, minced
- 1 egg
- 1 1/2 teaspoons canola oil
- 1/4 teaspoon salt
- 1/4 cup milk powder
- 1/4 cup grated cheese, cheddar, Swiss, or Jack

Heat oven to 350°F (180°C, or gas mark 4). Oil a small ovenproof dish. Put bread crumbs in a small bowl. Add grated potato, onion, carrot, garlic, egg, oil, salt, and milk powder, and stir well. Pour mixture into oiled dish and bake for 30 to 40 minutes, until firm. Carefully remove the dish from the oven. Stir in cheese and bake for 5 more minutes.

YIELD: *Makes 1 adult and 1 toddler serving*

EACH WITH: 221.0 calories; 10.3 gm total fat; 4.9 gm saturated fat; 92.4 mg cholesterol; 406.1 mg sodium; 22.1 gm carbohydrate; 1.9 gm dietary fiber; 10.2 gm protein; 215.7 mg calcium; 1.4 mg iron; 2299.0 IU vitamin A; 13.6 mg vitamin C.

Greek Vegetable Stew 👪

Serve with whole-wheat bread and peach sorbet for dessert.

- 1/4 cup (60 ml) olive oil
- 1 medium onion, peeled, and finely chopped
- 1 large fresh tomato, washed
- 3 cups mixed vegetables, cleaned and cut into pieces about 1 x 1 inch (2.5 x 2.5 cm) (*Always use potato and carrots, then add any of the following vegetables: zucchini, green beans, cauliflower, eggplant, or okra.*)
- 1/2 cup (30 g) chopped flat leafed parsley
- Salt and pepper to taste
- 1/2 cup (75 g) crumbled feta cheese

Heat oil in a large heavy-bottomed pot. Add onion and sauté until soft. Grate tomatoes into pot, using the large holes of the grater. Add vegetables, parsley, salt, and pepper. Add enough water to cover vegetables by 1 inch. Bring to a simmer and cover. Cook until vegetables are very well done and have formed a thick sauce (30 to 45 minutes). Stir occasionally and add more water if necessary. Serve topped with crumbled feta cheese.

YIELD: *Makes 2 to 3 servings*

EACH WITH: 79.0 calories; 5.9 gm total fat; 1.6 gm saturated fat; 5.6 mg cholesterol; 80.9 mg sodium; 5.0 gm carbohydrate; 1.4 gm dietary fiber; 1.8 gm protein; 42.8 mg calcium; 0.5 mg iron; 1304.7 IU vitamin A; 8.6 mg vitamin C.

Spinach, Cheese, and Mushroom Pie 👪

This can be served either for lunch or dinner. Serve with sweet, seedless, grapes. Halve the grapes for your toddler. This dish is also nice to take to a potluck or on a picnic.

- 1 pound (455 g) fresh spinach, or two 10-ounce (280 g) packages frozen, chopped spinach
- 2 tablespoons (28 ml) olive oil
- 1½ cups (195 g) finely chopped onion
- 1½ cups (150 g) cleaned and sliced mushrooms
- Salt and pepper to taste
- 3 eggs, well beaten
- 2 cups shredded Jarlsberg, or a mixture of Jarlsberg, cheddar, and Parmesan (1 + ¾ + ¼ cup)
- One 9-inch (22.5-cm) deep dish piecrust, home-made or frozen (uncooked)

◎ ▣ Preheat oven 400°F (200°C, or gas mark 6). Wash and stem spinach, and with the water clinging to the leaves, steam in a covered pot on low for five minutes. Drain in colander. (If using frozen spinach, defrost in a colander.) Heat oil in a frying pan, and sauté onion until transparent. Bring heat to medium high, and add mushrooms. Season with salt and pepper, and fry the mushrooms until lightly browned.

Combine well-drained spinach, mushrooms, onion, eggs, and 1½ cups of the cheese in a large bowl. Mix well and pour into the piecrust. Sprinkle remaining ½ cup of cheese over the pie. Place on a baking sheet, and bake in the center of the oven for 15 minutes. Reduce heat to 325°F (170°C, or gas mark 3), and bake for an additional 30 to 45 minutes. Cool on a rack.

YIELD: *Makes 8 servings*

EACH WITH: 297.8 calories; 21.7 gm total fat; 9.8 gm saturated fat; 114.0 mg cholesterol; 360.9 mg sodium; 13.4 gm carbohydrate; 1.8 gm dietary fiber; 13.4 gm protein; 313.2 mg calcium; 1.8 mg iron; 4585.3 IU vitamin A; 10.9 mg vitamin C. .

DINNER

Hamburgers 👫

I use ground turkey for my patties, but low-fat ground beef works well also. Serve with Sweet Potato Fries (page 101) and pitted, halved cherries for dessert.

- 1 pound (455 g) ground turkey
- Salt (optional)
- Pepper (optional)
- 1 teaspoon olive oil
- 4 hamburger buns, split
- 4 teaspoons ketchup
- 4 lettuce leaves
- 1 large tomato cut into 4 slices
- 4 onion slices (optional)

◎ With your hands, divide the turkey and gently shape into 4 patties. Season with salt and pepper. Heat the oil in a frying pan over medium heat. Place the patties in the pan and cook, turning often, until an instant-read thermometer inserted into the center of the patties registers 160°F (70°C). Lightly toast the buns and spread each half with ketchup. Place the lettuce and tomato on half a bun; add an onion slice, if you like. Top with the hamburger patty and cover with the other half of the bun.

NOTE: The hamburger patties can also be cooked on a grill. Be sure to use the thermometer to check that the meat is adequately cooked.

YIELD: *Makes 4 hamburgers*

EACH WITH: 309.4 calories; 12.5 gm total fat; 3.2 gm saturated fat; 89.6 mg cholesterol; 373.7 mg sodium; 24.6 gm carbohydrate; 1.9 gm dietary fiber; 24.0 gm protein; 63.1 mg calcium; 2.8 mg iron; 2066.3 IU vitamin A; 16.1 mg vitamin C.

Red Beans and Rice 👨‍👧

- 1 cup (235 ml) chicken or vegetable broth
- ¼ cup (50 g) rice, well rinsed
- ½ cup (56 g) shredded cheddar cheese
- 1 cup (225 g) cooked or canned kidney beans with liquid, mashed or processed

◎ Bring broth to boil in a small saucepan over high heat; add the rice, stir, and cover. Reduce heat to low and steam rice 20 minutes. Stir in the cheese until melted. Stir in the mashed beans. Serve your toddler ¼ cup.

VARIATION: Use black-eyed peas instead of the red beans.

YIELD: *Makes 2 cups; 8 toddler servings OR 4 adult servings*

EACH WITH: 77.9 calories; 2.6 gm total fat; 1.5 gm saturated fat; 7.4 mg cholesterol; 208.2 mg sodium; 9.5 gm carbohydrate; 1.5 gm dietary fiber; 4.2 gm protein; 65.8 mg calcium; 0.7 mg iron; 70.8 IU vitamin A; 0.5 mg vitamin C.

Poached Salmon 👨‍👧

Salmon (with the exception of farm raised) is one of the healthiest fish you can eat. It is high in omega-3 fatty acids (beneficial to your health) and it has no detectable mercury. The traditional Norwegian way of poaching salmon is one of the simplest and tastiest ways to prepare it. Poached salmon can be served hot or cold. If serving hot, garnish with fresh dill and sliced lemon.

- 4 cups (940 ml) water
- 2 tablespoons (35 g) kosher salt
- 12 peppercorns (optional)
- 2 teaspoons vinegar (optional)
- 4 salmon fillets (without skin and bones), 8 ounces (225 g) each

◎ Bring the water and salt to a boil in a large pot. If you plan on serving the salmon cold, add the peppercorns and vinegar. Carefully add the salmon fillets and immediately reduce the heat to low (the fish should never boil). Poach 10 minutes, until the fish flakes easily when tested with a fork.

YIELD: *Makes 4 servings*

EACH WITH: 184.7 calories; 5.5 gm total fat; 0.9 gm saturated fat; 82.7 mg cholesterol; 3594.8 mg sodium; 0.1 gm carbohydrate; 0.0 gm dietary fiber; 31.7 gm protein; 22.8 mg calcium; 1.3 mg iron; 186.0 IU vitamin A; 0.0 mg vitamin C..

Macaroni Casserole 👨‍👧

You can use homemade tomato sauce, but a good commercial brand is fine too. (I occasionally use Classico pasta sauce with tomato and basil.) Serve with steamed or microwaved Broccoli, and Rice and Apricot Pudding (page 103) for dessert.

- 2 cups (300 g) elbow macaroni
- 2 cups (475 ml) Tomato Sauce (page 174)
- 1 tablespoon (14 ml) olive oil
- 1/2 cup (65 g) finely chopped onion
- 2 garlic cloves, minced
- 1 pound (455 g) ground turkey
- Salt, pepper, and paprika to taste

◎ Bring 8 cups (2 liters) of water to boil in a large pot over high heat. Add the macaroni, stir, and cook uncovered 10 minutes, or until macaroni is just tender. Drain and transfer to a microwave-safe lidded casserole. Add the tomato sauce and stir.

Meanwhile, heat the oil in a frying pan over medium heat. Add the onion and sauté 5 minutes. Add the garlic and stir for another minute. Add the ground turkey and cook, stirring to break into small pieces, until the pink color has disappeared. Stir often, so the meat will cook evenly. Add the meat to the macaroni and tomato sauce, and stir until well blended.

▭ Cover, place in the microwave and cook for 5 minutes, or until the casserole is warmed through.

▣ Place in a 350°F (80°C, or gas mark 4) preheated oven, and bake 30 to 45 minutes, until heated through. Serve your toddler 1/4 cup.

YIELD: *Makes 4 servings*

EACH WITH: 413.8 calories; 14.5 gm total fat; 3.3 gm saturated fat; 89.6 mg cholesterol; 427.0 mg sodium; 45.1 gm carbohydrate; 5.3 gm dietary fiber; 28.4 gm protein; 65.0 mg calcium; 4.0 mg iron; 133.0 IU vitamin A; 5.7 mg vitamin C. .

Halloween Stew in a Pumpkin

This recipe was in the first edition of The Baby Cookbook, *more than two decades ago. A dear friend has made it every Halloween since then, at the request of her two sons, who are now in their twenties. The stew can also be cooked ahead of time in a Crock-Pot; then you need only to bake the shell on Halloween night. Serve with freshly baked whole-wheat or sourdough bread. For dessert offer small cupcakes decorated with orange frosting, white ghosts, and black witches. Or serve persimmons with black grapes (halved and seeded)*

- 2 tablespoons (28 ml) olive oil
- 2 onions, chopped
- 2 cloves garlic, minced
- 1 cup (120 g) all-purpose flour
- 1/2 teaspoon salt
- $1/4$ teaspoon pepper
- $1^1/2$ pounds (680 g) stewing beef, cubed
- 4 cups (940 ml) nonfat chicken broth or water
- 2 white potatoes, scrubbed and cubed
- 2 sweet potatoes, peeled and cubed
- 2 green or red bell peppers, seeded and dice
- 1 cup (150 g) sweet corn (fresh, frozen, or canned)
- 4 tomatoes, peeled and chopped
- 1 cup (115 g) cubed pumpkin (optional)
- $1/2$ cup (85 g) diced fresh or canned peaches (optional)
- 1 pumpkin, 15 inches (37.5 cm) in diameter
- Chopped fresh parsley

Heat the oil in a large, heavy-bottomed pot over medium-high heat. Add the onion and garlic and sauté until golden. Combine the flour, salt, and pepper in a large, clean brown paper bag. In batches, add the beef and shake to coat lightly. Add the beef to the pot and brown the meat on all sides. Stir in the broth or water. Add the potatoes, sweet potatoes, peppers, corn, tomatoes, and pumpkin and peaches if desired. Bring to a boil over medium heat, stir, reduce the heat, cover and simmer $1^1/2$ to 2 hours, until the meat is tender. Check and stir a couple of times during cooking, adding more liquid if needed. Season to taste with salt and pepper.

Preheat the oven to 375°F (190°C, or gas mark 5). Cut a lid-size piece from the top of the pumpkin and remove the seeds and pulp, but leave firm flesh intact. Pour 2 inches of water in a large baking dish, place the pumpkin and "lid" in the dish, and steam in the oven for about 1 hour, until the pumpkin is tender, but still firm. Transfer to a serving plate and keep warm. When the stew and pumpkin are cooked, carefully add the stew to the pumpkin and garnish with parsley.

YIELD: *Makes 4 toddler servings AND 4 adult servings*

EACH WITH: 312.3 calories; 16.5 gm total fat; 5.9 gm saturated fat; 42.0 mg cholesterol; 305.1 mg sodium; 28.0 gm carbohydrate; 3.3 gm dietary fiber; 13.7 gm protein; 24.9 mg calcium; 2.5 mg iron; 904.9 IU vitamin A; 64.5 mg vitamin C.

Super Moist Cornbread 👫

* 2 large eggs
* 1 cup (235 ml) milk
* 1 can (16½ ounces, or 683 g) creamed corn
* 1 cup (120 g) yellow cornmeal
* ¼ cup (30 g) all-purpose flour
* ¼ cup (50 g) sugar
* 1 teaspoon salt
* ½ teaspoon baking powder
* ½ teaspoon baking soda
* 1 cup (115 g) grated cheddar cheese
* 4 tablespoons (½ stick, or 55 g) butter, melted

◎ ▣ Place a 9-inch (22.5-cm) cast-iron skillet or 9-inch (22.5-cm) square baking pan in the oven and preheat the oven to 375°F (190°C, or gas mark 5).

Beat together the eggs, milk, and corn in a large bowl. In a smaller bowl, stir together the cornmeal, flour, sugar, salt, baking powder, and baking soda. Add the dry ingredients to the wet ingredients and stir to combine. Add the cheese and stir well. Stir in 3 tablespoons (42 g) of the butter.

Carefully remove the skillet or baking pan from the oven (it will be very hot). Add the remaining 1 tablespoon (14 g) butter and swirl to coat. Add the batter to the skillet. Return the skillet to the oven and bake about 45 minutes, or until the cornbread is golden.

VARIATION: For spicy cornbread, add chiles to the batter when you add the cheese. Use 1 (7-ounce, or 196 g) can jalapeños (drained) or 3 chopped fresh jalapeño chiles.

YIELD: *Makes 8 servings*

EACH WITH: 288.1 calories; 13.3 gm total fat; 7.7 gm saturated fat; 86.0 mg cholesterol; 690.4 mg sodium; 35.0 gm carbohydrate; 2.5 gm dietary fiber; 9.2 gm protein; 165.7 mg calcium; 1.5 mg iron; 492.8 IU vitamin A; 2.8 mg vitamin C.

Corn and Butter Beans 👪

Serve this as a complete meal with a baked potato or as a topping for a baked potato. Serve avocado on the side and a peeled and pitted tangerine for dessert. The corn and butter beans can also be served as a side dish with fish or chicken.

- 1 teaspoon olive oil
- 1/2 cup (65 g) chopped onion
- 1 cup (240 g) canned butter beans, drained
- 1 cup (160 g) frozen corn
- 1/2 cup (90 g) chopped tomato
- 1/2 to 1 cup (120 to 235 ml) water
- 1 tablespoon (14 ml) lime juice
- Salt
- Pepper
- Chopped fresh cilantro

◎ Heat the oil in saucepan over medium heat, add the onion and sauté until soft. Add the beans, corn, tomato, and water. Bring to a boil, cover, reduce the heat, and simmer 20 minutes. Remove from heat and mash the beans to give the dish a saucy texture. Add the lime juice and salt and pepper to taste and garnish with cilantro.

YIELD: *Makes 2 servings*

EACH WITH: 126.8 calories; 2.9 gm total fat; 0.4 gm saturated fat; 0.0 mg cholesterol; 161.1 mg sodium; 23.2 gm carbohydrate; 4.3 gm dietary fiber; 4.6 gm protein; 33.4 mg calcium; 1.4 mg iron; 561.5 IU vitamin A; 17.7 mg vitamin C.

Linguini with Clam Sauce 👪

This is a quick, easy, and tasty meal. Clams provide a good supply of iron. Serve with a salad and a favorite fruit sherbet for dessert.

- 1 package (1 pound, or 455 g) dried linguini
- 1/4 cup (60 ml) olive oil
- 1 clove garlic, minced
- 1/4 cup (60 ml) water
- 2 teaspoons fresh or 1/2 teaspoon dried oregano
- 2 tablespoons (8 g) finely chopped parsley
- 1/2 teaspoon salt
- 1/4 teaspoon pepper
- 1 can (6.5 ounces, or 182 g) chopped clams in clam juice

◎ In a large pot, bring 4 quarts of water to a boil, add linguini, stir and cook for 6 to 8 minutes or until al dente (firm to the bite). Drain linguini and return to the pot. Add a little olive oil, and stir well until linguini is coated. In a small pan, heat oil and garlic over low heat. Slowly and carefully add 1/4 cup (60 ml) of water (hot oil may splatter). Stir in oregano, chopped parsley, salt, and pepper. Add the clams with the juice, stir and cook for one minute. Put a serving of linguini in a pasta bowl and add some clam sauce.

YIELD: *Makes 4 servings*

EACH WITH: 472.3 calories; 15.0 gm total fat; 2.1 gm saturated fat; 4.1 mg cholesterol; 597.3 mg sodium; 75.6 gm carbohydrate; 0.1 gm dietary fiber; 15.3 gm protein; 64.2 mg calcium; 4.3 mg iron; 210.1 IU vitamin A; 4.2 mg vitamin C. .

Penne Pasta with Tomatoes and Mushrooms 👪

If in season, use fresh plum tomatoes instead of canned. For dessert, half-ripe papaya, seeded, and filled with your favorite ice cream.

- 1 can (28 ounces, or 784 g) whole, peeled tomatoes.
- 2 tablespoons (28 ml) olive oil
- 1/2 onion, chopped
- 1 garlic clove, minced
- 1/2 pound (225 g) mushrooms, cleaned, and thickly sliced
- Salt to taste
- 1/4 cup (15 g) chopped parsley
- 1/4 cup (15 g) fresh basil, chopped
- 1/4 teaspoon red pepper flakes, optional
- 3 cups (1/2 pound, or 225 g) whole-wheat penne pasta
- 1/2 cup (50 g) grated Romano or Parmesan

◉ Drain tomatoes (save juice), coarsely chop the tomatoes, and set aside. Heat oil in a large frying pan, add onion and garlic, and sauté over medium heat for 3 to 4 minutes, or until the onion is soft. Increase heat to medium-high, add mushrooms, and sprinkle with a little salt. Stirring frequently, sauté until mushrooms give off their liquid and are lightly browned (about 5 minutes). Reduce heat to low and add tomatoes, 1/2 cup (120 ml) of the reserved tomato juice, parsley, basil, and red pepper, if desired. Salt to taste, and simmer for 15 to 20 minutes, adding more juice if needed.

Bring 4 quarts of water to boil in a large pan. Add pasta, stir and cook for 10 to 12 minutes, until al dente, or follow package instructions. Drain the pasta. Transfer to a large, warm bowl and stir in the tomato-mushroom sauce. Serve with grated cheese.

YIELD: *Makes 6 servings*

EACH WITH: 279.3 calories; 7.8 gm total fat; 2.2 gm saturated fat; 7.3 mg cholesterol; 175.6 mg sodium; 43.9 gm carbohydrate; 5.5 gm dietary fiber; 12.5 gm protein; 137.0 mg calcium; 2.8 mg iron; 471.1 IU vitamin A; 8.6 mg vitamin C.

Penne Pasta with Shrimp and Feta Cheese 👨‍👩‍👧

This is a quick dish to prepare when using peeled shrimp. Remove tails, if desired. Cut the shrimp and pasta into small pieces for your toddler.

- 3 cups (450 g) whole-wheat penne pasta
- 3 tablespoons (40 ml) olive oil
- 2 cups (400 g) shelled and deveined shrimp, fresh, or frozen and defrosted
- 1 teaspoon minced, fresh garlic
- 1/2 cup (65 g) green onion, sliced
- 1/2 cup (75 g) feta cheese
- 2 tablespoons (8 g) chopped fresh parsley, washed
- 1 tablespoon (4 g) chopped fresh oregano, washed
- Freshly ground pepper, optional

◎ Bring 2 quarts of water to boil in a large pot. Add the pasta and cook until al dente (8 to 10 minutes). Drain and save 1 cup (235 ml) of the cooking water. Stir in 1 tablespoon (14 ml) olive oil to prevent the pasta from sticking. Heat 2 tablespoons (28 ml) olive oil on medium hot in a large stir-fry pan and add shrimp and garlic. When the shrimp start to turn pink, add the green onion, and stir. Cook 2 to 3 minutes until the shrimp are cooked through. Stir in the cheese, parsley, and oregano. Combine the shrimp and pasta. If the sauce needs some more liquid, stir in 1/4 to 1/2 cup (60 to 120 ml) of the saved cooking water (or more if needed). Serve with a grind of black pepper, if desired and additional crumbled feta cheese on the side.

YIELD: *Makes 4 to 6 servings*

EACH WITH: 761.3 calories; 18.1 gm total fat; 4.4 gm saturated fat; 700.2 mg cholesterol; 817.0 mg sodium; 45.2 gm carbohydrate; 4.8 gm dietary fiber; 101.8 gm protein; 334.9 mg calcium; 13.4 mg iron; 1093.1 IU vitamin A; 12.7 mg vitamin C. .

Halibut 👪

Serve with rice and steamed asparagus. Finish with a peach for dessert.

- 3 (1-inch, or 2.5-cm, thick) fresh halibut fillets, skin and bones removed
- 1 tablespoon (14 ml) light olive oil
- Juice from 1/2 lemon
- 2 tablespoons (8 g) minced parsley
- Salt and pepper to taste

▭ Place the 3 fish fillets in an 8 x 8-inch (20 x 20-cm) microwave-safe dish and brush the fillets with olive oil. Cover with a lid and microwave 6 to 8 minutes on high, until fish is opaque all the way through. Remove dish to the table. Sprinkle lemon juice and parsley evenly over the fish. Salt and pepper to taste.

▦ Preheat oven to 400°F (200°C, or gas mark 6). Place halibut in ovenproof dish, sprinkle with 2 to 3 tablespoons (28 to 40 ml) of olive oil and a little salt. Cover and bake for 10 to 15 minutes, or until the fish is opaque throughout. Remove from oven and sprinkle with lemon juice and fresh parsley.

YIELD: *Makes 3 servings*

EACH WITH: 267.1 calories; 9.2 gm total fat; 1.3 gm saturated fat; 65.3 mg cholesterol; 111.8 mg sodium; 0.8 gm carbohydrate; 0.1 gm dietary fiber; 42.6 gm protein; 100.0 mg calcium; 1.9 mg iron; 535.2 IU vitamin A; 7.0 mg vitamin C.

Fish Casserole with Leeks 👪

Leeks have a delicate and mild flavor, are an excellent source of folate, and contain some iron. Serve with mashed potatoes and broccoli.

- 2 leeks, white parts only, washed and finely sliced
- 1 stalk celery, washed and thinly sliced
- 1 pound (455 g) fresh or defrosted cod, sole, or halibut fillets (without skin and bone)
- Salt and pepper to taste
- Small dots of butter
- 2 tablespoons (10 g) grated Parmesan
- 2 tablespoons (28 ml) half-and-half

▦ Heat the oven to 375°F (190°C, or gas mark 5). Lightly oil a lidded ovenproof casserole dish. Layer half of the sliced leek and celery in the casserole dish. Top with fish and lightly season with salt and pepper, except for the toddler's portion. Dot with butter and cover the fish with the remaining leek and celery. Add the cheese. Pour half-and-half around the edges of the casserole. Cover and bake in the center of the oven for 30 minutes.

YIELD: *Makes 1 adult and 1 toddler servings*

EACH WITH: 214.5 calories; 5.4 gm total fat; 2.6 gm saturated fat; 82.7 mg cholesterol; 200.5 mg sodium; 9.4 gm carbohydrate; 1.3 gm dietary fiber; 31.1 gm protein; 115.4 mg calcium; 1.9 mg iron; 1188.1 IU vitamin A; 10.2 mg vitamin C. .

BIRTHDAY PARTIES

Although your baby will not be aware of all the grandeur that goes along with her first birthday, it will be a special day. With any luck, all the important people in his young life will be there, and at the end of the day you'll have some priceless photos and memories.

By the time her second birthday rolls around, she'll most likely be able to understand the basic idea of her birthday if you explain it to her. The options available to parents for birthday party foods, games, and entertainment can be daunting. But, keep in mind that little ones get tired and overwhelmed quickly, so a couple of hours should be plenty of time to have fun.

Summertime is perfect for a garden party; or choose a spot at your favorite park. (You may need a permit to decorate.) You'll have much less clean up and fewer worries outside.

If you have an indoor party, make sure that flowers, forks, balloons, glassware—anything that might be grabbed by little ones—are safely out of reach.

A picnic table covered in butcher block-paper (stapled underneath) works well outside. Have mommies and daddies help each child trace their hands in bright non-toxic crayons on the paper, and then get as creative as they like. Even the shyest toddler will have fun, and spills won't matter.

Play some of your little one's favorite music, lay out a buffet of delicious food for both adults and children, and little else is needed at this age. (Some wonderful celebration foods follow.)

Clowns and puppets can be scary; most games are too competitive and complex for two-year-olds; and "moon bounces" and other party equipment can cause accidents, so save those for later years. The birthday cake will be the *pièce de résistance.*

Consider these tips for keeping things simple and safe:

BALLOONS: Do not use latex balloons around small children. They may be swallowed and choked on. If you really want balloons, get the helium-filled Mylar type (although these aren't environmentally friendly).

PAPER VS. PLASTIC: Paper plates and bowls are safer for children, but buy the heavy-duty type that won't collapse under cake and ice cream. Plastic spoons are fine; again, the sturdier kind are best, but don't give little ones plastic knives or forks. If parents are concerned about party clothes getting spoiled, provide bright, inexpensive bibs.

PARTY FAVORS: At this age, party favors mean little to the child. You can create memories for everyone by providing a hand/footprint kit, or have single-use cameras for parents to take home after they have taken pictures. Little hard page books, a music tape, or age-appropriate toy would also be appropriate. Leave candy at the store. Gifts don't need to be wrapped; just write the recipient's name on a bright ribbon tied around the gift.

For your toddler's birthday parties, keep the portions of birthday cake, cookies, chocolate, and ice cream small. To complement the sweets, fill ice cream cone cups with small pieces of the birthday child's favorite fruit. You can also use grated apple, grated carrots, grated cheese, or animal crackers. In place of chocolate sauce, puree a favorite berry or fruit to put over yogurt or ice cream. Serve milk or 100 percent fruit juices rather than sugary drinks or soda. Homemade Strawberry Lemonade (page 288) is delicious and full of vitamin C. From the time my children were very young, they got to choose their favorite food and cake on their birthday. I would start off the day with a special tray (sometimes served in bed) with their breakfast of choice, nice dishes, cloth napkin, a small vase with flowers, and a small present. This gave them the feeling of having a special day that was just for them.

For the grown-ups, I have included my favorite party recipes.

BRUNCH

Strawberry Lemonade

👪

- ½ cup (120 ml) freshly squeezed lemon juice
- ¼ to ⅓ cup (50 to 65 g) sugar (according to taste)
- 1 cup (260 g) frozen (or fresh) unsweetened strawberries
- 2 cups (470 ml) water
- 1 cup ice

Place the lemon juice, sugar, strawberries, water, and ice in a blender and process until blended (about 30 seconds).

YIELD: *Makes 5 cups*

EACH WITH: 54.5 calories; 0.1 gm total fat; 0.0 gm saturated fat; 0.0 mg cholesterol; 0.5 mg sodium; 14.4 gm carbohydrate; 0.7 gm dietary fiber; 0.3 gm protein; 6.7 mg calcium; 0.1 mg iron; 8.3 IU vitamin A; 29.1 mg vitamin C.

HORS D'OEUVRES

Smoked Salmon Spread

👪

Serve on Crostini (page 289) or on cucumber slices.

- 1 cup (115 g) cream cheese
- ½ cup (113 g) smoked salmon, coarsely chopped
- 1 tablespoon (14 ml) lemon juice
- 1 teaspoon Worcestershire sauce
- 5 drops Tabasco sauce
- 2 tablespoons (8 g) chopped chives

Combine cream cheese, salmon, lemon juice, Worcestershire, and Tabasco sauce in a food processor. Blend until smooth. Add chopped chives, and pulse a few seconds until blended.

YIELD: *Makes 1½ cup*

EACH WITH: 90.4 calories; 7.6 gm total fat; 4.4 gm saturated fat; 25.6 mg cholesterol; 440.8 mg sodium; 0.7 gm carbohydrate; 0.0 gm dietary fiber; 4.9 gm protein; 18.6 mg calcium; 0.4 mg iron; 299.2 IU vitamin A; 0.7 mg vitamin C..

Crostini 👪

This crispy bread goes well with a variety of savory spreads, or as an accompaniment to pasta or salads.

* 1 French baguette (bread) cut into ⅓-inch thick slices
* Olive oil
* 1 or 2 large garlic cloves, peeled and halved, optional

🔲 Preheat the oven to 375°F (190°C, or gas mark 5). Lightly brush both sides of the bread slices with olive oil, and place on a baking sheet in the center of the oven. Bake from 1 to 3 minutes, until the edges are golden. Turn the slices, and bake until golden, but still soft on the inside (1 to 2 minutes). Rub one side of the bread lightly with garlic, if desired.

YIELD: *Makes 1 serving*

EACH WITH: 131.5 calories; 5.4 gm total fat; 0.8 gm saturated fat; 0.0 mg cholesterol; 195.5 mg sodium; 17.6 gm carbohydrate; 1.0 gm dietary fiber; 3.0 gm protein; 29.5 mg calcium; 0.9 mg iron; 0.0 IU vitamin A, 0.9 mg vitamin C.

Goat Cheese Spread 👪

Serve on Crostini (left)

* 4 ounces (115 g) mild goat cheese
* 1 teaspoon olive oil
* 1 garlic clove, minced
* 1 tablespoon (14 ml) lemon juice
* 1 tablespoon (4 g) chopped parsley
* Dash of cayenne, optional

Place goat cheese, olive oil, garlic, lemon juice, parsley, and cayenne in a food processor and pulse until smooth.

NOTE: This can be topped with a half, pitted Greek olive, a slice of roasted red bell pepper, and a sliver of sweet, red onion.

YIELD: *Makes ½ cup*

APPROXIMATE SERVING SIZE: .5 cups. **EACH WITH:** 29.4 calories; 2.4 gm total fat; 1.4 gm saturated fat; 4.4 mg cholesterol; 35.3 mg sodium; 0.3 gm carbohydrate; 0.0 gm dietary fiber; 1.8 gm protein; 14.3 mg calcium; 0.2 mg iron; 124.7 IU vitamin A; 0.8 mg vitamin C.

Prosciutto with Figs 👪

* 6 fresh figs
* About ¼ pound (115 g) prosciutto, very thinly sliced

Wash, stem, and halve the figs. Wrap each half in a thin slice of prosciutto.

YIELD: *Serves 12*

EACH WITH: 47.7 calories; 2.3 gm total fat; 0.8 gm saturated fat; 7.4 mg cholesterol; 78.3 mg sodium; 5.3 gm carbohydrate; 0.7 gm dietary fiber; 2.0 gm protein; 9.4 mg calcium; 0.2 mg iron; 35.5 IU vitamin A; 0.5 mg vitamin C.

Roasted Red Peppers 👪

See page 126 for roasting, or buy ready roasted red peppers.

- One roasted, sliced, red pepper serves 4 to 6

Cut the peppers into 1½-inch (3.75-cm) strips. Top each strip with pieces of feta cheese, slices of fresh mozzarella and chopped fresh basil, or a thin anchovy fillet.

YIELD: *Serves 12*

Roquefort Spread 👪

Serve on Crostini (page 289) or spread on slices of fresh, ripe pears. (You can also use blue cheese or Gorgonzola).

- 4 ounces (115 g) of Roquefort cheese
- 2 tablespoons (28 g) butter
- 1 teaspoon minced garlic
- ½ teaspoon Worcestershire sauce
- Fresh ground pepper

Place Roquefort, butter, garlic, and Worcestershire sauce in the food processor. Pulse until blended.

YIELD: *Makes ½ cup*

EACH WITH: 78.8 calories; 7.2 gm total fat; 4.6 gm saturated fat; 20.4 mg cholesterol; 264.2 mg sodium; 0.5 gm carbohydrate; 0.0 gm dietary fiber; 3.1 gm protein; 96.2 mg calcium; 0.1 mg iron; 237.9 IU vitamin A; 0.2 mg vitamin C.

Lemon Mousse 👪

- Juice from two fresh lemons, about ½ cup (120 ml)
- 1 envelope Knox unflavored gelatin
- 1 cup (200 g) sugar
- 1 pint (475 ml) whipping cream
- Peel from one lemon, finely grated
- One can (11-ounces, or 310 g) mandarin orange segments, drained
- One non-stick bundt cake pan

Sprinkle gelatin over half of the lemon juice (¼ cup, or 60 ml). Let stand for 1 minute. Add remaining lemon juice (¼ cup, or 60 ml) and sugar to a saucepan. Stir over very low heat until sugar has melted. Add lemon-gelatin mixture to the saucepan, and stir until gelatin has completely melted. Remove from heat and cool. Whip the cream and add grated lemon peel. Slowly pour the cooled lemon-gelatin mixture into the cream and stir well. Rinse the bundt cake pan with cold water to prevent sticking, and pour in the cream mixture. Place in refrigerator until the mixture has stiffened. When the mousse is completely firm, quickly dip the form in very hot water (about 2 seconds). Place a serving dish on top of the bundt pan and quickly turn it onto the serving dish. Fill the mousse with drained mandarins.

YIELD: *8 servings*

EACH WITH: 258.3 calories; 11.0 gm total fat; 6.9 gm saturated fat; 40.8 mg cholesterol; 62.9 mg sodium; 40.4 gm carbohydrate; 0.6 gm dietary fiber; 1.8 gm protein; 26.5 mg calcium; 0.1 mg iron; 932.6 IU vitamin A; 20.9 mg vitamin C. .

Norwegian Birthday Cake 👫

This is so delicious, I was asked to make a large version for my very special friend and co-author's wedding. It has also been a frequent request for my family's birthdays.

INGREDIENTS FOR CAKE:

- 6 eggs
- 1 cup (200 g) sugar
- 1 1/2 cups (175 g) all-purpose flour, sifted
- 1/2 teaspoon baking powder
- 1/4 teaspoon salt

INGREDIENTS FOR FILLING:

- Two 12-ounce (340 g) bags frozen, sweetened red raspberries
- 2 cups (220 g) fresh raspberries
- 1 tablespoon (14 ml) frozen orange juice concentrate
- 1 pint (475 ml) real whipping cream
- 1 teaspoon pure vanilla extract

Preheat oven to 350°F (180°C, or gas mark 4). Butter and flour a 9-inch (22.5-cm) round spring-form cake pan. Defrost frozen raspberries and reserve the juice. Mix orange juice concentrate with raspberry juice, and set aside. In a mixer, beat eggs and sugar together until airy, pale, and tripled in volume. Combine flour, baking powder, and salt. Using a rubber spatula, gently fold the flour mixture into the beaten eggs. Pour cake batter into the greased springform pan, and place in the center of the oven.

Bake 30 to 45 minutes, or until a toothpick comes out clean when inserted in the middle of the cake. While the cake is baking, whip cream until it peaks, and add vanilla. When the cake is done, place it on a rack to cool. Once cooled, carefully remove the form, and put the cake on a serving plate. Cut the cake in half, and soak both layers with reserved raspberry-orange juice. Cover the bottom layer with the defrosted and drained raspberries, and one cup of fresh raspberries. Cover the berries with half of the whipped cream. Add the second cake layer, and cover with the remaining cream. Decorate with the remaining fresh raspberries.

YIELD: 8 servings

EACH WITH: 391.0 calories; 14.8 gm total fat; 7.9 gm saturated fat; 180.3 mg cholesterol; 161.9 mg sodium; 57.9 gm carbohydrate; 4.2 gm dietary fiber; 7.9 gm protein; 71.3 mg calcium; 2.2 mg iron; 637.9 IU vitamin A; 17.2 mg vitamin C.

REFERENCES

Achterberg, Cheryl, PhD.; Elaine McDonnell, MS, RD; and Robin Bagby, MEd, RD. "How to put the Food Guide Pyramid into Practice." *Journal of the American Dietetic Association* 94, no. 9 (September 1994).

Agostoni, Carlo; Enrica Riva; and Marcello Giovannini. "Dietary Fiber in Weaning Foods of Young Children." *Pediatrics* 96 (November 1995).

Alliance for a Healthier Generation. "A Nation at Risk: Obesity in the United States." **www.healthiergeneration.org**

American Academy of Pediatrics. "Calcium Requirements of Infants, Children, and Adolescents." *Pediatrics* 104, no. 5 (November 1999): 1152–1157.

American Council on Science and Health. "Scientists Assure Parents: Commercial Baby Food is Safe and Nutritious." **www.acsh.org/news/newsID.529/news_detail.asp**, April 4, 1997.

American Dietetic Association. "Role of Dietary Fiber in Children's Health." **www.eatright.org/child/roleoffiber.html.**

American Dietetic Association. "Vegetarian Infants." *Vegetarian Nutrition*, 1998.1997 American Dietetic Association Position Paper on Vegetarianism. ADA NFS: Feeding Your Baby the Vegetarian Way. USDA–FDA- More People Trying Vegetarian Diets. ADA Vegetarian Nutrition: Vegetarian Infants - Vegetarian Toddlers and Preschoolers.

American Dietetic Association. "Position of the American Dietetic Association: Dietary guidance for healthy children 2 to 11 years." *Journal of the American Dietetic Association* 99, no. 1 (January 1999).

American Dietetic Association. "The flavor of food? It's all in your head! How the chemosenses taste and smell let us savor flavor." (Interview with Valerie B. Duffy, PhD, RD.) *Journal of the American Dietetic Association* 96, no. 7 (July 1996).

American Dietetic Association. "Position of The American Dietetic Association: Dietary guidance for healthy children aged 2 to 11 years." *Journal of the American Dietetic Association* 99, no. 1 (January 1999).

American Heart Association. "Nutrition and Children." *Circulation* 95, no. 9 (May 6, 1997).

American Heart Association. "Dietary Guidelines for Healthy Children." **www.americanheart.org/Heart_and_Stroke_A_Z_Guide/dietgk.html.**

American Heart Association. "Fat." **http://www.americanheart.org/presenter.jhtml?identifier=4582.**

Birch, Leann L., and Jennifer O. Fisher. "Development of Eating Behaviors Among Children and Adolescents." *Pediatrics* 101 (March 1998).

Brink, Pamela J.; Kristi Ferguson; and Anju Sharma. "Childhood Memories About Food: The Successful Dieters Project." *Journal of Child and Adolescent Psychiatric Nursing* 12 (January 1999):17.

Burger King Corporation. "Great Taste Table," August 1998.

CNN. "Study: Americans fatter than ever and getting even fatter." May 28, 1998, **www.cnn.com/HEALTH/9805/28/obesity/index.html.**

Cox, Dana R., MS, RD; Jean D. Skinner, PhD, RD; and Betty Ruth Carruth, PhD, RD. "A Food Variety Index for Toddlers (VIT): Development and Application." *Journal of the American Dietetic Association* 97, no. 12 (December 1997).

Dennison, B.A. "Fruit juice consumption by infants and children: a review." *Journal of the American College of Nutrition* 15, 5 Suppl (October 1996):4S–11S.

Dennison, B.A.; H.L. Rockwell; and S.L. Baker. "Excess fruit juice consumption by preschool-aged children is associated with short stature and obesity." *Pediatrics* 99, no. 1 (January 1997):15–22.

Department of Health and Human Services, Food and Drug Administration. "Bottled Water. Final rule." RIN 0910-AA11 (lrd/n095-323.txt), **http://www.cfsan.fda.gov/~lrd/n095-323.txt.**

Dietz, William H., MD, PhD, FAAP, and Loraine Stern, MD, FAAP, eds. *American Academy of Pediatrics Guide to Your Child's Nutrition.* Villard, 1999.

Environmental Protection Agency. "Children and Drinking Water Standards," http://www.epa.gov/safewater/kids/kidshealth/booklet_text.html.

Faine, Mary, and Donna Oberg. "Survey of dental nutrition knowledge of WIC nutritionists and public health dental hygienists." *Journal of the American Dietetic Association* 95, no. 2 (February 1995).

Farley, Dixie. "More People Trying Vegetarian Diets." *FDA Consumer,* January 1996.

Fisher, Edward A., MD, PhD, MPH; Linda Van Horn, PhD, RD; and Henry C. McGill, MD.

Fitzsimons, Dina, Johanna Dwyer, Carole Palmer, and Linda Boyd. "Nutrition and oral health guidelines for pregnant women, infants, and children." *Journal of the American Dietetic Association* 98, no. 2 (February 1998).

Forgac, Marilyn T., MS, RD. "Timely Statement of the American Dietetic Association: Dietary guidance for healthy children." *ADA Reports* 95, no. 3 (March 1995).

Herbert, Victor, MD, FACP, and Genell J. Subak-Sharpe, MS, eds. *Total Nutrition: The Only Guide You'll Ever Need.* New York: St. Martin's Press, 1995.

Jarvis, Judith K., and Gregory D. Miller. "Fat in infant diets." *Nutrition Today* 31, no. 5 (September/October 1996): 182.

Jacobson, Michael F., PhD. "Liquid Candy: How Soft Drinks are Harming Americans' Health." Center for Science in the Public Interest. www.cspinet.org/sodapop/liquid_candy.htm.

Juttelstad, Ann. "The Best of the Wurst." *Design Elements,* May 1999.

Kimm, Sue Y.S., MD, MPH. "The Role of Dietary Fiber in the Development and Treatment of Childhood Obesity." *Pediatrics* 96 (November 1995).

Lino, Mark, PhD. "Report Card on the Diet Quality of Children." *Nutrition Insights,* USDA Center for Nutrition Policy and Promotion, October 1998.

McBride, Judy. "Vegetarians Can Get Enough Zinc and Other Minerals From Food Alone." USDA Agricultural Research Service, March 25, 1998, http://www.ars.usda.gov/is/pr/1998/980325.htm.

McBride, Judy. "What Americans Eat — For Better, For Worse." *Food & Nutrition Research Briefs,* April 1995, http://www.ars.usda.gov/is/np/fnrb/fnrb495.htm#eat.

McDonald's Nutrition Information Center. "McDonald's Nutrition Facts," August 1998.

Mennella, J.A., and G.K. Beachamp. "Early flavor experiences: research update." *Nutritional Revue* 56, no. 7 (July 1998): 205–211.

Murphy, Anne S., PhD, RD; June P. Youatt, PhD; Sharon L. Hoerr, PhD, RD; Carol A. Sawyer, PhD, RD; and Sandra L Andrews, PhD, RD. "Kindergarten students' food preferences are not consistent with their knowledge of the Dietary Guidelines." *Journal of the American Dietetic Association* 95, no. 2 (February 1995).

National Institutes of Health. "Helping Your Overweight Child." NIH Publication No. 97-4096, January 1997, http://win.niddk.nih.gov/publications/over_child.htm.

National Institutes of Health. "Statistics Related to Overweight and Obesity." NIH Publication No. 96-4158, July 1996, http://win.niddk.nih.gov/statistics/index.htm.

Nicklas, Theresa A. "Dietary Trends Among Children." Based on "Dietary studies of children: The bogalusa Heart Study experience." *Journal of the American Dietetic Association* 95, no. 2 (February 1995).

Nicklas, Theresa A., PhD; Rosanne P. Farris, MS; Leann Myers, MS; and Gerald S. Berenson, MD. "Dietary fiber intake of children and young adults: The Bogalusa Heart Study." *Journal of the American Dietetic Association* 95, no. 2 (February 1995).

Picciano, Mary Frances; Lois D. McBean; and Virginia A. Stallings. "How to grow a healthy child: a conference report." *Nutrition Today* 34 (January 1999): 6.

Ross, Emma. "Study: Soft Drinks Lead to Obesity." Associated Press, February 15, 2001.

Saldanha, Leila G., PhD, RD. "Fiber in the Diet of US Children: Results of National Surveys." *Pediatrics* 96 (November 1995).

Saltos, Etta, PhD., and Shanthy Bowman, PhD. "Dietary Guidance on Sodium: Should we take it with a grain of salt?" *Nutrition Insights*. USDA Center of Nutrition Policy and Promotion, May 1997.

Skinner, Jean D., PhD, RD; Betty Ruth Carruth, PhD, RD; Kelly S. Houck, MS; Frances Coletta, PhD, RD; Richard Cotter, PhD; Dana Ott, PhD; and Max McLeod, MS. "Longitudinal study of nutrient and food intakes of infants aged 2 to 24 months." *Journal of the American Dietetic Association* 97, no. 5 (May 1997).

Smith, M.M., and F. Lifshitz. "Excess fruit juice consumption as a contributing factor in nonorganic failure to thrive." *Pediatrics* 93, no. 3 (March 1994):438–43.

Stallone, Daryth D., Ph.D., M.P.H., and Michael F. Jacobson, Ph.D. "Cheating Babies: Nutritional Quality and Cost of Commercial Baby Food" *CSPI Reports*, http://www.cspinet.org/reports/cheat1.html.

Stedronsky, Frances M., MBA, MA. "Child Nutrition and Health Campaign: A member update." *Journal of the American Dietetic Association* 98, no. 7, (June 1998).

Stehlin, Dori. "Feeding Baby Nature and Nurture." *FDA Consumer* U.S. Food and Drug Administration, September 1990, updated March 1991.

Wood, Marcia. "What Carotenes Do for You." *Agricultural Research*, November 1996.

U.S. Department of Agriculture. "Choose a diet with plenty of grain products, vegetables, and fruits." warp.nal.usda.gov/fnic/dga/dga95/grains.html.

U.S. Department of Agriculture. "Eat a Variety of Foods." warp.nal.usda.gov/fnic/dga/variety.htm.

U.S. Department of Agriculture. "Focus on Ground Beef." September 2001, www.fsis.usda.gov/oa/pubs/focusgb.htm.

U.S. Department of Agriculture. "Focus on Chicken." September 2000, www.fsis.usda.gov/Fact_Sheets/Chicken_Food_Safety_Focus/index.asp.

U.S. Department of Agriculture. "USDA Nutrient Database for Standard Reference Release 12." www.nal.usda.gov/fnic/foodcomp/Data/SR12/sr12.html.

U.S. Department of Agriculture, "What and Where our Children Eat—1994 Nationwide Survey Results," news release, April 18, 1996, www.usda.gov/news/releases/1996/04/0197.

U.S. Department of Agriculture, Agricultural Research Service. "Making Calcium More Available." *Food & Nutrition Research Briefs*, January 2002, www.ars.usda.gov/is/np/fnrb/fnrb102.htm.

U.S. Department of Agriculture, Center for Nutrition Policy and Promotion. "The Food Guide Pyramid." *Home and Garden Bulletin*, no. 252 (October 1996).

U.S. Department of Agriculture, Center for Nutrition Policy and Promotion. "Is fruit juice consumption dangerous for children?" *Nutrition Insights*, March 1997 http://www.cnpp.usda.gov/InsgtM97.html.

U.S. Department of Agriculture, Center for Nutrition Policy and Promotion. "Is Total Fat Consumption Really Decreasing?" *Nutrition Insights*, April 1998.

U.S. Department of Agriculture, Center for Nutrition Policy and Promotion. "Profile of Overweight Children." *Nutrition Insights*, May 1999.

U.S. Food and Drug Administration. "Bottled Water: New Trends, New Rules," *FDA Consumer*, June 1991.

Williams, Christine L., MD, MPH, and Marguerite Bollella, RD. "Is a High-fiber Diet Safe for Children?" *Pediatrics* 96, no. 5 (November 1995): 1014–1019.

Wijn, J.F. "Obesity in children. Feeding pattern in relation to the possible development of obesity." *Tijdschr Kindergeneeskunde* 49, no. 6 (December 1981):214–20.

RECIPE INDEX

GENERAL INDEX

Acknowledgments

Thank you to my daughter, Mirabai, whose love, computer savvy, intelligent editing, sage advice, and thoughts on content and language have helped me over many hurdles in this new book.

I am blessed to have had the resources of Harriet Eichenholz, chef supreme and good friend. Her exquisite taste and delicious recipes, many of which are included in this book, were there for sharing.

My son, William, whose expertise in computers surpasses most, has dug the manuscript and me out of many deep technological holes. Without his help this book may well never have been written. His patience and humor have been endless, and I am as grateful for that as I am for his input and for creating a software program for the nutritional analyses of the recipes

To Katya, *tusen takk* for being in my life and for your wonderful cooking and great recipes.

Many thanks to friends and family who offered suggestions and encouragement, most especially to Helena Hoas and Ken Lockridge for their motivation and printer; to Lynne Shaara, who read every page of the manuscript and came up with thoughtful ideas; and to

Greg Patent, writer of fine cookbooks, who read my manuscript and willingly shared his broad knowledge of the publishing world with me.

My love and appreciation to my husband, Bob, whose confidence in the book and in me has never wavered. He has been my food-taster (right down to the pureed stuff), dishwasher, courier, house cleaner, and gentle ear.

Thank you, Kim Darling, for your diligent editing and your helpful advice.

To my critique group, Karen Buley, Kathleen Snow, and Carla Heitz, I cannot thank you enough for your support, encouragement, and help through all my times of despair, disappointment, and misery. And when all went well, still being there for me, to share my joy and happiness. I don't know how I would have made it without you guys.

Thank you to Robert, Stacie, Michael, and all my friends who loved my food and waited patiently for this book to be published so they could have my recipes.

And then, there is my wonderful literary agent, Linda Konner. Thank you so much, Linda, you are the best, ever. I really am so lucky to have you.

About the Authors

KARIN KNIGHT, R.N., worked as a registered nurse for twenty-five years in her native country, Norway, and in California before turning her passion for cooking into an occupation. As a chef, she planned meals and catered events honoring film industry luminaries. Karin also coauthored *The Baby Cookbook*, which has over 43,000 copies in print. She currently resides in Montana with her husband and three children.

JEANNIE LUMLEY was born England and spent six years as an editor and writer at a major press agency on London's Fleet Street. She worked for nine years in the editorial department of a large California-based entertainment company and handled public relations for its chairman. Jeannie has written two other cookbooks, including *The Baby Cookbook*, which she coauthored with Karin Knight. She lives in Ventura, California.